STUDIES ON MODERN ASIA
AND AFRICA

Volume 2

FAMILY LAW IN ASIA
AND AFRICA

FAMILY LAW IN ASIA AND AFRICA

Edited by
J. N. D. ANDERSON

Routledge
Taylor & Francis Group

LONDON AND NEW YORK

First published in 1968 by George Allen & Unwin Ltd

This edition first published in 2022
by Routledge
2 Park Square, Milton Park, Abingdon, Oxon OX14 4RN

and by Routledge
605 Third Avenue, New York, NY 10158

*Routledge is an imprint of the Taylor & Francis Group, an informa
business*

British Library Cataloguing in Publication Data
A catalogue record for this book is available from the British Library

ISBN: 978-1-03-215171-7 (Set)
ISBN: 978-1-00-324754-8 (Set) (ebk)
ISBN: 978-1-03-215260-8 (Volume 2) (hbk)
ISBN: 978-1-03-215273-8 (Volume 2) (pbk)
ISBN: 978-1-00-324339-7 (Volume 2) (ebk)

DOI: 10.4324/9781003243397

Publisher's Note
The publisher has gone to great lengths to ensure the quality of this
reprint but points out that some imperfections in the original copies
may be apparent.

Disclaimer
The publisher has made every effort to trace copyright holders and
would welcome correspondence from those they have been unable to
trace.

FAMILY LAW
IN ASIA AND AFRICA

EDITED BY

J. N. D. ANDERSON

*Director of the Institute of Advanced Legal
Studies and Professor of Oriental Laws at the
School of Oriental and African Studies
in the University of London*

London

GEORGE ALLEN AND UNWIN LTD

RUSKIN HOUSE   MUSEUM STREET

PRINTED IN GREAT BRITAIN
in 11 *on* 12 *point Fournier type*
BY SIMSON SHAND LTD
LONDON, HERTFORD AND HARLOW

TO ALAN GLEDHILL
M.A. (Cantab.), LL.D. (Lond.)
Indian Civil Service, 1920–46
Judge, High Court at Rangoon, 1946–8
School of Oriental and African Studies, 1948–66
Professor of Oriental Laws in the University of London, 1955–63

FOREWORD

This volume represents a collaborative work by members of the Department of Law at the School of Oriental and African Studies, together with a number of distinguished visitors. It is based on a series of lectures under the same general title given during the academic year 1965/6. The lectures given by Haji Ahmad Ibrahim (then Attorney-General of Singapore) and by Professor Falk (of the Hebrew University of Jerusalem) were University Lectures given at the School of Oriental and African Studies under the auspices of the Board of Studies in Laws of the University of London. The remainder were lectures directly sponsored by the School of Oriental and African Studies, some of them given by distinguished guests (Professor Freedman, of the London School of Economics, Professor Hahlo, of the University of Witwatersrand, Professor Irani, then of the University of Bombay, and Professor Rocher, of the Free University of Brussels), and others by members of the Department of Law at the School.

The arrangement of the papers has been based on their subject matter rather than on the geographical area to which they refer, because the major interest of a work such as this probably lies in the basis it provides for comparative study.

The theme of the first group of papers is marriage, divorce and matrimonial causes. In the first two Mr Cotran and Dr Morris discuss respectively the changing nature of African marriage and attempted reforms in the law of marriage in Uganda. Then the focus of interest moves to the Far East, with Professor Freedman describing the rout of custom in Chinese family law in Singapore, and Mr McAleavy certain aspects of marriage and divorce in Communist China. Finally, Professor Rocher concerns himself with India, and describes the theory of matrimonial causes according to the Dharmaśāstra.

The next section is concerned with family property and the law of succession. Under this heading Professor Allott discusses family property in West Africa, Professor Hahlo the matrimonial régimes of South Africa, Professor Derrett 'family arrangements' in developing countries, Haji Ahmad Ibrahim the law of matrimonial property among Muslims in Malaysia and Singapore, and Professor Gledhill community of property in the marriage law of Burma.

The last section is somewhat more general in character. I have taken as my subject the eclipse of the patriarchal family in contemporary Islamic law; Professor Falk has contributed a paper on religious law and the modern family in Israel; Mr Rubin has discussed contemporary family law in Southern Africa; and Professor Irani has examined the juristic basis and content of the family law of the Parsis in India.

No attempt has been made radically to change the style of these lectures as they were given, since it was felt that any resulting gain would be more than matched by a corresponding loss.

I am indebted to my colleagues, Mr Henry McAleavy and Mr Eugene Cotran, for assistance in arranging these lectures and in preparing the material for publication.

J. N. D. ANDERSON

CONTENTS

PART THREE

GENERAL

PART ONE

MARRIAGE, DIVORCE
AND MATRIMONIAL CAUSES

I

THE CHANGING NATURE OF
AFRICAN MARRIAGE

EUGENE COTRAN

Lecturer in African Law
School of Oriental and African Studies

'Marriage' was defined in the old English case of *Hyde v. Hyde*[1] as 'the voluntary union for life of one man and one woman to the exclusion of all others'.

Now it has rightly been observed[2] that almost every single word of this Christian definition of marriage is inapplicable to marriages contracted under the traditional African customary law. It is argued, first, that in many African societies marriage was not a voluntary union, especially as far as brides were concerned; secondly, that the union was not for life since it might be easily dissolved without the intervention of a court; thirdly, that the marriage was not so much a union between a man and a woman, as an alliance between two family groups; and finally, that far from being a union to the exclusion of all others, all customary marriages were potentially polygamous.

So much for the negative aspects. What of the positive ones? Can one define marriage under African customary law? I shall certainly not enter into the old controversy here of whether marriage should be regarded as a status, an institution, a contract, a religious bond or purely a civil engagement. Nor shall I be as bold and ambitious as some writers who have tried to define marriage, not only to cover customary law, but also to cover marriage as recognized all over the world. Indeed, I would say that it is impossible to put forward a definition which would cover marriage as recognized and known under the multitude of African customary laws, differing and conflicting as they do in such material respects as their political and social structure, kinship groupings, descent systems, economic way of life and so on.

On the other hand, I think it is possible, despite this diversity, to trace some broad uniformity in certain basic principles, and to show

[1] (1866) L.R. 1 P. & D. 130.
[2] Allott, *Essays in African Law*, p. 213.

that African customary marriages, as compared with European Christian marriages, have certain distinguishing features and characteristics.

The present paper, as its title suggests, will be concerned with showing how these traditional characteristics have undergone a radical change through such agencies as religion, social and economic advancement, education and statutory intervention. But I must, even at the risk of boring you with repetition of what many others have said before me, restate briefly the traditional characteristics before discussing their changed or changing nature.

GENERAL CHARACTERISTICS OF AFRICAN MARRIAGE

Before going into the general characteristics of African customary marriage, let me say at the outset that I make no apology whatever for referring to the institution as 'marriage'. I reject the notion adopted by many writers, judges and even governments, that simply because African marriage differs in certain material respects from a Christian or European-type marriage, then it would be wrong to use for them both a common term of description. Such terms as 'wife purchase' (used by Chief Justice Hamilton in the old Kenya case of *R. v. Amkeyo*[1] in 1917, and surprisingly approved by the East African Court of Appeal as recently as 1963[2]), 'concubinage' (used by many of the old writers on African marriage), and 'customary unions' (used in South African legislation and surprisingly in the recent customary law legislation in Tanzania), apart from being politically objectionable, I would submit are manifestly wrong. Professor Phillips, in his excellent introductory essay to the *Survey of African Marriage and Family Life*,[3] gives at least six reasons for concluding that 'African customary marriage has sufficient in common with marriage in other parts of the world (including European marriage) to warrant the usage of describing it by the same generic term marriage'. I would only like to add one more justification which I give from my own experiences in investigating the laws of marriage of the Kenya tribes, namely that in all the customary laws I investigated, there is a definite distinction made by the people themselves between a regular marriage, regular in the sense that it is entered into according to all the requirements of the law, and irregular unions, where the customary requirements have not been complied with. This distinction, when translated into vernacular terms, would

[1] 7 E.A.L.R. 14.
[2] *Abdul Rahman Bin Mohamed and An. v. R.* [1963] E.A. 188.
[3] pp. xii–xiii.

result in giving one term for the regular marriage, and other terms, such as concubinage, elopement, etc., for the irregular unions.

Reverting now to the characteristics of traditional African marriage, one can detect at least seven distinctive features:

The first and most obvious is the polygamous, or rather polygynous, nature of African marriage. All customary laws in Africa, without exception, allowed, indeed encouraged, a man to have as many wives as he pleased. There is no legal restriction in number, as for example in Islamic law, where the maximum is four. The possession of several wives was regarded as a mark of importance and prestige, and it has been known for rich men or chiefs to have as many as fifty or even a hundred wives simultaneously.

The second outstanding characteristic of traditional African marriage is the role played by the spouses' families at almost every stage of the matrimonial relationship—what has been described as the 'collective' aspect of the marriage transaction, or the 'alliance' between two family groups. This is not only a fact of social importance, but has important legal implications and consequences. Thus we find that it is the spouses' families and not the spouses themselves that negotiate and conclude the marriage agreement; that the consent of the spouses' families is a legal pre-condition to marriage; that the domestic and property relations between husband and wife are closely linked with those of their families; and that just as the conclusion of the marriage agreement is the concern of the families rather than the spouses, so is its dissolution of divorce primarily their affair. Indeed, generally speaking, the dissolution of a marriage, especially on the part of a wife, would be virtually impossible without the co-operation of her family.

The third feature of African marriages is the complex formalities and ceremonial associated with it. These vary greatly from one society to another and may include a series of rituals and ceremonies lasting many months. The importance of this, from a legal point of view, is that it is often difficult to determine first which of these ceremonies are legal requirements and which are purely of a social character, and secondly at precisely what stage the marriage comes into existence.

A fourth distinctive feature of African marriage is its provision for the payment of goods or services by the bridegroom or his family to the wife's family before, or at the time of, or after the marriage—the institution commonly known as 'brideprice'.

There has been considerable controversy as to the significance or object of this payment. The older view was that it was striking proof that customary marriage was no more than 'wife purchase', but I think that in this connection it has rightly been observed that 'the idea that an African buys a wife in the way that an English farmer buys cattle is the result of ignorance, which may once have been excusable but is so no longer, or of blind prejudice, which is never excusable in those responsible for governing an African people'.[1]

Other theories are that brideprice is a compensation to the woman's family for the loss of one of its members; that it is a security for the good treatment of a wife; that it is a security for the maintenance of the marriage by the respective families; that it is merely a symbol to seal the marriage contract; or that brideprice is no more than child price, i.e. a compensation for the transfer of a woman's reproductive capacity and her issue to the husband's family.

These alternative theories have prompted writers to use expressions other than brideprice, such as 'childprice', 'dowry', 'marriage payment', 'marriage cattle', 'bridewealth', 'marriage consideration' and so on.

It seems unnecessary to join in this controversy. My conclusion about this matter is that each theory and each term suggested may be perfectly right for the one tribe or group of tribes that the particular writer was investigating, but that none of them could possibly be right for all customary laws in general. For example, to speak of compensation or bride *wealth* when the brideprice may only be a token such as a hoe is obviously wrong, and to speak of a symbol or seal when it consists of 50 or 100 head of cattle is equally absurd. Indeed it may even be possible by reference to one tribe only to justify the use of the term 'brideprice'. For example, amongst the Meru tribe of Kenya, I am informed that there are common terms of description for the verb 'to marry' and 'to buy'. However, I can assure you that I certainly do not justify my use of the term by reference to the Meru language, but on the ground that, since it is not possible to give a term which is an accurate description of the institution for all customary laws, it is necessary to use some sort of label which avoids confusion with other similar institutions.

What is more important than to search for adequate terms, at least for my purpose, is to find out the legal implications of the payment, and here I would agree with Professor Radcliffe-Brown that, in most African marriages, brideprice 'is an essential part of the establishment of legality'.[2] In other words, with very few exceptions, the payment of

---

[1] Radcliffe-Brown, Introduction to *African Systems of Kinship and Marriage*, p. 47.
[2] ibid., p. 46.

brideprice was traditionally not a mere compensation, but the means or one of the means by which a marriage became legally valid.

The fifth general feature of African marriage which I would like to mention is its emphasis on the procreation of children as the prime end of marriage. Now it may well be that this aspect is not peculiar to African marriages. However, the extent to which African law goes in establishing ingenious devices for procreation where the usual methods are absent shows how striking this feature is in African law, and provides an explanation of customs which would otherwise appear most puzzling. The desire for procreation, for example, finds expression in such practices as (i) polygamy, (ii) the fact that in some societies the final marriage ceremony is not performed until the wife conceives, (iii) the existence in some societies of elaborate magical rites and sacrifices which are performed as remedies against the barrenness of a wife or impotence of a husband, (iv) such institutions as the levirate union, widow-inheritance, sororate unions, and woman-to-woman marriages, and (v) the fact that most matrimonial disputes involve the major issue of custody or 'ownership' of the children.

The sixth feature of African marriage is the social and legal inferiority of the wife's status as compared with that of the husband in the marriage relationship. The practices already referred to such as polygamy, the payment of brideprice, the relative unimportance of a woman's consent to the marriage, and the levirate union are all examples of this inferior status. But quite apart from these, I think it can be stated as a general principle for most customary laws that, traditionally at any rate, a wife's authority and rights over her children, her rights of ownership and disposal of property, her right to sue and be sued in her own name, were very limited.

The seventh and final feature of customary marriage that I want to deal with is the question of divorce. Some writers have implied that ease of dissolution is a characteristic of African marriage. Husbands, they say, may turn away their wives at their will and pleasure. I would disagree with this, and venture to say that, where this occurs, it is the exception rather than the rule. Certainly, my own detailed researches into the marriage laws of several tribes in East Africa have revealed that, far from being an easy matter, divorce was traditionally either unknown altogether or only resorted to in very exceptional circumstances, e.g. where there were no children of the union. Further, that it was complicated by the fact that, since the marriage was an alliance between the family groups (as we have already seen), its dissolution and the question of the return of the brideprice and the custody of the children was very much the concern of the families. The suggestion, therefore, that a customary marriage can be dissolved 'at the will of the husband' could scarcely be further from the truth.

There are, however, two factors which certainly distinguish divorces in customary law and in English or European law. The first is the provision in customary law for conciliatory machinery and arbitration, and the fact that if this fails the marriage can be dissolved by inter-family arrangement without judicial pronouncement. The second is the fact that in most customary laws, although there must be grounds for divorce, these grounds are not as rigid and clear-cut as those recognized in English law. Furthermore, whereas, under English law, the establishment of grounds is the only factor taken into account, under most customary laws it is but one of the many factors, which may include, *inter alia*, the existence and number of children, the ability of the wife's family to return the brideprice, and the availability of remedies other than divorce.

So much for the traditional characteristics of African marriage. Let me now pass to consider the substantive part of my subject, namely, to what extent and how these characteristisc have undergone a change. I think that, broadly speaking, these changes can be considered under two separate headings:

(a) Changes due to what I shall call indirect methods. Under this head I include the influence of religion, economic influences such as the introduction of money, the establishment of modern systems of transport and communications, the opportunity of employment outside the tribe, urbanization, educational and social advancement, contact with Europeans and the outside world, and culture contact generally.

(b) Changes due to direct legislative interference by governments.

CHANGES DUE TO INDIRECT CAUSES—
RELIGION AND CULTURE CONTACT

Before embarking upon the various changes in the customary laws of marriage which I feel are attributable to this head, I should like to stress that the extent of these changes varies tremendously from one part of Africa to another, and sometimes even within different districts of the same African country, depending on the degree of contact with the outside world and the extent to which the influences of religion, education, etc., have been applied to the particular district. It goes without saying, for example, that the traditional laws of marriage of the Masai of East Africa will have changed very little as compared with the marriage laws of the advanced Kikuyu of Kenya or the Ganda of Buganda.

In determining the extent of the changes in the nature of African marriage under this head, the following matters deserve special mention.

The first is what may be termed the gradually dying influence of the family or kinship group in the marriage relationship, and the movement towards individualism. From a legal viewpoint, this is reflected in many aspects of marriage. First, in regard to consent, I think it is now true to say that generally speaking the choice of partner is left to the spouses. The custom of infant-betrothal is on the decline and, even where practised, would now be subject to the consent of the spouse upon reaching majority. Furthermore, since young men can now often provide their own brideprice, the hold that their family previously had in refusing to pay the brideprice in respect of a bride of whom they did not approve has gone. Nowadays, men often marry without the consent of their family. Secondly, since brideprice is in many instances today a cash transaction, the significance of its traditional nature as a continuing bond between the spouses' families is so no more. Thirdly, in regard to dissolution, spouses, especially wives, are no longer satisfied with family arbitration, and in many areas have defeated the family's traditional function in this respect by resorting to judicial divorces by the courts.

The second aspect of customary marriage that has undergone a marked change is the institution of brideprice. The most obvious one, to which I have already referred, is the transformation of its character from a payment of goods or services into a cash transaction. This has certainly had a marked effect on the detailed rules relating to the method of payment, replacement and return of brideprice on death or divorce, especially amongst people where the bulk of the brideprice was formerly payable in cattle.

But equally important is the fact that in some areas brideprice rates have gone up so high that there is a resulting dissatisfaction with the custom, especially amongst the younger generation. The consequence of this is that in many places, today, payment of brideprice is by agreement either postponed indefinitely or dispensed with altogether. One can foresee here that, if this practice becomes more widespread, the payment of brideprice may gradually become more of a social than a legal requirement.

A third discernible change in the customary law of marriage relates to the curtailment or total omission of the complex and long-winded formalities and ceremonial associated with the marriage. Such customs as the 'capture of the bride', the ceremonial defloration of the bride, the feasting, presentations, etc., have either become completely obsolete, or been varied substantially, and this is specially so among urban communities.

Yet a fourth change relates to the status of women. Now the complete legal emancipation of women is, of course, an extremely long and difficult process, but there are signs that African women are no less adamant and active in fighting for their rights than their European sisters. The growth of women's organizations in recent years in Africa has certainly contributed to the elimination of some of the legal restrictions applicable to women in the matrimonial relationship. For example, one of the principal reasons for the establishment of the Commission on Marriage, Divorce and the Status of Women in Uganda (to which I shall be referring later) was the constant and persistent nagging of the Uganda Council of Women!

The specific aspects of the marriage relationship where changes in this field can be detected are:

(i) that a woman's consent is now always obtained before a marriage is entered into;

(ii) that the custom of the levirate or widow-inheritance is breaking down and, where it is practised, the consent of the widow is invariably obtained;

(iii) that women can now sue and be sued in African or Local Courts, and that, so far as divorce is concerned, a wife may thus obtain the divorce without the assistance of her family.

This leads me to the last change I should like to mention under this heading—the question of divorce. Unfortunately, the changes that have occurred in the customary law on this subject have not altogether been changes for the better. There is no doubt, for example, that the rate of divorce has gone up considerably, and it has been argued with some justice that this is the result of European influence. Secondly, as I have already indicated, the role played by families in conciliation and arbitration is becoming less important, and this is certainly a most unfortunate aspect. Thirdly, the Local or African Courts are increasingly imitating the superior courts in looking at the question of divorce in terms of establishing rigid 'grounds', rather than using the more sensible traditional methods at looking at all the circumstances of the case.

CHANGES DUE TO DIRECT CAUSES—
GOVERNMENT POLICY AND LEGISLATION

I now pass to consider the changes in the nature of African marriage due to the direct policy of governments and the legislation passed to put those policies into effect. In this context, I shall be dealing only with the African common-law or Commonwealth countries. I shall treat first the position in the colonial period, and secondly developments since independence.

The Colonial Period
The British colonial policy in regard to customary marriages is best summed up by Professor Phillips, who, if I may quote him again, says:

> 'Hitherto, the predominant tendency of governments has been to avoid, as far as possible, any interference with the traditional pattern of domestic relations and to limit the intrusion of external authority into this sphere to matters which involve, not merely a conflict with European ideas and codes of behaviour, but a violation of the universal precepts of justice and morality.'[1]

But one must remember of course that this policy came into sharp conflict with the general object (or at least one of the declared objects) of a colonial power, that is of a civilizing mission. How was it possible not to interfere with the traditional pattern of customary marriage, differing as it did so materially from the European or Christian or 'civilized' (as it was often termed) pattern of marriage? In effect the answer of the British administration was to carry out the civilizing mission in this respect indirectly and gradually, that is, by expressly giving recognition to customary marriages subject to the repugnancy principle, but in addition making provision for persons, hitherto subject to customary law, to marry under an enactment providing for a monogamous or English-type marriage. The hope was that the existence side by side of the two marriage systems would gradually influence African public opinion, and that, through education and missionary influence, the monogamous type of marriage would finally prevail.

But it was natural that this policy of gradual evolution should be beset from the very start with acute problems that find expression in the marriage legislation of the ex-British colonies in Africa. Thus most

---

[1] Phillips (ed.), *Survey of African Marriage and Family Life*, p. xix.

Colonies and Protectorates had in their statute book a Marriage Ordinance regulating marriage in accordance with the general principles of English law. This form of marriage was open to all persons irrespective of race or religion. In some territories the Ordinance provided for a simplified procedure when the parties were African Christians, and in two territories, namely Kenya and Uganda, a special procedure was provided for converting a customary marriage into a monogamous marriage. Whilst these Ordinances generally gave specific recognition to marriages contracted under customary law, they emphasized that the option given to Africans to marry under the Ordinance did not merely involve the obligations of monogamy, but also acceptance of all other aspects of the English law relating to marriage. Thus Africans who married under the Ordinance were subjected to the same rules of English law relating to age, prohibited degrees, consents and form. Moreover, they were incapable, during the continuance of the Ordinance marriage, of contracting marriages under customary law under penalty of five years' imprisonment. In other words, the law of bigamy was extended to include a customary marriage following a monogamous marriage. Furthermore, it was expressly or impliedly provided that Africans who contracted a monogamous marriage were subjected to the same law of divorce as non-Africans (the divorce law again being based on English law). Even more absurd was the provision in certain African territories, such as Nyasaland (now Malawi) and Nigeria, to the effect that where a person, hitherto subject to customary law, contracted a statutory marriage and then died intestate, the English law of succession would be applied to the distribution of his property. Indeed, dicta in certain West African cases, exemplified by the old case of *Cole v. Cole*,[1] suggested that the marriage of Africans under the Ordinance 'clothed the parties with a status unknown in native law', and that the Ordinance marriage negatived the application of customary law to them in all matters relating to personal status.

There were two other disturbing aspects of the legislation affecting customary marriage. The first was that even though customary marriages were expressly recognized, the legislature (and indeed the judges of the superior courts) went out of their way to emphasize the superiority of a statutory marriage over a customary marriage. Mention has already been made of the dicta of certain judges stressing that customary marriages were no marriages at all; but, over and above that, certain statutory provisions stressed the same fact. For example, the

[1] (1898) 1 N.L.R. 15.

African Christian Marriage and Divorce Act of Kenya[1] provides that when a registrar addresses parties to a customary marriage who wish to convert that marriage into a statutory one, he should say, 'Whereas you, A.B. and you C.D. profess that you have been heretofore married to each other by African law and custom, and whereas that marriage does not bind you by law to each other as man and wife so long as both of you shall live, and whereas you desire to bind yourselves legally each to the other as man and wife so long as both of you shall live. . . .'

The second disturbing feature was that, for the purposes of certain legislation enacting general territorial law, a marriage under customary law was not a marriage within the meaning of the particular enactment. For example, some Penal Codes, such as the Penal Code of Uganda, provided that for the purpose of the Code—the general criminal law of the territory—a wife married under customary law was no wife at all, and hence the rules of criminal law relating to such things as conspiracies, compulsion, etc., did not apply to those so married.

It is unnecessary for me to go into a detailed criticism of this conflicting marriage legislation, except to mention that its introduction resulted in going far beyond the original intention of providing Africans with the option of monogamy. Needless to say, many aspects of the relevant laws were ignored, or not enforced. Indeed, if the object of the legislation was primarily to encourage a move from polygamy to monogamy, it was a failure since Africans who married under such Ordinances almost invariably took subsequent wives under customary law, and the penal provisions regarding this aspect of bigamy were never enforced.

Perhaps the most unfortunate aspect of the legislation has been the inculcation in the African mind of the notion of the superiority of the Ordinance marriage and the inferiority of the customary marriage. Africans themselves, especially amongst the educated class, have got to the stage where, although unwilling to dispense with customary law marriage they regard marriage under the Ordinance as a sign of prestige and respectability. It is important to stress, however, that the reason for this was not that one was monogamous and the other polygamous but that the authorities seemed to regard the Ordinance marriage (or the 'Government marriage' as Africans called it) as more important.

Another method by which an attempt was made to regulate the application of the customary marriage law in the colonial period was through local legislation. This again was directed not so much at the content of the marriage law, as at the imposition of additional admini-

[1] Cap. 151.

strative measures. The best examples are measures to enforce the registration of customary marriages and divorces, and attempts to control the payment of brideprice.

Provisions for registration of customary marriages were thus introduced in various territories such as Tanganyika, Kenya and the Rhodesias. Some of these were voluntary, and did not affect the validity of the marriage. Others were compulsory, and the sanction of nullity was imposed in default of registration. Generally speaking, however, whether voluntary or compulsory, the legislation was ignored and ineffective.

Attempts to limit brideprice by local legislation have met with equal failure. Even in areas where brideprice had reached alarmingly high rates, the legislation was ignored. The most recent list of failures comes from Southern Nigeria where I understand nobody takes the slightest notice of the imposed limit of £30.

Before leaving the colonial period, let me say that, apart from the measures I have indicated, it is generally fair to say that the era—as compared with the comparatively short era of independence—is characterized by the lack of governmental initiative in the major problems arising out of the application of the customary laws of marriage and the relationship of these latter with the statutory laws of marriage. Thus, apart from sporadic attempts by individuals or organizations, there was no governmental initiative for the systematic study or recording of the customary marriage laws, which remained to a very large extent unwritten and were treated in the courts as a matter of fact rather than of law.

The Period of Independence

With the attainment of independence by many of the ex-colonial territories in the late 1950s and early 1960s, we find a new approach to the question of the customary laws of marriage. Unlike the colonial governments, which were inhibited by the fact that they were a foreign power and should not directly interfere with the domestic life and laws of the people they were governing, the independent African governments adopted policies of direct interference in these matters. The extent of this interference in the laws relating to marriage has varied from one country to another, but broadly speaking the action taken by the various African governments can be classed under three categories:

(a) Restatement of the Customary Law of Marriage

First, there are those countries that have taken the view that the greatest defect in the customary law of marriage lay in the fact that it was unwritten and hence difficult to ascertain; that it would not be possible to initiate sound reform before such laws were ascertained; and that consequently the first step was to initiate projects of recording or restating the different customary marriage laws in the country. Countries included in this category are Tanzania, Kenya, Malawi, Zambia, Bechuanaland, Swaziland, Basutoland, Sierra Leone and Eastern Nigeria. In this connection, special mention must be made of the work undertaken by the Restatement of African Law Project of this School under the direction of Professor A. N. Allott. Indeed, most of the countries I have mentioned have undertaken the work of recording in close collaboration with this Restatement Project.

(b) *Unification of Customary Laws of Marriage*

Most of the countries included in the first category have not got beyond the stage of restatement. But there is one country, namely Tanzania, which has moved into a second stage, that of unification of its different customary marriage laws. I do not wish to go into details in describing this Unification Project here, as this has been adequately covered by myself and others elsewhere. Briefly, the original intention was to start with the first stage that I have described, i.e. the restatement of each customary law by a group of experts, before going on to the second stage of preparation of a unified draft based on the restated laws. Unfortunately, however, the Government was so anxious that unification should be achieved as quickly as possible that the project gradually changed character, and the unification in the later stages consisted in persuading the different ethnic groups to accept an already unified draft without prior detailed investigation and restatement. The result of this unification, so far as the law of marriage is concerned, is contained in a Schedule to the Local Customary Law Declaration Order, 1963, which deals with the subjects of bridewealth, marriage, divorce and the status of children. It has now been adopted by all the patrilineal tribes of Tanzania, and is gradually being extended or 'sold' (as Professor Allott aptly puts it)[1] to the matrilineal tribes.

The most interesting part of this document is that, although it purports to be a mere unification of different customary laws, it in fact introduces major reforms and rules unknown to any of the customary laws which it purports to unify. Let me give you a few examples of the new provisions:

[1] See Allott, *Towards the Unification of Laws in Africa*, I.C.L.Q. Vol. 14, p. 367 at p. 376.

(1) Although a girl requires parental consent to marry before she is 21 years of age, she is free to marry without parental consent after that age.

(2) Payment of bridewealth is not essential to the validity of a marriage.

(3) Customary ceremonies connected with marriage cannot legalize the union. No customary marriage is valid unless it is registered.

(4) No customary divorce is valid unless it is registered and a divorce certificate obtained.

It may well be, of course, that these reforms are sound and necessary in Tanzania, but the question remains, firstly whether this was the right way of introducing reforms, i.e. by pretending that they merely represent a unification of the different customary laws, and, secondly, whether in any case the unified version will in fact be followed or will merely exist on paper. It is unfair to prejudge this issue, since the unifications have not been in operation for long enough. The reports I have received, however, do indicate that many people have either never heard of these unifications or, if they have, seem to think that they apply in neighbouring districts, but not in their own!

(c) *Unification of Statutory and Customary Laws of Marriage*

The third category or method of reform of the marriage laws consists not merely in restating or unifying the customary laws, but in introducing a new law of marriage which attempts the integration or unification of the different systems of marriage within a country whether statutory, customary or religious. This type of reform has been suggested or attempted in two Commonwealth African countries, namely Ghana and Uganda.

In Ghana the first step in this direction came in May 1961 when the Government published a White Paper which was intended 'to provoke discussion on the question of marriage and divorce and the related problem of inheritance'. 'These questions' (the White Paper continued) 'touch the very roots of Ghanaian society and it is the Government's intention that they should be freely and dispassionately discussed.'

This was followed a year later by the publication of the Marriage, Divorce and Inheritance Bill, which broadly speaking contained the suggestions outlined in the White Paper. It proposed that a man might register only one marriage, and would thus accord public recognition only to the wife whose name appears on the Register. But the Bill was not designed to abolish polygamy, in the sense that there would be nothing to prevent this man from marrying subsequent wives by customary law. Only the registered wife, however, would be entitled to inheritance under the Bill.

The Bill preserved the concept of arbitration and attempted reconciliation in divorce matters. Thus a husband or wife could petition any High Court Judge for a divorce. On receipt of the petition, the Judge was to appoint a divorce committee, of which he should be Chairman, to arbitrate in the matter and attempt a reconciliation. The object of the Bill was clearly to discourage divorce, and the Memorandum to the Bill stated that 'it is considered that Ghana should set an example by approaching marriage in a constructive way. The proposed legislation would accentuate the aim of reconciliation and the sanctity of marriage. Divorce would be treated as a last resort.'

But apart from dealing with these two major matters, and also imposing a new scheme of intestate succession, and making provision for the making of wills, the Bill was not a complete code of the law of marriage and divorce, and left out any matters such as the question of consents, prohibited degrees, payment of brideprice and details of formalities. The Bill, however, made provision for these matters to be dealt with by Ministerial regulations.

When this Bill was first introduced in May 1962, it aroused such opposition from so many quarters that it was withdrawn. Another attempt at introducing it, with minor amendments, was made in January 1963. One of the more important of these admendments was that the new version laid down a minimum age of 16 for all marriages. But, again, there was much opposition, and the Bill was withdrawn once more. Yet a third attempt to introduce it was made in June 1963, when, for the third time, the opposition was so great that the Bill was withdrawn, probably for the last time.

The abortive history of the Ghana Bill clearly demonstrates the difficulties in trying to introduce revolutionary changes in the laws of marriage. The moral to other countries is quite plain—that no matter how important and desirable African governments feel it to be necessary to unify and reform their marriage laws, such ends cannot be achieved if they are ahead of public opinion.

Turning to Uganda, in January 1964, a Commission was appointed by the President with the following terms of reference:

'To consider the laws and customs regulating marriage, divorce and the status of women in Uganda, bearing in mind the need to ensure that those laws and customs while preserving existing traditions and practices, as far as possible, should be consistent with justice and morality and appropriate to the position of Uganda as an independent nation and to make recommendations.'

The Commission was composed of six members, including one woman and including Mr V. C. R. A. C. Crabbe, a Ghanaian lawyer working for the Government of Uganda as Legal Draftsman. Mr Crabbe, as well as being a member, was the Secretary to the Commission. I mention this specifically since the fact that Mr Crabbe was a Ghanaian is rather important.

On July 30, 1965, one year and a half after its appointment, the Commission presented its report to the President, and this was duly published.[1]

The Report is a document of 133 pages. Chapter I is an introduction explaining the work of the Commission; Chapter II, entitled 'Marriage', examines the different systems of marriage existing in Uganda under the statutory law, customary law, Hindu law and Islamic law, and offers some criticism of the existing state of affairs; Chapter II, entitled 'Divorce', again examines divorce under the different systems; Chapter IV, on the status of women, criticises this status under customary law; Chapter V is entitled 'Dowry' and examines very briefly its nature and the problems which arise therefrom; and, finally, Chapter VI contains the Recommendations of the Commission.

Now in the ordinary course of events I should have spent much time examining these recommendations in detail. If, however, I did that you would, I think, find that I would be repeating myself, for the recommendations on marriage and divorce, and to some extent on inheritance, are closely modelled on the provisions of the abortive Marriage, Divorce and Inheritance Bill of Ghana.[2] Why Ghana, in particular, I think no one can answer but Mr Crabbe!

Now, of course, there is nothing uncommon about one country's adopting the ideas of another. Indeed, in colonial times, most government draftsmen looked for precedents in other colonial territories, but I feel that this method may not work so well when one is trying to legislate on a subject like marriage and its unification, in which the problems in each country may be different. There is no doubt that many of the problems in this field are particular to Ghana or Uganda. For example, one of the principal problems in Ghana arises out of the

[1] Report of the Commission on Marriage, Divorce and the Status of Women 1965, Government Printer, Entebbe.

[2] For assessment of Recommendations, see Morris, *Report of the Commission on Marriage, Divorce and the Status of Women* [1966] J.A.L. pp. 3–7.

fact that many tribes are matrilineal and there is a growing dissatisfaction with the matrilineal system. None of the Uganda tribes, however, is matrilineal. Another example is that, whereas in Uganda the
question of brideprice constitutes an acute problem in certain areas
where the rates are rising, there is no such problem in Ghana. In the
Uganda report, the Commissioners do recognize the problem and
raise it in their chapter on 'Dowry', but the recommendations have
nothing to say on this topic. Even if the problems of Ghana and
Uganda in this field of marriage were the same, it seems to me totally
unnecessary to appoint a Commission to investigate the matter for
one year, and a half, to receive evidence from all sorts of people and
organizations, only to come up with recommendations adopted in
many cases verbatim from proposed legislation in another country,
which itself proved unsuccessful and was finally abandoned.

The Uganda Report is now under consideration by the Uganda
Government and, as it has only been published recently, it is too early
to assess how it has been received. My own feeling is that it will have
precisely the same fate as its Ghana counterpart, but we shall simply
have to wait and see.

The Future

I should like to conclude this paper by offering some thoughts, rather
than suggestions, for the future.

It is obvious, I think, from what I have said so far, that the laws of
marriage inherited from the colonial period by the African countries are
badly in need of reform. I do not think that anybody would quarrel
with this statement, and there is no doubt that most African governments recognize this fact. What is more controversial is first the method
that should be adopted for reform, and secondly what the reformed law
should contain.

As regards methods, I feel that those countries which have taken
the view that the initial need is to ascertain, and authoritatively restate,
the different customary laws of marriage, have certainly taken the
first step in the right direction. It is a truism to say that you cannot reform the law without knowing what it is. I feel this is well demonstrated in the Uganda marriage report, where the Commission purports
to describe in Chapter II the customary laws of fifteen districts in
about eight pages. In some cases only one or two paragraphs are
devoted to a whole tribe.

But I also feel that the authoritative restatement of the customary
laws of marriage should only be the first step. The restatements might,

for example, reveal that there is a very wide scope for unification. Such unification should certainly be accomplished where feasible, provided care is taken that it should not amount to an imposition—as seems to have happened in the later stages of the Tanganyika unification project.

The next stage should be that of reform, where I feel the reformer, whether he be a Commissioner or one of several Commissioners, or a draftsman or a legislator, should sit down and suggest reforms not only to the restated or unified customary laws but also to the introduced English law.

The next question is what the new law should contain. I have already warned against the danger of generalization here, and shown how, for example, the problems in Ghana and Uganda are different. We have also seen that legislation, such as that attempted in Ghana, which tries to unify the laws of marriage and produce reforms unacceptable to the people, is a non-starter.

The answer must surely lie in the introduction of what has been referred to as an 'integrated' rather than a 'unified' law of marriage, by which is meant a law that would bring together under one enactment the different marriage and divorce laws, customary and non-customary, with a view to laying down rules governing all marriages and divorces, where feasible, and leaving the matters where unification cannot at present be achieved to the personal law of the parties.

We have seen earlier that the customary law of marriage has developed sufficiently in certain fields to make it feasible for it to be unified with the statutory law without much difficulty. Such matters as procedural requirements, minimum age, the question of consent, can and should be unified. On other matters such as monogamy or polygamy, the payment of brideprice and the prohibited degrees, no complete unification is possible, and the integrated law should provide that these must be left to the personal law of the parties. The personal law would not be difficult to ascertain, because, as I have indicated, a pre-condition for this type of reform is that the customary laws will already have been authoritatively recorded. Rather than perpetuate the different status of wives according to whether they were married monogamously or polygamously, as the Ghana Bill attempted to do by distinguishing between a registered and a non-registered wife, a new integrated law should ensure that, whether a marriage is monogamous or polygamous, it should enjoy the same legal status and have the same legal consequences.

On the question of divorce, I feel much can be learnt from the abortive Ghana Bill. As I have indicated earlier one of the unfortunate trends of customary divorce is the weakening of the family system of reconciliation and arbitration. If the concept of family arbitration can be revived and made the basis of divorce in a new integrated law, then perhaps one could justifiably point to this valuable concept to show how a reformed law of marriage and divorce could as usefully draw from the good aspects of customary law as it does from the imported English law, to produce a law which is more in line with the requirements and conditions of the people of Africa.

Postscript

Since delivering this paper a Commission to review the law of marriage has been set up in Kenya with the following terms of reference:

'To consider the existing laws relating to marriage, divorce and matters relating thereto.

'To make recommendations for a new law providing a comprehensive and, so far as may be practicable, a uniform law of marriage and divorce applicable to all persons in Kenya, which will replace the existing law on the subject comprising customary law, Islamic law, Hindu law and the relevant Acts of Parliament and to prepare a draft of the new law.

'To pay particular attention to the status of women in relation to marriage and divorce in a free democratic society.'

The Commission consists of fourteen members under the Chairmanship of Mr Justice Spry. The writer is a member of, and Secretary to, the Commission.

2

MARRIAGE LAW IN UGANDA:
SIXTY YEARS OF ATTEMPTED REFORM[1]

H. F. MORRIS

Lecturer in African Law
School of Oriental and African Studies

In January 1964, the Uganda Government set up a Commission with the following terms of reference:

> 'To consider the laws and customs regulating marriage, divorce and the status of women in Uganda, bearing in mind to ensure that those laws and customs while preserving existing traditions and practices as far as possible should be consistent with justice and morality and approprite to the position of Uganda as an independent nation and to make recommendations.'[2]

The establishment of this Commission represents the latest development in a lengthy, if somewhat leisurely and singularly unsuccessful, battle fought during the last sixty years in an attempt to rationalize what virtually all bodies of opinion in Uganda agree to be a particularly inept body of statutory law on the subject of marriage and divorce. It is proposed in this paper to review this period of gentlemanly warfare.

It all began with a dispatch from the Marquess of Lansdowne, the Foreign Secretary, in 1902 to the effect that 'the time has come to provide facilities for the intermarriage in Uganda of parties neither of

[1] The material for this paper has been obtained largely from the Entebbe Secretariat records. Of the file series consulted, the most important to this subject are the following: the unnumbered 'Special Files' entitled 'Marriage 1902–4' and 'Divorce', D.177/1, D.177/4, D.221 and 473.

[2] Since this paper was delivered, the Commission has published its recommendations. These recommendations follow closely the provisions of the Ghana Marriage, Inheritance and Divorce Bill first introduced in the National Assembly of that country in 1962, subsequently modified and finally withdrawn. The Uganda Government has invited the public to comment on the Commission's recommendations. For an assessment of the recommendations see E. Cotran, *The Changing Nature of African Marriage*, pp. 30, 31 above. See also H. F. Morris, *Report of the Commission on Marriage, Divorce and the Status of Women* [1966] J.A.L. pp. 3–7.

whom is a British subject under forms and ceremonies which (would be valid in) English law . . . The accompanying draft Ordinance based on a Colonial Office model . . . may be promulgated.'

Colonel Hayes Sadler, the Commissioner, did not at first appreciate the full significance of the dispatch for he assumed, not unreasonably, that the draft Ordinance was intended to apply only to non-Africans, and the Ordinance was, accordingly, duly promulgated. The Ordinance followed the usual pattern for colonial territories and was the lineal descendant of the Gold Coast Marriage Ordinance of 1884. Provision was made for the registration of marriage before registrars after the completion of certain formalities, such marriages being valid only if they complied with the English law in such matters as kindred and affinity; to contract a further marriage either under the Ordinance or by native law and custom was a criminal offence. If was also an offence to marry under the Ordinance while married under native law and custom to another person. Succession to the property of persons married under the Ordinance was to be in accordance with the English law of succession. But Hayes Sadler was mistaken in thinking that the Ordinance was not to apply to Africans and a storm of protest broke about his head, directed by Alfred Tucker, the Bishop of Uganda. It must, of course, be remembered that in the early years of the Protectorate the Missions, and in particular the Church Missionary Society, played a vital part in the framing and implementing of Protectorate policy, and the Anglican Bishop of Uganda was, in practice, in the position of honorary adviser to the Commissioner. To attempt to implement legislation against the wishes of the Bishop, particularly on such a matter as marriage, would have been unthinkable.

Tucker had various objections to the legislation. In the first place, the procedure was cumbersome, burdensome and impracticable, and the fees were too heavy. In the second place, the Ordinance was, in his opinion, in breach of the Buganda Agreement in that the English law of intestate succession was to be substituted for customary law and the imposition of a fee was, he felt, a form of interior taxation which the Agreement did not permit the Protectorate Government to levy without Buganda's consent. But what apparently worried the Bishop most was that the Ordinance legalized marriage between a man and his deceased wife's sister; and it is this objection which will first be considered, though it is perhaps rather hard for us today to understand the heat which this particular issue engendered. In 1902, when the Secretary of State sent his draft Marriage Ordinance, marriage with a deceased wife's sister was still unlawful in England, but, since a change in this respect was then contemplated, the draft Ordinance anticipated the change and stated specifically that the rules regarding kindred and affinity were to be those under English law except that a man could marry his deceased wife's sister or her niece. It may be mentioned here that there was bitter opposition in England to these changes and that marriage with a deceased wife's sister was legalized only in 1907. In many African societies, marriage to a wife's sister is not merely permitted but is considered to be particularly desirable. This was the position which the Christian missions had found in Buganda, and for the previous forty years they had exhorted their converts to abandon this anti-canonical practice. But here was the Government undermining their good work and not merely countenancing such unions but proclaiming specifically that such marriages were valid. It was hardly surprising that the Bishop was incensed, and indeed Hayes Sadler fully sympathized with him. After nearly a year of correspondence with the Foreign Office and the Commissioner of the East Africa Protectorate, who had received a similar draft Marriage Ordinance but, without a Bishop Tucker at his elbow, was at a loss to understand what all the fuss over deceased wives' sisters was about, Hayes Sadler hit on a rather extraordinary compromise. Africans would be excluded from this form of marriage available to those of other races: thus Europeans, who for centuries had been prevented from contracting such marriages, would be allowed to do so, but Africans, who for at least as long a time had been accustomed to such marriages, were to be prevented from contracting them. The matter, however, was decided in England. The question was discussed with heat in the House of Commons and in the House of Lords, where the Archbishop of Canterbury expressed his grave concern at such legislation being enacted in African territories, and the Commissioner was instructed to repeal the section concerned.

Bishop Tucker's other objections to the original Ordinance were also met to the Bishop's satisfaction. A separate Native Marriage Ordinance was enacted providing for the formalities preliminary to marriage to be dispensed with in the case of African Christians marrying in Church; and marriage fees were substantially reduced, although the Commissioner could not agree that the imposition of such fees was a form of interior taxation contrary to the Agreement. Perhaps the most important change was that the section imposing succession by English law was repealed and a Succession Ordinance based on the Indian Succession Act was introduced soon afterwards, but with application only to non-Africans.

The Secretary of State's original dispatch had suggested that the enactment of the draft ordinance he had enclosed would probably necessitate a Divorce Ordinance, and the Judge in Uganda accordingly drafted one on the model of the Indian Divorce Act of 1869. This Ordinance, which was enacted in 1904, in fact reflected very closely the English law of divorce as it stood at that time: that is to say, divorce could only be obtained if the respondent were guilty of adultery and, if the petitioner were the wife, then adultery by the husband was not in itself sufficient but had to be coupled with some other form of wrongdoing such as cruelty. The introduction of the Ordinance was accepted by the Missions with resignation, Bishop Tucker writing to the Commissioner as follows: 'As you very rightly observe, it will not be popular with the Missions! I feel, however, that it is no use struggling against the inevitable and the law of England being what it is I look upon a Divorce Act out here as one of those things which must come sooner or later.'

With the passage of the Marriage and Divorce of Mohammedans Ordinance in 1906, the body of marriage law was completed—apart from the addition of a Hindu Marriage and Divorce Ordinance in 1961—and has remained in force almost unchanged to the present day. That this body of laws is in many ways highly unsatisfactory has for many years been generally recognized. Since its defects have, on several occasions, been explored and discussed,[1] I do not propose to dwell on this aspect of the subject. In order to throw light on later developments, however, some of the major defects and problems must be briefly listed. First, there is the general question of conflict between the statutory and customary law of marriage, since Africans marrying under the Marriage Ordinances have almost invariably coupled their statutory marriage with a customary marriage contract, paying the customary marriage consideration. Then there has, in the past, been the question of whether the native courts should have any jurisdiction in respect of the customary law side of such 'dual marriages' and, in particular, whether, on the parties separating without a divorce under the Divorce Ordinance, a native court should have the power to order the return of the marriage consideration. Then there is the fact that, although it is a criminal offence to marry another wife by customary law during the existence of a statutory marriage, this practice is widespread and the penal section of the Marriage Ordinance has practically never been invoked. There is also the question of whether the law

---

[1] See Morris and Read: *Uganda: the Development of its Laws and Constitution*, pp. 395-9.

provides adequate safeguards for the welfare of a wife or widow. Finally, there is the fact that the law of divorce has remained virtually unchanged since 1904, and is now very different from the law in England and in most African common law countries.

These, and other similar problems, became apparent in the succeeding years, but during the decade immediately following the enactment of these Ordinances there was little criticism of the law as it stood. Those were days when administrators, as well as missionaries, believed that the inherent virtues of Christianity and Western civilization would soon lead to the replacement of indigenous customs such as polygamy. The outlook of the administrator of the inter-war period, however, tended to be very different. Unlike his pre-war counterpart, he was not likely to be a regular churchgoer, and frequently had little sympathy with either the missionaries or their activities. It was the period we associate with the doctrine of 'indirect rule', although it was not so much a doctrine that was involved here as an attitude of mind, an attitude which had a profound effect on the outlook of the average administrator towards matters such as family law. The pre-British, or rather pre-missionary, period tended to be idealized by many of these officers who, like the Irish Celtic revivalists of a slightly earlier period, often built up for themselves a somewhat synthetic and romanticized version of what the way of life in the old society had been. Institutions such as bridewealth, and the mystical symbolism believed to be associated with it, appeared to many European administrators to be more attractive than the often rather forbidding and puritanical tenets of the missionaries, who were at times accused of having undermined customary virtues and brought about the destruction of established values rather than the substitution of higher ones. It was, accordingly, from the ranks of the administration that the existing body of marriage law came under attack during this period. As far as articulate African opinion was concerned, this, certainly in Buganda and the Western Kingdoms, tended, as expressed through the native governments, to side with the Missions. Attention in this period was first focused on the question of marriage law when an extraordinary judgment was delivered by Mr Justice Guthrie Smith in 1923. Although this case, *Bishan Singh v. R.*, aroused widespread criticism and was later described by the Governor of Uganda 'as hopelessly and utterly wrong', and although it in fact lay like a shadow over the administration for more than a decade, it has never been reported, and it therefore seems to merit discussion in some detail. A Muganda Roman Catholic had married a Mugwere Protestant by Bagwere custom and the trial court was satisfied that a marriage valid by customary law had taken place. A little later the wife left her husband to live with Bishan Singh, a Sikh. The husband thereupon instituted proceedings against the Sikh for adultery under the Indian Penal Code, which was then in force in Uganda, and the trial magistrate convicted him. Mr Justice Guthrie Smith, however, allowed his appeal, giving judgment in the following terms:

'The magistrate convicted the Sikh because the woman left her husband's house and went to live with him. Such an application of the rigours of the Penal Code to the protection of a mere casual and temporary liaison strikes one as startling and contrary to British ideas of morality. . . . The Native Marriage Ordinance of 1903 provides that marriages between native Christians may be celebrated by a minister of the religion of the parties and without formalities as to notice prescribed by the Marriage Ordinance 1902. The combined effect of these Ordinances is that marriages valid from the British point of view can only be effected under the Ordinance of 1902 except that native Christians may if they please marry under the Ordinance of 1903. The Ordinances are silent as to marriage of pagans; hence if two pagans marry by native custom they will have all the rights which flow from such a marriage under native law. The Ordinances are, however, imperative as to native Christians and so a marriage between Christians celebrated according to native custom is a nullity and no rights can be acquired thereby. Applying this to the present cast the marriage between the complainant and the woman was invalid and so no offence was committed by the Sikh in taking her away from him. Another argument leading to the same conclusion is that when people cease to be pagans and profess a religion which teaches monogamy and the sanctity of marriage, they must be taken to have abandoned the right to contract non-permanent unions such as are recognized and permitted under pagan customs.'[1]

It is certainly hard to see how a law which provides facilities for persons of a certain religion to have their marriages celebrated and registered can be interpreted as denying the right to contract any other form of marriage and, as has already been mentioned, there was a storm of protest from the administration. Indeed few judgments can have had so much time and ink spent on them by law officers of the Crown as had Guthrie Smith's. At one time it was proposed to get the

[1] Uganda High Court Criminal Appeal No. 13 of 1923.

judgment over-ruled, and at another to pass legislation vitiating it; but eventually, in the late 1930s, it was allowed to die a natural death. At the time, however, it had to be taken seriously and district commissioners sent out instructions to their native authorities that no Christian could marry by customary law and that, if he purported to do so, no rights could be enforced as a result. Some maintained that as a result of this judgment the penal sections of the Marriage Ordinance, making it an offence to marry another woman by native custom after a statutory marriage or to contract a statutory marriage during the existence of a customary marriage to another woman, were now in practice nullified, since Africans contracting statutory marriages would normally be Christians and would, therefore, be incapable of a customary marriage. If, therefore, after a marriage in Church an African *purported* to marry another woman by customary law, this could only be a merely adulterous liaison and could not come within the scope of the penal section. Although this view was derided by certain law officers, it was apparently held by Abrahams, the Attorney-General (later Chief Justice) who informed the Bishop of Uganda, in a case where a Muganda had married by native custom and then married another woman in church and the Bishop wanted criminal proceedings to be taken against him, that the Muganda had committed no offence since, being a Christian, there had been no marriage with the first so-called wife, the relationship being that of mere concubinage.

A problem which in particular perplexed the administration was that of the jurisdiction of the native courts in marriage matters. Under the Courts Proclamations the native courts had no jurisdiction in matters concerning statutory marriage. This was generally held to exclude from their jurisdiction cases concerning claims for return of the customary marriage consideration where the parties had contracted an ordinance marriage and had parted company without getting a divorce under the Divorce Ordinance. There was, however, considerable doubt and much high feeling on this matter and many conflicting opinions were given during the years by the law officers. The matter was finally solved by the Native Courts Ordinance of 1940—an ordinance originally conceived in 1929 as a full-blooded declaration of the independence of the native courts from judicial control on the Tanganyika model and in accordance with the purest principles of indirect rule, but which appeared on the statute book only after a decade of negotiation and in the most emasculated form. It did, however, establish the principle that native courts had jurisdiction even in cases of statutory marriages in matters concerning brideprice and adultery.

This now brings us to the question of adultery. In the 1920s it had been thought in some districts that the provisions in the old legislation preventing native courts from dealing with statutory marriages meant that they could not even deal with cases of adultery where had been such a marriage. This had not mattered so much while the Indian Penal Code had been in force in Uganda and adultery was a criminal offence under the territorial law, but the change-over to the new Penal Code based on English law in 1930 had meant the disappearance of this crime from the code—for, despite strong protests from all the East African governments, the Secretary of State had, with curious obstinacy, refused to depart from strict English law in this respect. So in Acholi District, where native courts carefully refused to hear adultery cases where there was an ordinance marriage, it was said that it had become the current pastime to commit adultery with women married by Christian rites. The pathetic story, indeed, became current of the Acholi Christian husband who had been shortsighted enough to commit adultery with a pagan and who was, as a result, languishing in the native administration gaol, with the chagrin of knowing that his wife was regularly sleeping with a neighbour and that he had no effective redress. The position at first, in fact, had appeared to be even more serious. The Chief Justice maintained that if—and he very strongly advised against it—adultery were to be omitted from the new Penal Code, then native courts would lose all jurisdiction to deal with adultery as a crime, since to do so would entail conflict with the territorial law in which adultery would no longer be so regarded. The ingenuity of the Attorney-General, however, came to the rescue on this point. Since the new Code stated that nothing in the Code should affect liability for offences against the common law, he was able to rule that 'the new draft Penal Code especially recognizes common law offences. "Common law" may be interpreted as "customary law" so native custom cannot be disregarded in native criminal courts.' It would be interesting to know how a court would have reacted to an argument that common law and customary law were apparently interchangeable terms; but however this may be, this was the answer the administration wanted.

The existence, but non-enforcement, of the penal section of the Marriage Ordinance against marriage by customary law to another woman during the duration of a statutory marriage, though irritating to the purist, was of little practical importance. It therefore came as a considerable shock to the administration when, in 1934, an attempt was made to apply the section. A Muganda lorry driver had married in

1914 under the Ordinance. In 1919, so it was said, 'he started marrying other women by native law and custom'. His legal wife apparently made no complaint and, indeed, appeared with her husband in some of the later wedding photographs. Then, in 1934, she started divorce proceedings—at the instigation, it was said, of the Church Missionary Society. The magistrate dismissed the petition on the grounds of connivance and condonation, but with surprising officiousness sent the papers to the Attorney-General for the institution of proceedings under the Ordinance against the husband. The matter was referred to the Chief Secretary and eventually to the Governor. 'I have never heard of a prosecution under this section,' one official minuted in alarm, 'and I am quite sure a prosecution would be the reverse of salutary from the point of view of enhancing the status of legal marriages in native eyes. Already it is difficult enough for the missions to persuade natives to marry according to Christian rites.' No prosecution was, accordingly, undertaken.

Problems such as these, and the high feeling which they aroused, were symptomatic of the wider and deeper unease which the administration felt about the existing legal position. Perhaps the prevailing mood, which was by no means confined to Uganda, could be fairly expressed in these terms. In the first place, it was felt that the original legislation had been framed, often under mission influence, without the acceptance, or indeed the knowledge, of the African population most affected by it. Secondly, just because a proportion of the African population had adopted Christianity and wanted their marriages blessed by their church, it was felt that this was no reason why the state should oust their own indigenous law, and impose upon them an alien body of law—alien not only in compelling monogamy, but also in introducing completely foreign rules as to how kindred and affinity permit or prevent marriage. Thirdly, if the Christian churches required their converts to follow rules of monogamy or other rules of moral behaviour, then, according to this argument, it was up to them to enforce this discipline by their teaching and precept without having to rely upon penal sanctions prescribed by the state. Marriage should, therefore, entail a purely civil ceremony, which for the vast majority of Africans would be the customary marriage contract for which provision for registration would have to be made, though a civil monogamous marriage under the Marriage Ordinance before a registrar of marriages would also be available for an African couple who specifically wanted it. Whatever the form of the civil marriage, the role of the Church in providing facilities for a Christian marriage ceremony would, from a legal point of view, be purely incidental. Those in East Africa who held this view naturally looked to Nyasaland as the pioneer and example. This territory originally had a Marriage Ordinance and a Christian Native Marriages Ordinance on the usual pattern. The Christian Native Marriages Ordinance, however, differed from the Uganda Native Marriage Ordinance on one— apparently small—point. It required the minister of religion celebrating the marriage to forward a certificate to the district officer stating that he was satisfied that, among other things, the parties to the marriage fully understood the grounds upon which they could obtain a divorce. Since the dominant missions in Nyasaland were high Anglican and Roman Catholic, to both of whom divorce was anathema, this requirement was particularly objectionable to them and their practice, therefore, was to ignore it and to celebrate marriages regardless of the law's requirements. It was for this reason, among others, that the Nyasaland Government decided in 1923 to repeal the Christian Native Marriages Ordinance and to replace it by the Native Marriage (Christian Rites) Registration Ordinance, which allowed ministers of religion to perform a ceremony of marriage between Africans which in itself had no legal consequences, it being presumed that the couple would also be united by customary law, to which they would be subject in their civil relations.

This Nyasaland expedient seemed so attractive to the prevailing frame of mind in administrative circles in the late 1920s and 1930s that the Ta nganyika Government got as far as putting forward a draft bill on the Nyasaland model,[1] and in Uganda it was felt that, if only mission ry opposition could be overcome, here the solution lay.

In the late 1930s increasing interest was being shown, in England and in international circles, in indigenous African institutions and in the rights of the individual—and in particular of the woman—thereunder. If these institutions had their champions in the colonial administrations of the day, they also had their powerful critics. The St Joan's Social and Political Alliance presented their Statement on the Status of the Women of Native Races to the League of Nations in 1937 and later joined issue with the Colonial Office on the question of forced marriages under customary law, maintaining that certain colonial administrations, including that of Uganda, had presented a misleading and unduly complacent statement of the existing position. It was at this time that Martin Parr, Governor of the Equatorial Province of the

[1] There was at first a good deal of support from the Tanganyika missions for the Bill, but opinion changed and the Bill was as a result withdrawn.

Sudan, carried out his investigation into the marriage and divorce of Christian members of African tribal communities with special reference to the position in Uganda. His report in fact typified the administrative officer's approach to the subject which has been outlined above and was highly critical of the existing legal position in Uganda.

The stage would seem to have been set, therefore, in the late 1930s for a reappraisal and comprehensive reform of the existing law in Uganda. Moreover, in 1935 Sir Philip Mitchell had come to Uganda from Tanganyika as Governor. Mitchell had not merely been associated as Secretary for Native Affairs with Cameron's policy of introducing (as he believed) indirect rule into East Africa, but had supplied much of the intellectual justification for many of the measures designed to strengthen or recreate what were thought to be indigenous institutions in Tanganyika. It was not, therefore, surprising that when promoted as Governor of Uganda he should have turned his attention to the existing marriage law in the Protectorate and have decided that a comprehensive review of the subject should be undertaken.

Mitchell's approach to the problem can best be described in his own words: 'My own conception is to provide for compulsory registration (either tribal or registry office) and voluntary religious "blessing". Divorce would then be by action in the courts directed only to the compulsory civil marriage. As to method I incline to favour a questionnaire circulated to the missionaries as well as to D.C.s, the native governments and native administrations, etc., to collect facts and data generally. Then a committee of inquiry largely native in composition. It may have to be in two parts (a) for the Nilotics and (b) for Buganda and the Bantu and advanced parts. It will have to comprise women and the proceedings may have to be in the vernacular: or a Women's committee might be set up—perfectly good Bantu custom.' The reaction of the Buganda Government to the suggestion of such a committee of inquiry was typical of that attitude towards Central Government proposals which was to become all too familiar during the next two decades, the Buganda Ministers informing the Resident: 'We would not welcome the setting up of a committee to investigate further into matters concerning native marriage in Buganda kingdom. As explained to you previously we have fears about the matter because we are aware that the results of such inquiry will undoubtedly make the position of native marriages more difficult than it has been before.' Despite this attitude from Buganda, the Governor went ahead and in 1938 a lengthy questionnaire was circulated, the answers to which provide a fascinating commentary not merely on the conditions at the time but on the conflicting views and often prejudices which were held on this subject.

As was to be expected, the views of the missionaries and of the Provincial Administration were on most points diametrically opposed, and it is not altogether surprising that Bishop Willis, writing in retirement to his successor as Bishop of Uganda (who had sent him the summary of the answers to the questionnaire), expressed his alarm at 'the almost frankly pagan outlook' of many of the administration. In general, the missions supported—if not with any great enthusiasm—the legal *status quo*. They were particularly on the defensive on the question of the treatment meted out, presumably with mission support, to discarded wives of converts to Christianity, for whom the administration maintained that conversion to Christianity and monogamous life on the part of their former husbands meant for them resort to prostitution. On the vexed question of the jurisdiction of native courts in claims for return of marriage consideration where there had been an Ordinance marriage, the missions were united in opposition, since a court order for return must in practice be tantamount to a divorce. So, too, on the general question whether the laws should be recast somewhat on the Nyasaland model, both the Roman Catholic and Protestant missions were adamant that this would be a disaster. It would be 'a retrograde step which would give the impression that government had withdrawn its support of Christian marriage and would be disastrous to the moral state of the country'; or again 'it would be tantamount to providing a lower state of morality for the African, who would resent such action, and the subsequent religious blessing in the church would be interpreted as a lame attempt by the church to retain its status'. On this point, as on most others, the native Governments of Buganda, Busoga and the western kingdoms, where Christianity had been longest established and mission influence strongest, supported the view of the missions, and those elsewhere opposed it.

As a result of the answers to the questionnaire and of long discussion with the Bishops, Mitchell decided in July 1939, in view of the irreconcilable differences of opinion, that the scope of any further inquiry should for the present be of a more limited nature than originally proposed and that the next step should be the setting up of a small committee of lawyers under the chairmanship of a High Court judge. The Government would then put to the committee questions as to whether the law was defective on certain points and get their recommendations as to reform. The missions and the native governments would be kept informed on the views of the committee and would be able to make any representations to it. But at this point war broke out and Mitchell moved to Kenya. The secretariat file on the subject is then silent from the entry of Mitchell's minute, in July 1939, just referred to, save for a short entry by way of epilogue three years later. 'I think we may well let the matter rest now until the war is over. The law office and Judiciary are neither in a position to devote the necessary attention to this highly controversial matter and we have had no communications from the mission as to how things are going.' So died Mitchell's ambitious venture.

A word must now be said about the Divorce Ordinance, which by this time had become archaic in many of its provisions. In 1923 the Matrimonial Causes Act in England put women on an equal footing with men as far as the grounds of divorce were concerned, and in 1924, at the suggestion of the Chief Justice, the Governor approached the Secretary of State to know whether the law in Uganda should be correspondingly altered. The Secretary of State replied that no general action was contemplated, but that there was no objection to Uganda amending its law if it wished to. No action was, however, taken, and three years later the Secretary of State was informed that this was because 'there does not appear to be any necessity in existing circumstances for any amendment'. In 1935 the Provisional Commissioners' Conference recommended that the grounds of divorce should be extended to include impotence, lunacy, desertion for two years and cruelty. The Attorney-General was unenthusiastic. 'Although the proposals would have the support of most divorce reformers,' he stated, 'I doubt if the Secretary of State would favour the provision of facilities so far in advance of existing English law and practice.' He did, however, belatedly recommend bringing the position of the wife into line with that of the husband as regards grounds for divorce. But once again nothing was done. In 1937 the Herbert Act was passed in England and in the following year a leading firm of Kampala advocates asked the Attorney-General that the Uganda law might be brought up to date. Again the response was negative. 'It is right and proper,' the Attorney-General minuted, 'that we should keep reasonable pace with the march of English law but too precipitate adoption of English law has its drawbacks. The general attitude of the Colonial Office is that the colonial dependencies should hesitate to adopt immediately any changes made in the law of England which are highly controversial or experimental in their nature. This view was strongly taken up, I remember, when certain colonies wished to rush into legislation to adopt the

Birkenhead Acts relating to the law of property and I am inclined to think that the arguments then used apply with even greater force in the case of the Herbert Act. There is little doubt in my mind that the Act will have to be amended in the light of experience and I should there-force prefer to wait.' Uganda is still waiting.

Although Mitchell's plan for a full-scale investigation was not revived after the war was over, nevertheless the Government remained conscious that reform of the marriage and divorce law must sooner or later be tackled. In fact, however, this had an inhibiting effect, since it made both the Secretariat and the Law Office even more reluctant to undertake piecemeal reform, and when, in 1947, it was once more suggested that the Divorce Ordinance should be brought into line with the Herbert Act, and certain amendments made to the Marriage Ordinance, the Attorney-General, while supporting the proposed changes, pointed out that the missions were not certain what they did want and that some more comprehensive decision on reform was needed.

Up till the mid-1950s, the Government had had to contend with the conflicting views of the missions and, to a much smaller degree, those of the African Local Governments. Now African opinion as such began to express itself: not, however, that of African men (who were, apparently, well content with the *status quo* as the law in practice operated), but of the women. Especially through the organization known as the Uganda Council of Women, and still very much through their European spokesmen, the view of progressively minded Christian women was put forward. This was, briefly, to the effect that customary law no longer provided adequate protection for a wife or widow; that the customary laws of succession (which applied, of course, under the existing law whether or not there had been an ordinance marriage) did not provide adequate provision for a widow; that these laws did not place her children in any better position than those of her husband's children by other wives whom he had married under customary law, even though the statute law forbade such unions; that the State connived at these illegal unions, since the penal provisions of the Ordinance were never enforced or even brought to the notice of the African husband; that there were no adequate provisions for the compulsory registration of customary marriages and divorces; that if a husband neglected his wife there were no adequate means whereby she could enforce a claim for maintenance; and that the divorce laws were unfairly discriminatory against the wife. The woman's point of view found an able champion in a Legislative Council member, Mrs Saben, the wife of a European businessman in Kampala. During the last few years of the colonial

47

régime Mrs Saben persistently ventilated the woman's case on these matters in the Legislative Council, urging reform and another comprehensive inquiry into, and review of, the whole legal position. With independence drawing close, and in view of the conspicuous lack of any great enthusiasm on the part of the African male members of the Council in urging any widescale reform, the Protectorate Government was determined not to embark at this stage on these dangerous waters, and put forward the plausible argument that this was a matter for the African people to decide once they had full responsibility for their own affairs. It now remains to be seen whether, as a result of the 1964 Commission, Uganda will find a rational and just solution acceptable to all the varying interests in the country, a solution which for sixty years eluded the Protectorate Government.

3

CHINESE FAMILY LAW IN SINGAPORE: THE ROUT OF CUSTOM

MAURICE FREEDMAN

Professor of Anthropology in the University of London

The situation before 1961

Since 1961 there has been no special Chinese family law in Singapore. The Women's Charter of that year subjected all non-Muslims resident or domiciled in the State (which is now a Republic) to a set of family rules that cannot in any sense be described as Chinese. Yet the Chinese form some nine-tenths of the non-Muslim population of Singapore (and about 75 per cent of the population as a whole), and it follows that, while there is no longer any specifically Chinese family law, there is a new body of family law for a predominantly Chinese population.

And yet, in the most literal sense of the word 'Chinese', there was no Chinese family law in Singapore before 1961 either. If we look at the Chinese diaspora we can, for the purpose of our present enquiry, divide the countries where overseas Chinese are domiciled into three classes. In the first (the outstanding example of which is Hong Kong) the family law governing the Chinese is the law of China—at least, as that law was before the Republic. In the second class, Chinese are subjected to a general family law that takes almost no account of their ethnic peculiarities. England is an obvious example. In the third class (to which the Singapore of pre-1961 belongs) Chinese family law as a whole is not admitted, but many principles peculiar to the Chinese are taken into account. We shall now see that, before the enactment of the Women's Charter, Singapore Chinese were governed by a family law that was *sui generis*, being in part Chinese, in part English, and altogether odd.

It developed in this fashion.[1] Founded as a British settlement in

---

[1] I dealt fairly fully with this matter in an earlier paper: 'Colonial Law and Chinese Society', *Journal of the Royal Anthropological Institute*, vol. LXXX, pts. I and II, 1950 (published 1952), although, were I rewriting that article now, I should want to revise a number of the arguments in it. For other points touched on here see my *Chinese Family and Marriage in Singapore*, HMSO, London, 1957; 'The Penhas Case: Mixed and Unmixed Marriage in Singapore', *The Modern*

1819, Singapore joined Penang, and was a few years later joined by Malacca, to form the trio that was eventually to become the Colony of the Straits Settlements. And for this reason we have, up to the Second World War, to treat Singapore law as part and parcel of the law of the Straits Settlements. The lawmakers and judges of these Settlements found themselves dealing with people of many religions and national traditions: Chinese, Muslims (chiefly Malays, Arabs, and Indians), Hindus, Christians, Parsis, and Jews. The list could be extended. It was natural, therefore, to suppose that each religious or ethnic community would be governed as to its family law by its own traditions. The Penang Charter of Justice of 1807, in the words of the first Recorder 'secures to all the native inhabitants the free exercise of their religion, indulges them in all their prejudices, pays the most scrupulous attention to their ancient usages and habits'.[1] But as the business of the courts built up on the basis of the Second Charter of Justice, 1826, it became clear that the judges thought themselves obliged to apply the law of England, although in such a way as to deal fairly with native custom. In a famous judgment of 1869 (*Choa Choon Neoh v. Spottiswoode*) Sir Benson Maxwell said: 'In this Colony, so much of the law of England as was in existence when it was imported here and is of general (and

Law Review, July 1953; and 'Chinese Kinship and Marriage in Early Singapore', *Journal of South-East Asian History*, vol. 3, no. 2, September 1962. For a recent survey of the treatment of Chinese family law in Singapore, see Richard C. H. Lim, 'Overseas Influence of English Law, Malaya and Singapore, Some Ancient Chinese Laws and Customs as Recognized by the Supreme Courts of the Federation of Malaya and Singapore', *The Solicitors' Journal*, vol. 105, nos. 38, 39, September 1961. I had the privilege of reading the typescript of a paper by Mr David C. Buxbaum, 'Chinese Family Law in a Common Law Setting: A Note on the Institutional Environment and the Substantive Family Law of the Chinese in Singapore and Malaysia', which later appeared in *The Journal of Asian Studies*, vol. XXV, no. 4, August 1966. In connection with the present paper I should like to acknowledge the help I received in Singapore in July 1963 from the following people: Dr Ahmad bin Mohamed Ibrahim, Mrs Jennie Chee, Mr E. H. D'Netto, Mr Richard C. H. Lim, Mr B. A. Mallal, Mr L. Rayner, Mr K. H. Tan, Mr and Mrs Harry Wee, and officers of the Marriage Registry and the Supreme Court. Both in Singapore in 1963 and during the writing of this paper I have greatly benefited from my wife's knowledge of the Singapore legal system. I am in debt·to the Solicitor General, Singapore (Mr Tan Boon Teik) for his courtesy in answering questions I put to him in a letter, and to the Singapore Trade Commissioner, London, for his making various official publications available to me. Finally, I have to thank Professor M. Ginsberg, Mr J. M. Gullick and Mr Buxbaum for their comments on the typescript of this paper.

[1] Quoted in V. Purcell, *The Chinese in Malaya*, London. 1948, pp. 49f.

not merely local) policy, and adapted to the conditions and wants of
the inhabitants, is the law of the land; and further, that law is subject,
in its application to the various alien races established here, to such
modifications as are necessary to prevent it operating unjustly and
oppressively on them.'[1] The term 'alien races' applied to all the non-
English,[2] but one section of the population had some claim to be considered indigenous: the Malays. And when British rule was extended
from the Straits Settlements to the Malay States in the last quarter of
the nineteenth century, the special positon of the Malays came to be
reflected in the Colony. It is for this reason that Islamic family law
became established almost in its entirety in the Straits Settlements
and that it is now the only special family law left in Singapore.[3] The
Chinese, unambiguously immigrant, were subjected to English law
modified to accommodate certain features of their institutional
life.

No statutes were enacted to lay down what that accommodation was
to be, and it was left to the judges to make the law as they went along.
They made it, to summarize its main points, by finding that the Chinese
were polygamous, that widows and daughters were entitled by English
rules to shares of an intestate's estate, that adopted sons were not entitled to such a share, and that property could not be tied up indefinitely in order to provide for ancestor worship.

The chief concession to Chinese principles was to acknowledge
that they were polygamous. But that polygamy so sanctioned was not
in fact an institution that the Chinese could recognize as their own.
For the law of the Straits Settlements turned concubines or secondary
wives into spouses of virtually equal status with major wives. The
rulings arose chiefly when decisions had to be made on the disposal
of intestate's estates.

---

[1] R. Braddell, *The Laws of the Straits Settlements, A Commentary*, 2nd edn.,
Singapore, 1931, p. 62.
[2] It would require a very detailed study to determine exactly how Muslim and
Chinese family law came to be treated differently in the courts. It is perhaps
relevant that in the rules laid down by Raffles (the founder of modern Singapore)
in 1823 it was stated that 'in all cases regarding the ceremonies of religion, and
marriages, and the rules of inheritance, the laws and customs of the Malays will be
respected, where they shall not be contrary to reason, justice, or humanity'.
Quoted in Ahmad bin Mohamed Ibrahim, *The Legal Status of the Muslims in
Singapore*, Singapore, 1965, p. 3. And cf. L. A. Sheridan, ed., *Malaya and
Singapore, the Borneo Territories, The Development of their Laws and Consti-
tutions*, London, 1961, pp. 14–19.
[3] See Ahmad Ibrahim, *Islamic Law in Malaya*, Singapore, 1965.

By the application of English law a widow on her husband's intestacy was granted a half or a third share of his property, depending on whether he left issue. This certainly was not Chinese law, for under that law a widow had no claims to an outright share, her rights being restricted by the fact that family property vested in males. And having admitted the wife to this right, the judges opened the same door to concubines, the widow's half or third share being divisible equally among all widows. Sir Benson Maxwell appears to have begun the series of relevant judgments in 1867. He said: 'The first wife is usually chosen by the husband's parents of a family of equal station, and is espoused with as much ceremony and splendour as the parties can afford: while the inferior wives are generally of his own choice made without regard to family connection. But that they are wives not concubines seems to me clear from the fact that certain forms of espousal are always performed and that, besides, their children inherit in default of the issue of the principal wife, and that throughout the Penal Code of China they are treated to all intents and purposes as well as the first.'[1] By the time of the spectacularly named Six Widows Case of 1908 there had been a series of judgments in which the Chinese had been held to be polygamous in this sense.

But how was a concubine to be distinguished from a mistress or (in the language of the Straits) a 'keep'? Rich men were sexually active; they made informal liaisons that were often fruitful of children. From the Chinese point of view, the legitimacy of offspring depended on a man recognizing them to be his children, and such recognition said nothing about the status of the mothers as the man's consorts. But to find that a child was a legitimate heir the Straits courts had to find that his mother was a wife; and while the judges seem to have begun by demanding that a marriage be proved by evidence of some ceremoney, they finished up in recent times by accepting that a secondary marriage could be found where there was merely intention to form such a union. In the 1930s the general test of a secondary marriage appears to have been whether there was cohabitation and repute, but since the Second World War intention has come to be taken as the crucial element. In 1965, when Singapore was still part of Malaysia (into which country it had ventured in 1963), the Federal Court upheld a Singapore judgment to the effect that, in order to prove a Chinese secondary marriage, it is necessary to show only that there was a common intention to form a permanent union as husband and wife and the formation of the union by the man taking the woman as

[1] *In re Lao Leong An: Straits Settlements Law Reports*, vol. 1, 1893, p. 2.

his secondary wife and the woman taking the man as her husband.[1] And that is how the law will presumably continue to be applied until all the secondary unions formed before 1961 have been exhausted by time.

But the doctrine of consensual marriage has not been confined to secondary unions. In the beginning the courts assumed that a primary marriage was formed by means of a complex series of rites; and as long as the Chinese in the Straits kept to some version of the traditional marriage procedure no serious problem could arise. But when the Chinese Empire came to an end and new forms of marriage ceremonial were copied from China by people in the Straits, it became less certain that the courts could with ease arrive at decisions about what was to constitute a primary marriage. Against this confused background, the Government of the Straits Settlements appointed a Committee in 1925 (the Chinese Marriage Committee) which reported the next year. The Committee was invited to submit *inter alia* 'proposals for legislation as to what forms or ceremonies should constitute a valid marriage and as to the registration of such marriages . . .'.[2] But the task proved very difficult. The evidence before them, in their view, disclosed to the members of the Committee that 'there were no essentials for Chinese marriages in the old style common to all the Districts of South China or to the locally-born descendants of emigrants from these Districts, while the new style of marriage does not require any particular form'.[3] The new-style form of marriage referred to was one in which, whether the wedding was held privately or publicly, a so-called wedding certificate (an unofficial document to be bought at a stationer's shop) was signed by the parties to the match, by their guardians, and by their 'Introducers'.[4]

The Committee recommended legislation to provide that the courts recognize marriages in the new style (on certain conditions), and a system of voluntary registration of both old- and new-style marriages.[5] Compulsory registration was out. 'The opposition among Chinese aliens to registration of Chinese marriages of any kind is practically unanimous; Chinese British subjects were divided in their opinions on this matter; . . . the supporters of compulsory registration consist

---

[1] *Re Lee Gee Chong Deceased: The Malayan Law Journal*, vol. XXXI, 1965, p. 102.

[2] *Chinese Marriage Committee, Proceedings of the Committee Appointed by His Excellency the Governor to Report on Matters Concerning Chinese Marriages*, Singapore, 1926, p. 1.

[3] op. cit., p. 11.

[4] op. cit., p. 23, and Freedman, 'Colonial Law and Chinese Society', p. 105.

[5] *Chinese Marriage Committee*, pp. 9f.

chiefly of Chinese ladies and a limited number of Chinese gentlemen of advanced views.'[1] Among the reasons for opposition the two most powerful were dislike of government interference in private affairs and the fear that registration 'would involve monogamy in the future'.

The Committee's recommendations were not acted upon and, in the same year in which it reported, the Chief Justice observed in court: 'I am not so sure that some day the Courts will not have to hold that the only real essential of the Chinese marriage of a principal wife is intention. . . . The whole question, in the absence of legislation, must, I think, be considered to be in the melting pot, and after the lapse of years the crystallization of essentials in the accurate sense of the word may eventuate. In my opinion there is no such accurate category in Singapore yet.'[2] Chief Justice Murison was right in his first prediction: since the Second World War it has been established in the courts that the doctrine of consensual marriage applies to all marriages among the Chinese.[3] Meanwhile, however, the forms of Chinese marriage had increased. To the old and the new style had been added a still newer form in which the marriage was made by a statement of intention placed as an advertisement in the newspapers.[4]

But if the law of marriage was obscure, what of the law of divorce? The Chinese Marriage Committee found that there was 'practically unanimous opposition among Chinese residents born in China to any divorce legislation, which is shared by many Chinese born in the Colony'. Chinese ladies of Penang were the only group solidly in favour of divorce 'as a means of obtaining the prohibition of concubinage'.[5] Yet the Chinese knew and practised divorce, and the courts were forced to take some account of it. In 1861 the Recorder had to decide in Penang whether a Chinese woman had been divorced, as she claimed to have been. The report says; 'Chinese witnesses were examined on the subject of Chinese law, but their evidence showed that their information was of the slightest character. On that point, however, the learned Recorder relied wholly on Staunton's translation of the Chinese Penal Code.'[6] He found the divorce proved. The Six Widows

[1] op. cit., p. 4.

[2] *Woon Kai Chiang v. Yeo Pak Wee and Others: Straits Settlements Law Reports*, 1926, vol. 1, p. 34.

[3] Freedman, 'Colonial Law', p. 120.

[4] op. cit., p. 107.

[5] *Chinese Marriage Committee*, p. 4.

[6] *Nonia Cheah Yew v. Othmansaw Merican and another*: J. W. N. Kyshe, ed., *Cases Heard and Determined in Her Majesty's Supreme Court of the Straits Settlements*, 1808–84, vol. 1, p. 160.

Case, 1908, recognized the possibility of a concubine being divorced, and the matter arose several times in later years. The position on the eve of the coming into force of the Women's Charter in 1961 was that, in the eyes of the courts, a Chinese secondary marriage could be terminated by the husband repudiating the wife. In 1935 a judge said: 'I accept with respect the reasoning of C. J. Shaw that just as in the case of the formation of a secondary marriage, its dissolution can be proved by intention and repute.'[1] There was no test case to decide whether the repudiation of a primary wife or the agreement to divorce between a man and such a wife was acceptable in law. And yet we know that divorces by mutual consent were quite common, some of them in fact being concluded with the help of a government agency— the Secretariat for Chinese Affairs, and, more recently (up to about 1954), the Department of Social Welfare.

The baroque muddle illustrated by the law of marriage and divorce could be elaborated by our considering the law of succession to property, adoption, maintenance of wives and children, and the tying-up of property for ancestor worship. Fortunately, I lack the space to go into these complications, for they would confuse my account intolerably. I shall close this section of the paper with a few general observations on the law as it existed up to 1961.

Some of the muddle arose from the attempt to adapt English law to certain Chinese principles. That is obvious. But some of it was due to the difficulty of knowing what precisely those principles were. During the nineteenth century and the early years of the twentieth, the courts sometimes looked at Staunton's translation of the Ch'ing Penal Code (a translation which is incomplete) and various digests of the law of China prepared by Westerners. In addition, evidence as to this law was taken from experts, both Chinese and British. No coherent and accurate picture of the law of China could be extracted from these sources. In the first place, the written sources, to be fully intelligible, would have needed to be subjected to a keen analysis, informed by sinological as well as legal skill, a point amply illustrated by Mr McAleavy's work on the parallel situation in Hong Kong.[2] In the second place, it cannot be taken for granted that the customary law which the parties to, and witnesses in, particular cases thought appropriate coincided with the written law of China. The Singapore Chinese

[1] *Lew Ah Lui v. Choa Eng Wan and Others: Straits Settlements Law Reports,* 1935, p. 179.

[2] H. McAleavy, 'Chinese Law in Hong Kong: The Choice of Sources', in J. N. D. Anderson, ed., *Changing Law in Developing Countries,* London, 1963.

were not all from one part of China (although nearly all came from the south-eastern provinces); local customs differed. And when the Chinese twentieth century opened, as it did in 1911, new legal ideas and new social rules were projected on to Singapore from China. The culmination of this source of confusion came in the 1950 Marriage Law of the People's Republic, which, as we shall see presently, was in part responsible for the Women's Charter eleven years later.

But we are not to assume that the confusion in the courts was exactly mirrored in the social life of the Singapore Chinese. For the great majority of them the law of the courts was irrelevant; they married, divorced, adopted, and disposed of their property according to the rules they recognized. When large properties were left by an intestate, some dissatisfied widow or child could invoke the law of the courts to secure a share; but most of the time family disputes were settled outside the framework of the legal system, narrowly defined, and by principles that the courts might well have refused to accept. It was only when law began to be thought of by Singapore Chinese as a desirable instrument of social change, and when law as an instrument of politics was placed in the hands of Singapore Chinese, that a new chapter opened in the history of family law.[1]

The Women's Charter, 1961

In the constitutional changes made after the Second World War, Singapore was separated from the rest of Malaya. In 1959 it graduated from the status of Colony to become an internally self-governing State. In its new form the State began life under the administration of the People's Action Party led by Mr Lee Kuan Yew. Mr Lee and his party may now seem to us no further to the political left than Mr Harold Wilson and the majority of the Labour Party, but at the time of

[1] It is interesting in this regard to compare the somewhat hesitant attitude expressed by Mr Lee Kuan Yew in 1957 (the context being a debate on proposals to register Hindu marriages) with the stand taken by his party a very few years later. After referring to the 'curious spectacle' in Singapore 'of the English law of intestacy of the eighteenth century embellished and embroidered to fit the polygamous institutions of China of the eighteenth century', Mr Lee went on: 'This is a matter which should receive comprehensive review. No single political party could brave the storm of religious protest and resistance, but if we made a serious attempt to reconcile religious practices with modern-day needs in a modern-day world, we might then first decide whether omnibus legislation covering all religions, except the Muslim religion which is an almost established church in the Federation (of Malaya), might not be a better answer than the proposal of the Member for Seletar.'—Legislative Assembly, Singapore, Sessional Paper No. Cmd. 37 of 1957, pp. 53f.

Singapore's independence the PAP was radically left, including in its ranks men and women for whom Communist China was a social model. When the Women's Charter Bill was introduced for the first time in 1960 one major change had already been made in Singapore family law; the Muslims Ordinance, 1957, had made provision for a Shariah Court and prohibited the registration of divorces other than those by mutual consent except by order of this Court. And in 1960 the Ordinance was amended severely to restrict Muslim polygamy.[1] Muslim family law having been put on the map of social reform, it was now the turn of the rest of the population, some nine-tenths of whom were Chinese.

The legal background of the proposed reform of 1960 has already been sketched in, but one further set of facts is required to make the provisions of the new Bill comprehensible. In 1960 many Chinese were already contracting registrable and monogamous forms of marriage. Since 1898 Christians had been barred from polygamy and obliged on marriage to enter monogamous registered unions (although the law was not as clear on this point as my summary makes it[2]). In 1960, 426 Chinese couples were married as Christians. In addition, it had been possible since 1941 for people to form monogamous unions under the Civil Marriage Ordinance; and in 1960, 3,082 Chinese couples married in this fashion. The total figure for monogamous Chinese marriages in 1960 was therefore 3,508. In 1941 it had been 470, in 1948 554, in 1957 1,751, and in 1959 2,490.[3] But a caution must be entered. By no means all the Chinese marriages registered in these years were, so to speak, fresh unions. Many involved couples already married by custom; and as the debates leading up to the new marriage law created a greater public awareness of the significance of registered marriage (for example, it was fairly clear that many Chinese women were under the impression that, once married in this form, they could get their husbands punished for keeping a mistress), the recourse to civil marriage increased. Of the 3,500 registered Chinese marriages in 1960 it would appear that about 1,000 were of couples already married by custom.

The 1960 Bill was not made law. It had been sent to a Select Committee and the Assembly prorogued before any further action could be taken. It was reintroduced the next year, sent to a second Select Com-

[1] Judith Djamour, *The Muslim Matrimonial Court in Singapore*, London, 1966, pp. 26ff.

[2] See David C. Buxbaum, 'Freedom of Marriage in a Pluralistic Society', *The Malayan Law Review*, December 1963.

[3] The marriage figures given here and later in the paper have been extracted from the *Singapore Monthly Digest of Statistics* and *Report on the Registration of Births and Deaths, Marriages and Persons*, Singapore, for various years.

mittee, and enacted. During the whole period of the debate there was
no opposition to it in principle in the Assembly and little sign of public
resistance. One or two voices were to be heard expressing themselves in favour of allowing polygamy to continue, but there was no
serious protest. At neither of the two Select Committees did any
effective opponent of the Bills put in an appearance, although a few
representations were made which opposed certain aspects of the new
law. It was not a time to be in favour of keeping the clock from turning
forward.

The Women's Charter Bill was deliberately so called in order to
convey the impression that a new deal for women was to be enacted.
There was to be monogamy and judicial divorce for all (except Muslims);
women's property rights were to be strengthened; and—which accounts
for the curious fact that both civil and criminal provisions were made
within one Ordinance—firmer measures were to be taken to protect
women and girls against sexual exploitation. I propose now briefly
to survey the second bill as it passed into law.

Part II of the Ordinance deals with monogamous marriages. It
begins (s.4) with the provision that nobody who on March 2, 1961,
is lawfully married 'under any law, religion, custom or usage to one or
more spouses' may, during the continuance of any such marriage,
validly contract a further marriage. Polygamists are called to a halt.
For people marrying after March 2, 1961, there will be monogamy.
And (s.6) penalties are laid down for bigamists. Henceforth (s.7) every
marriage shall continue until it is dissolved by death or by a judicial
decree.

In Part III the Ordinance deals with the solemnization of marriage.
Marriages may be solemnized by the Registrar of Marriages or by any
person to whom an appropriate licence has been granted. Parties to a
marriage must be 18 years of age or older unless a special authorization
is granted. The degrees of relationship within which marriage is prohibited are set out (s.10); they are virtually the prohibited degrees of
English law. But, by s.10 (5), the Minister may in his discretion grant a
licence for a marriage to be solemnized 'notwithstanding the kindred or
affinity of the parties, if he is satisfied that such marriage is valid under
the law, religion, custom or usage applicable to the parties' (a curious
provision, it has been pointed out,[1] since it seems to presuppose the
continuing validity of systems of marriage which the Ordinance otherwise wipes off the slate). The remainder of Part II deals *inter alia* with

[1] L. W. Athulathmudali and G. W. Bartholomew, 'The Women's Charter',
University of Malaya Law Review, vol. 3, no. 2, December 1961, p. 320.

the consent to a marriage required in the case of a minor, the notice required for a marriage, and the form of the marriage ceremony. Every marriage must be solemnized in the presence of at least two credible witnesses. The person solemnizing the marriage must be satisfied that both parties freely consent to it. No further ceremonial requirements are made, except that a form of marriage is laid down in the case where the Registrar performs the marriage. And it is provided that religious rites may be added at will. Finally, it is lawful for a religious rite of marriage to be performed when a person 'is under the expectation of death', but such a rite 'shall not be deemed to be a solemnization of marriage for the purposes of this Ordinance'.

Part IV opens (s.24) with the provision that every marriage solemnized henceforth must be registered. Methods of registration are laid down. But an escape clause is inserted: 'Nothing in this Ordinance or rules made thereunder shall be construed to render valid or invalid merely by reason of its having been or not having been registered any marriage which is otherwise invalid or valid.' To round off the provisions for registration and its effects we may jump to s.166 in Part XI, a section which provides that nothing in the Ordinance affects the validity of marriages created before March 2, 1961, and that such marriages if valid under the law, religion, custom, or usage under which they were solemnized shall be deemed to be registered and shall continue until dissolved by death or by a judicial decree. Taking Parts II and III together with s.166 we can see that it is the intention of the Ordinance that all future marriages should be registered, that they should be solemnized only by people licensed to do so, and that all past extant marriages should be treated as though they had been registered.

Part V makes certain provisions for the solemnization and registration of marriages. I need draw attention only to s.35 where freedom of marriage is entrenched by the rule that 'Any person who uses any force or threat (a) to compel a person to marry against his will; or (b) to prevent a person who has attained the age of 21 years from contracting a valid marriage' commits a punishable offence.

Let us jump to Part IX which deals with divorce. Roughly, this Part extends the provisions of the now repealed Divorce Ordinance (which applied only to monogamous marriages) to all marriages registered or deemed to have been registered, including polygamous unions formed before March 2, 1961. The English derivation of the provisions is plain in nearly every section, and is made explicit in s.81 where it is laid down that, subject to the provisions in this Part, 'the court shall in all suits and proceedings hereunder act and give relief on principles which in the opinion of the court are, as nearly as may be, conformable to the principles on which the High Court of Justice in England acts and gives relief in matrimonial proceedings'. By s.83 a petition may not normally be presented until three years after the marriage. Before determining an application for an early petition, the court may refer the parties to a Conciliation Officer. (Mention of this officer is first made in s.46, where it is provided that the Minister may appoint as Conciliation Officers such public officers as he thinks fit, and that where there are differences between spouses one or both may refer the differences to an Officer for his advice and assistance.) The grounds for divorce (s.84) are adultery, desertion for three years, cruelty and incurable insanity. These grounds are common to husband and wife, but the wife may offer two further grounds: that since her marriage her husband has gone through a form of marriage with another woman, and that since her marriage her husband has been guilty of rape, sodomy, or bestiality. Now, the first of these two additional grounds at first sight seems otoise, but it would appear to have been inserted to make it possible for a woman married before March 2, 1961, whose husband validly contracted a further marriage before that date, to petition for her own marriage to be dissolved. Thus, if a man was married to several wives before March 2, 1961, all of them except the last now has grounds for divorce.

At s.91 we come to nullity suits. I shall comment on only one of the many grounds specified. S.92 (1)(c) provides that a decree of nullity may be made on the ground that 'the former husband or wife of either party was living at the time of the marriage and the marriage with such former husband or wife was then in force'. *Prima facie*, the last of the wives of a polygamous husband validly married before March 2, 1961, who cannot like her co-wives sue for divorce under s.84, can, under s.92, sue for a decree of nullity. S.92 specifies for some other grounds set out, but not for this one, that a decree shall not be granted unless *inter alia* the petitioner was at the time of the marriage ignorant of the facts alleged.[1]

Petitions for judicial separation and for restitution of conjugal rights are dealt with in ss.96–104. We may now turn back to Part VI. It opens at s.45:

'(1) Upon the solemnization of the marriage the husband and the wife shall be mutually bound to co-operate with each other in safe-

---

[1] As far as I know, however, no divorces have been sought on the ground mentioned at the end of the last paragraph and no petition for nullity has been made on the ground mentioned in this paragraph.

guarding the interests of the union and in caring and providing for the children.

'(2) The husband and the wife shall have the right separately to engage in any trade or profession or in social activities.

'(3) The wife shall have the right to use her own surname and name separately.

'(4) The husband and wife shall have equal rights in the running of the matrimonial household.' It seems very doubtful whether any specific legal rights and duties flow from these provisions—at least in the case of (1), (2), and (4); and the right asserted in (3) seems to be legally established quite independently of this Ordinance. The legislators had their attention drawn to the vagueness of the section; perhaps the fact that it has passed into law is a sign that the Women's Charter was intended to be a demonstration of sexual equality even in realms where that equality was unenforceable.

S.46, as we have seen, provides for Conciliation Officers. The remainder of the Part deals with the property rights of married women, generally re-enacting the provisions of the repealed Married Women's Property Ordinance.

Parts VII and VIII provide for the maintenance of wives and children and for the enforcement of maintenance orders. Here the general effect is to re-enact the provisions of the repealed Ordinances dealing with maintenance, but there is an important difference in the new treatment of illegitimate children. Whereas in the old legislation a limit was fixed in respect of the maintenance that could be awarded for illegitimate children, under s.62 legitimate and illegitimate children are treated alike (the court having discretion to decide the amount); and the assimilation of rights seems to have been prudently enacted when, by the banning of polygamy, the Women's Charter may be expected to increase the population of bastards.

It is worth pointing out that a possible measure to provide for wives and children is conspicuously absent from the Ordinance: no restraint is placed on a married man willing away his property. So while wives and children are protected during a man's lifetime, his widow and orphans are not. An attempt to remedy this defect was made in 1963 when the Inheritance (Family Provisions) Bill was given a second reading; but this piece of reform got lost during Singapore's membership of Malaysia, and has only just now (March 1966) reappeared. The Bill, which seeks to enact the provisions of the English Inheritance (Family Provision) Act, 1938, as amended by the Intestates' Estates Act, 1952, gives the court the power to vary dispositions of property in order to provide for the maintenance of dependants. It will not apply to Muslims.

Part X of the Women's Charter generally re-enacts the repealed Women and Girls Protection Ordinance; it is concerned with criminal offences (prostitution and traffic in women and girls) of no relevance to family law. As for Part XI, the only section of interest to us, s.166 has already been discussed.

The discussions regarding the Women's Charter Bills
The atmosphere in which the Charter was brought to birth and the attitudes and considerations motivating its sponsors and supporters are conveyed by the debates in the Legislative Assembly and the discussions with witnesses before the two Select Committees. I think it is worth referring to these valuable historical sources. They reveal, in the first place, that for many of the legislators the Charter was an important first step towards the good society in which women would be placed on a basis of equality with men. Full equality would come only with the consummation of a socialist society; meanwhile, as much as possible was to be done, even within the limits of a still backward community, to secure a good measure of female emancipation. Listen to the words of Miss Chan Choy Siong (translated from Chinese): 'This Charter as drafted has incorporated some of the provisions of a number of Ordinances. It has also adopted those of the existing laws of China which have some merits. . . . The marriage system provides for monogamy to enable both the husband and the wife to enjoy equal status in their matrimonial life. The previous evil custom will vanish with the coming into operation of this Charter. The passing of this Women's Charter will not only enable women to be safeguarded in law but will also bring about a revolutionary change in society on a practical basis. . . . The problems of women are the result of an unreasonable society. Men take women as pieces of merchandise. The inhuman feudalistic system has deprived women of their rights. In a semi-colonial and semi-feudalistic society, the tragedy of women was very common. Man could have three or four spouses. Men are considered honourable, but women are considered mean. It was common in those days to regard having more than one female in a Chinese family as being very despicable. Women in our society are like pieces of meat put on the table for men to slice. The PAP Government has made a promise. We cannot allow this inequality in the family to exist in this country. We will liberate women from the hands of the oppressor.'[1]

[1] *Singapore Legislative Assembly Debates*, vol. 12, no. 7, April 6, 1960, cols. 442f.

The indignation at the abuse of women was probably coupled in the minds of many radicals with a puritanical resentment of the opportunities afforded to men in Singapore to exercise their sexual capacities to the full. Dr Lee Siew Choh expressed the point with elegance. ' . . . as our country is just on the threshold of a new era and will need all the energy and help from all quarters—male as well as female—in the gigantic task of nation building, it might be advisable for those who are blessed with more zest and vitamins in their system than may be good for them to re-channel their exuberant energy into other socially useful and non-population-increasing types of productive occupations. The practice of the noble art of sexual sublimation will serve as a shining example for our future generations and will also lighten very much the burden of the Family Planning Association. It is a long cry, sir, from primitive communism and polygamy as has been practised throughout the ages in various parts of the world. Customs die hard but, in all progressive countries, the one man one wife system of marriage is the recognized social order.'[1]

But alongside the left-wing ideological pronouncements there lay technical discussions on matters of detail and procedure. I shall deal with three such points: the registration of marriage, the rights of husbands and wives, and the rules of divorce. The first matter arose because, while in the charter as it passed into law all extant marriages formed before March 2, 1962, were deemed to have been registered, in the 1960 bill they were required to be registered. Within a fixed period of the new law all marriages not already registered under some previous ordinance were to be reported to a Registrar, upon whom was to fall the task of deciding in each case whether a valid marriage existed. An appeal was to lie to the High Court. It emerged that certain major disadvantages attached to this procedure. First, the administrative burden would be very heavy indeed, for nearly every existing marriage would need to be registered and there was likely to be a great number on which the Registrar would have to spend time before pronouncing on their validity. Second, from the point of view of the public, wholesale registration would be a great nuisance, many men would be embarrassed to report their plural marriages and some women would be too shy to come forward to register marriages that their husbands had neglected to report. But there was more to it than that: the post-registration of customary marriages was likely in the most dramatic fashion to highlight the conflict between the stand taken by case law

[1] op. cit., col. 454. Dr Lee became Chairman of the newly formed Barisan Sosialis party in August 1961.

on the nature of Chinese polygamy and the attitudes and values of a great part of the Chinese population.

Let me cite the evidence given before the first Select Committee by Mrs Lee Cheng Hiong, the Chairman of the Singapore Women's Council. Mrs Lee suggested that a separate register be kept for concubines. The Chairman of the Select Committee asked Mrs Lee what she meant by a concubine, and she replied: 'When a young man has a first girl friend and they get married, then that girl is considered to be the legal girl. And the women in any subsequent marriages of this man are termed "concubines".' The Chairman: 'But before this Bill was introduced, it was a recognized thing, shall we say, for the Chinese to have more than one wife; is that correct?'—'We do not have the phrase "more than one wife" in our vocabulary. If there is more than one woman, we call her a concubine. According to Chinese custom, there is only one wife.' The Chairman: 'Is the Women's Council then suggesting that a man, who now has five wives—using the term "wife" in that sense—has, in effect, in the eyes of the Women's Council, one legal wife and four mistresses? Is that what the Council means?'— 'Yes. We do not consider the mistresses as wives.' The Chairman: 'If you understand me, of course, that is against the common law as we find it in Singapore. Do you understand that our courts have, in fact, recognized that these other wives are, in fact, secondary wives and not mistresses? Do you realize that?'—'The men who have more than one wife say that those women are their wives. But according to proper Chinese custom, such women cannot be called wives. That is impossible.'[1] It then became clear that the ladies represented by Mrs Lee wanted to deprive the concubines of rights to their intestate husbands' estates; in other words, virtually to make the monogamy rule retrospective. It was the cruel plight of the wife that apparently weighed with Mrs Lee, not that of the deprived concubines.[2] 'My suggestion is to protect those women who are on the legal side. They are the righteous and decent ones. You cannot protect such women as well as those women who are on the wrong side. There must be some difference.'[3] And since the Charter as it has become law dispenses with post-registration, only a few disputed marriages will ever come before the courts (although in somewhat greater numbers than before, because the new divorce provisions now embrace past customary marriages), and Singapore was spared the spectacle of numerous wives contesting

[1] First Legislative Assembly, State of Singapore, *Report of the Select Committee on the Women's Charter Bill*, L.A. 16 of 1960, cols. 13f.

[2] op. cit., cols. 15ff.   [3] op. cit., col. 20.

the claims of their husbands' concubines before a harassed Registrar.

We have seen that in the Charter s.45 sets out the rights and duties of husbands and wives under four heads. The last head in the first bill read: 'The husband and wife shall have equal rights in the running of the matrimonial household and in the ownership and management of the family properties.' The clause as a whole came under fire, but sub-clause 4 was shown to be particularly weak. In the Assembly Mr Rajah confessed himself not to understand it. He went on: 'The implications of this sub-clause could be very drastic. Some of the phrases used are such that they cut across the whole conception of property and opera-tion of law in Singapore.' He then quoted the sub-clause, asking what it meant. (A member interjected: 'Half the bed!'[1]) In this debate the clause was defended (it was said to be taken from the Swiss Civil Code[2]), but in the end sub-clause 4 was modified, 'as it was suggested that it might be inconsistent with the provisions relating to the property rights of married women'.[3] The legislators had found themselves torn between giving married women securer rights to 'family property' and protecting their rights as individuals.

We come to the question of divorce which, as we have seen, now rests on English principles ('framed on the basis of Protestant theology', as a lawyer critic asserted before the second Select Committee).[4] A case was put by witnesses before both Select Committees for introduc-ing divorce by mutual consent; and it was inevitable that somebody should cite the model of the new law in mainland China (or rather, what that law was taken to mean).[5] At the first Select Committee, the Minister for Labour and Law, Mr Byrne, said that he and his colleagues had taken a close look at the Chinese law, concluding, first, that it had been made in conditions very different from those in Singapore ('there were a lot of forced marriages in China') and, second, that it appeared that it had become very difficult to obtain a divorce in China in respect of marriages formed after the installation of the new régime.[6] And in

[1] *Singapore Legislative Assembly Debates*, op. cit., col. 458.

[2] There is in fact a strong resemblance between the first sub-clause and Article 159 of the Swiss Civil Code, but it could hardly be the case that the second, third, and fourth sub-clauses were modelled on anything in that Code.

[3] *Singapore Legislative Assembly Debates*, vol. 14, no. 16, March 22, 1961, col. 1,199.

[4] First Legislative Assembly, State of Singapore, *Report of the Select Committee on the Women's Charter Bill*, L.A. 10 of 1961, col. 12.

[5] *Report of the Select Committee*, 1960, cols. 55ff., and *Report of the Select Committee*, 1961, cols. 8ff.

[6] *Report of the Select Committee*, 1960, col. 63.

the final debate Mr Byrne said: 'The Bill is not as revolutionary as some people would like it to be. In particular, the provisions relating to divorce follow closely similar provisions in the English Divorce law.... It was felt, however, that to allow a marriage to be dissolved by mutual consent or under the Chinese custom by a unilateral public act by the husband would be to defeat the basis on which the Women's Charter was framed. The Bill seeks, on the one hand, to make it as easy as possible to enter into the contract of marriage and, on the other hand, to make it as difficult as possible to contract out of it. It is especially necessary, in a situaion where existing polygamous marriages are recognized and where monogamy is to be enforced for the future, that the institution of marriage should be safeguarded and that too easy divorces should be prevented. For otherwise, it would be very easy for an unscrupulous husband to divorce his existing wife or wives and take for himself another wife. Thus the very basis of the legislation would be demolished and instead of raising the status of women, the Charter would further lower it. It may be that when the women of Singapore are more advanced and more aware of and more in a position to exercise their rights, it would be possible to go further in liberalizing the law of divorce—but for the present it is felt that it would be better to work on the existing law, which has been in force in Singapore since 1912, and which has been found on balance not to have operated unsatisfactorily.'[1]

It will by now have become clear how paradoxical the Women's Charter is. A left-wing political party felt itself under an ideological compulsion to raise the status of women from the lowly level to which, according to the then current political analysis, colonialism and feudal institutions had condemned them. At the same time the new legislators were working within British parliamentary forms and on the basis of an English legal system, so that the reforms had to be couched in an idiom which was far from being revolutionary. Indeed, we may say that the Women's Charter brought to full fruition the colonial introduction of English law by making the law of marriage and the family a close replica of the relevant law of England—divorce law and all. The courts and the legislators of the Straits Settlements and colonial Singapore had in some measure respected Chinese custom; on independence a largely Chinese party threw out custom to claim the heritage of post-colonial modernism: English law justified by the principles of Asian socialism.[2]

[1] *Legislative Assembly Debates*, vol. 14, no. 20, May 24, 1961, col. 1,546.
[2] It is possible (as has been pointed out to me) that an important reason for

The consequences of the Women's Charter

It is clear that the legislators responsible for the Women's Charter looked to it as a means both of propagating new norms (that is to say, new ideal standards of conduct) and of enforcing new rights by legal sanctions. At the same time, they obviously recognized that rule-making in a complex society is not simply a matter of positive law but also of education in the broadest sense. The State has in fact forgone the opportunity to press home by penal action a crucial reform: to date (March 1966) there has not been a single prosecution for the irregular solemnization of marriage.[1] It was assumed, perhaps, that the new law would gradually take root by the operation of self-interest.

As was to be expected, registered marriage, which was on a steadily rising curve before the Women's Charter came into law, has climbed higher still since 1961. Registered Chinese marriages for the years 1961 to 1964 were respectively 3,508, 4,229, 4,769, and 5,476. And these figures have increasingly represented new marriages; in 1963 the four and three-quarter thousand registered Chinese marriages included only fifty-five marriages of couples already married by custom. The problem is how to interpret these figures. The population increased from just over a million in 1957 (when Chinese registered marriages numbered one and three-quarter thousand) to about a million and a third in 1964 (when Chinese registered marriages were five and a half thousand), and some of the rise in registered marriage must be attributed to the growth in the numbers of young people reaching marriageable age. Clearly a great number of marriages must still be taking place outside the provisions of the new law. When I wrote about the Singapore Chinese as I knew them in 1949–50, I hazarded the guess that a total of 7,000 primary marriages were formed each year,[2] registered marriages making up about 8 per cent of them. (The population was

---

introducing the Women's Charter may well have been the growing need in a modern state to ensure clear definitions of the status of wife, husband, and children. In taxing and providing social services, a modern bureaucracy must know the precise standing of its citizens.

[1] And there have been only six prosecutions for bigamy in the years 1961–5 (nine cases in all having been reported). Of course, the lack of prosecutions for the irregular solemnization of marriage may perhaps have been due to a difficulty lying in the term 'solemnization'. Many Chinese marriages, it might reasonably be contended, are formed without elements of such rites as are implied by the English word 'solemnization'. Can a marriage made by a declaration be said to have been solemnized?

[2] Freedman, *Chinese Family and Marriage*, p. 114.

then just over three quarters of a million.) Can we now assume that some 12,000 marriages are taking place annually? If so, only a half are being registered.

There are in fact some indications that the couples entering registered marriage come disproportionally from the richer and better educated elements in the population. In a sample drawn from marriage licences taken out by Singapore Chinese in 1962, a sociologist found the mean ages of brides and grooms to be 24·25 and 28·35 respectively;[1] and these figures suggest that we are dealing with a biased group. Of the 1,335 husbands only sixty-one had had no education, and a total of 535 had been educated at the secondary level (Chinese or English).[2] Again, only 518 husbands were in unskilled and semi-skilled jobs, while 367 were in superior occupations and 459 in skilled jobs.[3]

Yet I think we may assume that there is steady progress towards universal registered marriage. It was already clear to me in 1949 and 1950 that Chinese were making increased use of civil marriage because of pressure exerted from the bride's side: after such a marriage there was no possibility of doubt about the woman's status and no means by which the husband could legally take a concubine. The insistence on civil marriage was part of the bargaining leading up to a match and sometimes the price paid for domestic peace by a man who had been party to a customary marriage. It is in the interest of women and their protectors to seek registered marriage, and the man as husband loses out to the man as father or brother of the bride. In a very few years from now, even without penal action by the State, nearly all new Chinese marriages will probably be registered.

One of the consequences of wholesale registration is that, in the eyes of the law, no Chinese marriage is dissoluble except by a judicial

[1] Stephen H. K. Yeh, 'Chinese Marriage Patterns in Singapore', *The Malayan Economic Review*, vol. IX, no. 1, April 1964, p. 104. (The average ages of brides and grooms in *all* registered marriages in 1963 were 23.9 and 27.6 respectively.)

[2] op. cit., p. 108.

[3] op. cit., p. 109. There is a peculiar feature of the figures for registered marriages. The Women's Charter provides for two kinds of marriage: in the Registry and by a person licensed to solemnize a marriage. We find that of the total of registered marriages in 1963 (the latest year for which I have the figures) 4,416 were solemnized in the Registry, 848 in churches, 51 in Hindu temples, and 51 in 'various other places'. The implication is that the Chinese are not taking the opportunity of converting the former 'new style' weddings (often held in public buildings or club premises) into registered marriages by getting the heads of associations and other leaders licensed as solemnizers. But is the heavy concentration on Registry weddings a cause or a consequence of the failure of large numbers of Chinese couples to marry by the rules of the Women's Charter?

process according to English principles. In the old days several hundred Chinese marriages must have come to an end in any one year. In 1951, 143 divorces (nearly all Chinese) were signed in the Department of Social Welfare by the informal procedure then current.[1] At the same time many divorces (but how many it is impossible to say) were signed with or without the help of lawyers.[2] And some marriages simply ended by one spouse quitting the other. There has certainly been a rise in the number of divorce petitions before the court in recent years, but it is equally evident that since 1961 Chinese marriages have not been legally dissolved in anything like the same proportion as in the earlier decade. In 1963, having the opportunity to go through the divorce files in the Supreme Court, I found that in the years 1959 to 1962 the numbers of petitions involving marriages both parties to which were Chinese were 40, 54, 54 and 72; they led to the following numbers of decrees: 35, 47, 49 and 48. In the first seven months of 1963, sixty-four Chinese petitions were before the court. Since that time the total number of petitions presented has gone up, the figure for 1965 being 156, but in this number Chinese cases are merged with all non-Muslim cases. Legal aid is available,[3] but there must still be some economic deterrent acting along with the formidable obstacles set up by a divorce system working by English rules. As the Minister of Labour and Law said in 1961, an immediate aim of the Women's Charter was to make marriage difficult to get out of. Clearly, the point was to prevent husbands shedding their wives; one may ask whether wives are not also being prevented from ridding themselves of undesirable husbands. Of the 220 Chinese petitions presented in the years 1959–62, 145 were petitions by wives.[4]

Of course, the new law of 1961 was concerned above all with sexual equality, and the extirpation of custom was to be a means to procure that equality. It was, after all, a Women's Charter. New nations

[1] Freedman, *Chinese Family and Marriage*, p. 182.

[2] op. cit., pp. 183f.

[3] In 1962, twenty-four applications for legal aid were made in respect of Chinese customary marriages, all but two of them being allowed. They 'produced' three decrees, nineteen pending at the end of the year. In the first six months of 1963, fifteen such applications were received, again all but two being granted.

[4] It will be recalled that the Women's Charter made provision for the appointment of Conciliation Officers, to whom the divorce court might in certain cases refer couples. There was one such Officer in mid-1963 (when I was in Singapore), but no case had been referred to him by the court. On the other hand, conjugal disputes are still brought to the Counselling and Advice Section (which in this matter is the successor to the Women and Girls Section) of the Department of Social Welfare.

emerging from the status of British possessions tend to carry into their new lives political and legal assumptions which, deriving from the institutions of modern Britain, presuppose enfranchized, property-owning, literate, independent women. In the case of the Singapore Chinese, high modernity has been inspired not simply by the direct British model, but also, and more importantly, by the version of Western ideals created in China during the past half-century. We come now to the sociological problem. What social conditions will facilitate or impede the realization of the ideals of sexual equality?

In fact, Singapore seems to enjoy the basic conditions likely to allow institutions to respond to the call of the new ideals. It is a country made up very largely of a city and dominated by urbanism. Its old economic function as a centre of trade and small industry is being partly replaced by the function of a large-scale manufacturing centre. Education is highly developed. Family planning is publicly and officially accepted as a means of limiting fertility. At the time of the 1957 census (which is the most recent) nearly a quarter of all Chinese women over the age of 14 had worked more than fifteen hours during the so-called 'reference week', only an eighth of these working women being 'unpaid family workers', and a half of all the working women being married. The literacy rate (per thousand) for Chinese females in the age group 10–14 was 580 and in the age group 15–19 496. The foundations of what passes for sexual equality in a modern society seem to have been laid. And I think we may safely assume that since 1957 the economic, political, and social roles of women outside the domestic sphere have both multiplied and been more largely filled.

What the precise implications of these general changes have been I cannot say, for I have not been able to repeat the observations I made in 1949–50 (my study in Singapore in 1963 was brief) and, although some other studies have been published,[1] they are neither comprehensive enough nor sufficiently up to date to make it possible for us yet to assess the manner in which the new law has meshed with general social change. We are left with a set of unanswered questions. Has

[1] For a fairly recent account of some relevant Chinese social institutions, see Ann E. Wee, 'Chinese Women of Singapore: Their Present Status in the Family and Marriage', in Barbara E. Ward, ed., *Women in the New Asia, The Changing Roles of Men and Women in South and South-East Asia*, Paris, 1963. See also Barrington Kaye, *Upper Nankin Street, Singapore*, Singapore, 1960; The Child Welfare and Social Work Section of Maris Stella Girls' School, *Teen-Age Girls' Family Problems, Singapore*, Singapore, 1965; and Barbara E. Ward, 'Men, Women and Change', in Ward, ed., op. cit.

polygamy declined *de facto?* Are the rich still able to maintain several households and procure their acceptance as Chinese families by drawing on the reserves of traditional attitudes and values? As Mrs Wee has pointed out,[1] for many educated young women secondary marriage to a rich man has hitherto been an honourable estate. Has the Women's Charter for them constituted a repeal of status? Is there now even less of a distinction in Chinese eyes between a concubine and a mistress? In the traditional Chinese view, as we have seen, the legitimacy of children depended upon their being recognized by their fathers. Has the new law led to a shift in values such that henceforth only the children of monogamously married wives will be socially acceptable? In a word, how are the norms enshrined in the Women's Charter being translated into the values and expectations of ordinary people?

In Singapore the norms of family life in a modern society have been stated in order to induce that family life. Industrialism and education may well push society along the road to the fulfilment of the new ideals, but it would be dangerous to assume that they will inevitably succeed in all particulars. It is true that the institutions of family and marriage all over the industrialized world tend to take on a common pattern; yet it would be unwise to imagine that every detail of the Chinese tradition will be flattened by the steamroller of modernity. Is it likely, for example, that the ideal of monogamous devotion (that we, looking out from Britain, take to be the hallmark of stable and satisfying family life) can be established where male sexuality has traditional licence and the women are categorized into humdrum mothers and alluring playmates? The left-wing puritanism that inspired the Women's Charter is not a set of religious values permeating society. It can dominate politics and law, as new economic opportunities can help women assert the rights that new ideology and new law create for them; but the responses of a complex society to legal and economic changes are not to be foretold by a few simple rules of prediction. It is certainly a pity that, as an anthropologist taking part in a legal symposium, I have had to pontificate on the law and be very hesitant about the fate of social institutions. Yet at least I shall have demonstrated how much remains to be done in the study of the politics and sociology of family law in Singapore. And, by implication, I am

---

[1] Wee, op. cit., pp. 401ff. Nobody knows how widespread has been the practice of plural marriage by the Chinese in Singapore; but it has certainly been fairly common, and not confined to the rich, although most noticeable among them. Cf. Freedman, *Chinese Family and Marriage*, pp. 119ff.

arguing the case for wider and comparative study. Quinquennial research budgets please copy.[1]

[1] It may be worth adding that I once looked forward from my experience of the Singapore Chinese in 1949–50 to the legal reforms that were yet to come. Happily, I made no predictions but, addressing myself to the colonial government of Singapore, I referred to three 'delicate' matters in the realm of Chinese marriage on which I was prepared to make recommendations. The first of these matters was secondary marriage. I wrote: 'There is a possibility, I suppose, that public and official opinion might eventually move against Chinese polygamy ...', but I was not very sure about it; and I went on to recommend some legal definition of secondary marriage in order to prevent 'a mistress slipping over the line into the territory of the wife'. I then made a case for the compulsory registration of Chinese marriages. Finally, I asserted that Chinese divorce required some proper basis in law. I wrote: 'With or without the aid of registration and with or without the intervention of the courts, it should be possible to legislate for some certainty in this field.'—*Chinese Family and Marriage*, pp. 228f.

4

SOME ASPECTS OF MARRIAGE AND
DIVORCE IN COMMUNIST CHINA

HENRY MCALEAVY

Reader in Oriental Laws in the University of London

On the Eve of 'Liberation'

Students of contemporary Chinese affairs, who seem condemned throughout the foreseeable future to derive their knowledge from propaganda sheets written on behalf of one side or the other, can hardly fail to look back with nostalgia to the days of the Nationalist régime, when even under the most rigorous government censorship the Chinese press, in contrast to its present fate, was comparatively free and unconfined. Among the magazines of that time, the Shanghai monthly *Hsi Feng* or *West Wind* occupied an honoured place. As its name suggests, its chief purpose was to introduce European literature and ideas to Chinese readers, but in addition it was much concerned with the general problems of Chinese society. In particular, it ran a correspondence column for readers in need of advice, and every now and then their letters and the answers they received were collected and published as brochures.

One such booklet which appeared in June 1948, precisely eleven months before the entry of the Communists into Shanghai, carried the following inquiry from a reader in Chengtu, capital of the western province of Szechwan:

'When I was nineteen years of age I married my wife Mei-chen. The following year my father's elder brother died without leaving a son, and I was appointed as his adopted heir, while retaining the succession to my own parents. My aunt, with the consent of my mother (note: who was clearly a widow), took for me as a second wife my first wife's younger sister, Chu-chen. Since the two of them were sisters, and also to show proper respect to my uncle, no distinction of status was made between them. Furthermore, on the advice of my family and friends, in order to mark the solemnity of the occasion I went through a ceremony of marriage with both of them together, and that evening the three of us shared a nuptial chamber. In the

73

twenty years that have passed since then, both my wives have accompanied me whenever I have had to make ritual visits of felicitation or condolence to my relatives and friends. Each of them has borne me sons and daughters. They are both old-fashioned women, gentle and well-mannered. I am very fond of them and have always treated both of them in the same way. We form a happy and united family.

'Recently, because of my work, we have moved to a house in town. Soon after our arrival a policeman called to ask me to fill in a form with particulars of my household. I was going to write down the names of my two wives when the policeman objected, and no matter how hard I tried to explain, he still wasn't satisfied. At last I asked him how he suggested I should fill in the form, to which he replied that I could enter the name of only one woman as my wife, and the other would have to go in as a "dependant". What am I to do? One wife was chosen by my mother, the other for my uncle. My mother, as well as my uncle, is now dead. How can I make a distinction between my two wives? If I were to do such a thing, all my family and friends would blame me. True, my wives did not receive a modern schooling, and indeed both of them have bound feet, but they are not on that account to be considered as un-educated; on the contrary they have a good grounding in Chinese literature, and often compose verses. If one of them is now com-pelled to pass as less than a concubine, as a mere "dependant", can you imagine what her feelings will be?

'I remember hearing that the law is not retrospective. Since the status of my two wives was long since legally recognized, why can the police now annul it? Can I seek redress through the courts? Or is there anything else I can do?'[1]

The appeal was in vain. The second marriage, said the *West Wind*, was bigamous, and the only advice which could be given to the un-fortunate husband was that if he insisted on according parity of treat-ment to his women he should declare both of them to be 'dependants'.

The form of marriage—known to the outside world chiefly by its survival, under the Cantonese name of *kim tiu*, in Hong Kong and among the Chinese communities in South-east Asia, has been described in an earlier volume of this series, and does not require further analysis here.[2] But it seemed useful at the beginning of this essay to quote the

[1] Huang Chia-yin, edit: *Mao-tun*, pp. 102–4, Shanghai 1948.
[2] See H. McAleavy: *Chinese Law in Hong Kong*, in J. N. D. Anderson, edit: *Changing Law in Developing Countries*, pp. 262ff. (*Studies on Modern Asia and Africa* 2), London 1964.

letter from Chengtu in order to throw light on the institution of marriage as it existed on the very eve of the Communist victory in China.
The inquirer, who seems to have been a reasonably intelligent and
educated man, is totally unaware, until the unlucky visit from the
policeman, that in taking two wives he has committed any infringement of the law, and his ignorance is shared by all his family and friends.
It is a far cry from the picture drawn by eminent Nationalist lawyers,
who assure us that concubinage was abolished as long ago as 1910,
and that the Nationalist legal system was so firmly rooted in mainland
China that its survival in Formosa since 1949 maintains 'the continuity
of the judicial life of the Chinese nation' and that 'based as it is on the
latest products of Western jurisprudence it cannot fail to forge a bond
between the East and the West, forming, at the same time, a golden
bridge through which they will meet'.[1] One may sympathize with the
loyalty which expresses itself in such statements, but the political and
social history of the Nationalist period becomes utterly incompre-
hensible if one imagines that the legislators of Nanking were able to
do much more, especially in matters of the family, than draft a blue-
print for the sort of China they hoped might somehow emerge into
the world. Leaving aside altogether the ruin caused by the Japanese
war from 1937 onwards, even in the brief heyday of the Nationalist
Government its writ scarcely functioned beyond the Yangtze Valley.
Elsewhere in the provinces theoretically loyal to Nanking, ex-warlords
turned governors administered justice in a decidedly idiomatic manner.
A sizeable part of the country was always in Communist hands.
Finally, the whole of Manchuria—then the centre of heavy industry—
was between 1931 and 1945 totally detached from Chinese control and
erected into a puppet State. Today, no doubt, the Empire of 'Man-
chukuo' is remembered, if at all, as a grotesque by-way of history, but at
the risk of being indiscreet one should in fairness mention that it was
granted *de jure* recognition by no less an authority than the Holy See,
and, what is more relevant in our context, was in due course provided
with its own system of law, which yielded nothing in point of merit to
the Nationalist codes and, like the latter, was almost entirely without
influence on the mass of the population.[2]

---

[1] Lone Liang: *Modern Law in China*, pp. 57 and 69; F. T. Cheng: *A Sketch of
the History, Philosophy and Reform of Chinese Law*, p. 45 (both in *Studies in the
Law of the Far East and South-east Asia*, Washington Foreign Law Society,
1956).

[2] K. Shimizu: *Kei no kenkyū*, p. 1, Tokyo, 1945.

The Marriage Law of 1950

When therefore the new rulers of China in September 1949 declared
the abrogation of all Nationalist laws the step was of little practical
significance to the people at large. The Marriage Law of the People's
Republic was promulgated on May 1, 1950, to come into effect immediately, and it is plain from the text that those who drafted it were
addressing themselves to a society still regulated by the unreformed
customary law. Article 1 proclaims the abolition of 'the feudal marriage system' and decrees that for the future marriage will be monogamous, while bigamy and concubinage are specifically prohibited in
the next article. So little credit was given to earlier Republican governments for any amelioration of manners that it was considered worth
while, under Article 13, to state that 'the drowning of infants and
similar crimes are strictly forbidden'.

Of the features of the traditional marriage system, the one most
offensive to the Communists was undoubtedly polygamy, using that
term in its most general sense to include both the rare *kim tiu* bigamy,
of which we have seen an example at the beginning of this essay, and
the far commoner concubinage. They hated it because it was peculiarly
redolent of class exploitation. There is some dispute among the lawyers
as to the precise effect on concubinage of the Nationalist Civil Code.
Certainly the taking of a concubine was equivalent to adultery and
gave the injured wife grounds for divorce. If, however, the latter
acquiesced in the arrangement, as she normally did, the best opinion
seems to be that the concubine enjoyed limited recognition as a family
'dependant'.[1] The debate, however, is of merely academic interest. The
decline in concubinage among certain classes of society before 1949
had nothing whatever to do with legal policy but was due to the influence of western ideas in intellectual circles. Loose morals in the
academic world were frowned upon, and if conspicuous would not
have been tolerated. Even incorrigibly Bohemian writers and artists
tended under the Republic to have their partners one at a time.
Similarly, government officials, especially those in international view,
would have thought it a solecism to follow the example of their prede-
cessors, the imperial mandarins, by maintaining a seraglio. Yet when
all is said and done these advanced opinions were confined to a very
small though influential section of the population. Few high-ranking
officers of the Nationalist army felt such inhibitions. Wealthy mer-
chants, including the compradores of the treaty-ports, thought concubines necessary to their social prestige. Most common of all was the

[1] Cheng Ching-yi: *Fa-lü ta tẓ'u-shu*, Vol. I, p. 688, Shanghai, 1935.

landlords' habit of taking the prettiest daughters of their tenants.

In prohibiting polygamy for the future, the Marriage Law of 1950 declared that existing unions of the kind would not be interfered with except on the application of one of the parties. But this easy-going doctrine was not adhered to in practice. The promulgation of the Marriage Law on May 1st in that year was followed on June 30th by the appearance of the famous Agrarian Law, of which Article 32 decreed:

'In the course of agrarian reform a People's Tribunal shall be set up in every county to ensure that it is carried out. The Tribunal shall travel to different places to try and punish, according to law, the hated despotic elements—whom the masses of the people demand should be brought to justice.'[1]

These words were already menacing enough, but the reality far exceeded what could have been anticipated. For before the end of 1950 China had intervened in the Korean War, and the People's Tribunals had become the instrument of a reign of terror, justified, like its precursors in France and Russia, by a foreign threat to the security of the revolutionary Government. In the space of eighteen months the landlord class had been thoroughly destroyed either by expropriation or by physical elimination. Estimates of the number of victims vary, but the slaughter was enormous, and it is hard to believe that less than one million people were put to death. To inflame the minds of the peasantry against their former masters, the homes of the landlords were in many places thrown open to public inspection and any trace of luxury and self-indulgence, especially of a sexual kind, dragged out into the light of day. When we add that in 1951–2 the People's Tribunals extended their sanguinary activities to the cities, and if we bear in mind the social pressure which in China even in the absence of legal process can be directed at a moment's notice against any person suspected of improper behaviour, it would clearly be a miracle if after 1952 a landlord lucky enough to escape with his life managed to retain the company of any young woman he might have taken as a concubine before the Communist victory. Middle-aged households, however, like that of our poor friend from Chengtu, if their social background did not stamp them as class enemies, would have been treated more indulgently, so that even today in so numerous a population there are bound to be many surviving examples of an institution which has at long last been given its death-blow.

[1] Robert Carin: *Agrarian Movement in Communist China*, Vol. I, pp. 33ff., Hong Kong, 1960.

Not perhaps such an outrage to Communist susceptibilities as polygamy, but still regarded as a great evil, was the old system of arranged marriages. In traditional Chinese law, as is well known, parents could contract a valid marriage on behalf of their children without the latter's consent, nor were the children freed from the duty of obedience so long as they had a father or mother alive: there was no legal age of majority in this sense. In addition, neither dynastic codes nor customary law prescribed a minimum age for marriage, and marriages of children were quite common. True, Republican governments had in their legislation attempted to check this by requiring the parties' consent; but in Chinese circumstances the seemingly reasonable provision of the Nationalist Civil Code, that men of 18 and girls of 16 could marry with their guardians' permission (Article 980), was found to provide a loophole for undue parental influence even among those restricted social groups which had regard for the newfangled statutes; and as we have seen most people never gave the Civil Code a thought. These facts serve to explain why the Marriage Law of 1950, after stipulating in Article 3 that the free consent of both parties is necessary, and in Article 4 that the minimum age is 20 for the man and 18 for the girl, makes no mention whatsoever of any possibility that younger persons may marry with their guardians' consent. The wishes of parents and other third parties are entirely excluded from consideration. Here it may be worth noting that Chinese Communist lawyers, basing their opinion on the experience of Chinese society, denounce not only the Nationalist Civil Code but the laws of capitalist nations generally for the infringement of personal freedom implied in permitting minors to marry with the consent of their guardians.[1]

The great majority of arranged marriages took place, of course, among peasants, to whom the system was part of the order of nature and who scarcely thought of repining at it. But even in the case of young people who had received a modern education and who had left home—sometimes to go abroad—in the course of their schooling or employment, there was one particular institution of the traditional law which was often effective in forcing them into a marriage from which all their reason and instincts recoiled. This was the contract of betrothal.

Betrothal

In the old China, where there was no State registration as part of marriage procedure, great attention was paid to the requirement of pub-

[1] N. Niida: *Chūka Jinmin Kyōwakoku konin-hō*, p. 28 (in K. Miyazaki, edit: *Shin hikaku konin-hō*, Tokyo, 1960).

licity, which in the absence of any religious intervention, as by a church, had to be manifested by the actions of the families concerned. The most striking example, familiar to anyone who has lived in China, was the conveyance of the bride, on the wedding-day, to her husband's house in a red sedan-chair accompanied by a party of musicians who ensured that nobody for a long way around could be unaware of what was happening. But even before matters had reached this final stage, the preliminary negotiations had to be conducted through the medium of a go-between, and not directly between the parties or their families. Then, when agreement had been reached on the main conditions, it was essential before the marriage itself could take place that there should be a solemn contract of betrothal. It frequently preceded the marriage by some years, but immediately the pair were declared affianced their status underwent a marked alteration. This was demonstrated by some odd rulings in the dynastic codes. For example, illicit sexual relations were in general an impediment to the subsequent marriage of the culprits; but if a betrothed coupled anticipated their nuptial privilege their conduct, though punishable as disobedience to parental authority, was not regarded as fornication and did not prevent their marriage. Then again, the dynastic laws provided that in the case of specially heinous crimes, such as treason, punishment should extend not merely to the criminal but also to members of his family. Yet, if the family of a betrothed girl incurred this penalty, she escaped on the grounds that she already to a certain extent belonged to another household. On the other hand, if it was her fiancé's family who were visited by the disaster she was not included in the list of condemned, as a wife would have been, but was permitted to claim her maiden status.[1]

After the fall of the Manchus in 1912, these regulations were simply of academic interest. What was important was the survival in popular custom of the ancient doctrine that a contract of betrothal was specifically enforceable. According to the imperial code even a purported ceremony of marriage between an affianced person and a third party was to be declared null and void at the suit of the injured partner.[2] It must be remembered, too, that prior to the concluion of the betrothal a substantial present would normally be made from the family of the bridegroom to that of the bride, and that such a present, in fact though not in name, would among the peasantry constitute a brideprice. True, the sale of brides was forbidden both by the Empire and the Republic —another instance of the immense gulf that separated theory from

[1] *Taiwan shihō*, Vol. II, Pt. 2, p. 304, Tokyo, 1911.
[2] ibid., p. 303, Tokyo, 1911.

79

practice—but even the Nationalist Civil Code by ruling, in Article 977, that on the cancellation of a contract of betrothal the party at fault must pay damages for any loss caused by such cancellation to the innocent party, especially since this ruling had been judicially interpreted to mean that 'when a contract is cancelled unilaterally, the cancelling party is responsible for indemnifying the other against losses received', had in fact condemned any poor person to the performance of an agreement of betrothal, however much against his will.[1] Nobody familiar with Chinese society will have any doubts on this point: the most cursory reading of the Chinese press before 1949 will produce examples by the score. Let one quotation suffice: it is from a letter written to the Shanghai People's Court and published in April 1950, just a month before the promulgation of the Marriage Law:

'As a child I was betrothed and sent to live in my fiancé's family. Later I had to leave and so came to Shanghai. Being dissatisfied at the proposed marriage, I put an announcement in a newspaper cancelling the betrothal. The other party has now made use of evil forces to seize my parents and hold them in custody.'[2]

The phrase 'evil forces' is extremely vague. As it may be assumed that the girl's parents lived in a remote country district, she may have been referring to the Nationalist magistrate and police, whom the Communist authorities had not yet had time to investigate or replace. She might equally well have meant a group of the ruffians who infested the countryside and were willing to act as hired bullies. At all events it can be seen what a hideous incubus this contract of betrothal was, and how it ruined many lives. We can understand therefore that the Communists were resolute in omitting any mention of betrothal in the text of the Marriage Law—a step which in China was a very substantial innovation. Nevertheless, an agreement to marry is an inevitable preamble to a wedding, and social custom as well as natural sentiments make it likely that the occasion will be marked by gifts, especially from the bridegroom to the bride. Even though the law frowns upon the slightest suggestion that a betrothal should be allowed to press anybody into a marriage against his will, yet would it not be offensive to all notions of justice if a blameless person were to forfeit what might be a valuable betrothal gift? Communist lawyers, though far from showing great eagerness to provide a remedy, have come to agree that 'so long as the money or the object is simply a present, the

[1] Niida: op. cit., p. 28.
[2] *Hun-yin fang-wu chai-wu-teng wen-t'i chieh-ta*, p. 24, Shanghai, 1950.

question should be decided according to the economic circumstances of the parties. If the donor is in special economic difficulties, while the recipient is fully capable of making restitution, then—always with the condition that the freedom of marriage must be safeguarded—according to the circumstances and at the discretion (of the Court) a part or the whole of the gift may be returned to the donor. In principle, however, the latter cannot demand such return (as of right).'[1]

Registration

The most basic condition for a reform of the marriage law was that there should come into existence a government able and ready to assert for itself a monopoly of force. It is well known to students of the old China that there were important areas of social activity over which even the strongest of the imperial régimes never seriously attempted to extend their control. In Manchu times, we are told, magistrates' offices commonly kept lists of powerful families in whose affairs it was inadvisable to interfere,[2] and in the humblest circles a son or daughter could not appeal to the State for help against the oppression of a parent. The political and administrative impotence of successive Republican governments had made things worse, until in 1949 there is no doubt that the mass of the population longed for the establishment of a central authority powerful enough to crush to the earth any jurisdiction other than its own. This explains why the term 'liberation', the expression used by the Communists to denote the occupation of a territory by the Red Army, seemed to many people by no means a misnomer. Not only so, but the People's Government by its Marriage Law of 1950 for the first time in Chinese history made registration by the State necessary condition to a valid marriage. In other words, from then on the reality of the parties' consent would be open to scrutiny by a public official, and child-marriage and other such practices could no longer shelter behind the wall of peasant tradition. More immediately, the innovation was welcome for another reason: it provided a cheap and convenient procedure, and one which furnished, through a readily obtainable certificate, the best possible proof that a wedding had legally been concluded.

---

[1] Niida: op. cit., p. 29. It should be noticed that among the regulations to protect the interests of members of the armed forces there is one which provides that an agreement to marry where one of the parties is in military service cannot be annulled during the period of such service without the soldier's consent. *Hun-ym-fa wen-ta*, p. 18, Hofei, 1964.

[2] Cf. *Hung Lou Meng*, chap. 4.

It was in fact an inevitable concomitant of the traditional marriage procedure whereby—leaving aside altogether the question of dowry and marriage price and the like—the entry of the bride to the connubial home was publicized by a procession with sedan-chair and musicians, not to mention a feast, that vastly more money should be spent than the parties could afford. The loans at usurious rates and all the attendant misery may easily be imagined. The Nationalist Civil Code required the simplest possible procedure. By Article 982 it was enough that there should be an open ceremony in the presence of at least two witnesses: the words 'open ceremony' were interpreted very loosely to mean any expression by conduct of the parties of their will to take each other as man and wife, in a place from which the public were not barred from entry. A lunch party in a restaurant, for instance, at which the guests would wear festive rosettes and would toast a couple's prosperity, would fulfil the requirement, and indeed a much less spectacular demonstration would do just as well. But in practice, lack of pomp and circumstance was felt to be bleak and unnatural, and throughout the Nationalist period the depressing phenomenon called a 'group-wedding', in which twenty or thirty couples would assemble in hired costumes, in a school hall or other such building, to be talked at by some local notability, was regarded as a smart way of cutting down expense. Even so, the cost was sometimes a burden and clearly any legislative or administrative action effective in leading young people to begin their life together by a simple visit to the registrar was a social benefit.

In an agrarian community, where everybody knew everybody else, the traditional marriage procedure was admirably designed to fulfil the purpose of publicity. Where, on the other hand, the plain requirements of the Nationalist Civil Code were taken at their face value difficulties often arose later when one of the parties found it necessary to establish proof of the marriage. To be sure, it commonly happened that on the wedding day a certificate of the marriage was executed in duplicate by the bride and groom, and countersigned by the witnesses, but such a document was never necessary, since it was thought sufficient if two of the spectators present could on occasion give oral testimony of what had passed. If, in fact, the witnesses were not available to give evidence when required, the situation might be serious. To complicate matters further there was a tendency among a small but increasing section of the urban population—especially in Shanghai—to imagine that they were more than meeting the needs of publicity by simply announcing a marriage in the press, even if they then went on to disregard the requirement of witnesses to the actual ceremony. Often indeed, especially during the 1930s, one read in the newspapers an announcement in which a man and woman declared that as from a certain date they were 'cohabiting'. Precisely what legal effect these peculiar advertisements were intended to have it is hard to say: from 1943 the press in what was then called Free China (meaning that part of the country under Chungking rule) at last refused to publish them. Today, it is unions of this kind that the Hong Kong Government seems especially to have in mind in its condemnation of 'Modern Chinese Marriages'.

To form an idea of the unhappiness to which such a state of affairs all too frequently led, we may take another look at the correspondence columns of the *West Wind* magazine. A further selection of letters, published in the same month of June 1948 as the one quoted at the beginning of this essay, carries the following appeal to the editor from a woman reader:

'I am only twenty but have been married for more than two years. Previously I worked in a store, where there was a man much older than myself who always treated me as a child, and was upset whenever I went to the cinema or for a stroll with any of my other workmates. For more than a year there was never any question of love between us, but as time went on I came to trust him, and when at last he wrote to me with an offer of marriage, I thought the matter over very carefully and accepted. In July of the year before last, just on the eve of the victory over Japan (note: the letter must have been written in 1947) we went to the country for a "honeymoon marriage". Since his mother was absent in Liuchow (in Kwangsi province) our wedding was as simple as possible: we dispensed with all ceremonial, certificates and the like, and contented ourselves with a honeymoon trip of a couple of months which we reckoned to be our wedding ceremony. More than two years have passed and we have a child nearly a year old. My husband has now gone elsewhere to carry on business, and I live with his mother and sister-in-law comfortably enough.

'But when I think matters over, I feel that I have been silly. How can one be certain that a man will always be faithful? If my husband does change in his affections, should I leave him? You see, I have no evidence of our marriage which I could rely upon if I went to a court, and I might well find myself destitute. I have been wondering whether it may still be possible to get him to sign a written acknowledgement of our marriage? Or is there some other way?'

The editor says she is quite right to be worried about the situation to which her imprudence has led her. He continues:

'These things are very delicate. If at the moment your relations are not all that they should be, your husband may refuse to go through a supplementary ceremony, or to acknowledge the marriage in writing; and such a request on your part may even make matters worse. If on the other hand you are still on good terms, and if he should return home, he may agree to give a little party on your wedding anniversary, at which a photograph could be taken. He may even be willing to sign a formal certificate of marriage.

'We may call this the method of frontal attack. Perhaps after all it may be more profitable to mount an offensive from the side. I mean by this that if you go through all the letters he has sent you since you were married, it is almost certain that somewhere in them you will find a reference to you as his wife. If, however, you have no such letters, then why not write to him in the hope of eliciting a reply which may contain the evidence you need? A photograph of you both after the wedding, preferably with the child, would be another item of proof. Again, if you do not have such a picture, you might arrange to have a family group photographed on his mother's birthday. If it includes him, so much the better, but even without him the fact that you and your child are included as family members would constitute evidence on your behalf.'[1]

The Marriage Law of 1950 decreed in Article 6 that a couple seeking to be married should go in person to the local office of the People's Government, where, provided there was no legal obstacle, their union would be registered and they would be issued with a marriage certificate. On May 16, 1950, or just over a fortnight after the promulgation of the Marriage Law, the Shanghai daily *Chieh Fang Jih Pao* stated in answer to a question: 'Since May 1st of this year, it is left to the parties to decide whether a marriage should be accompanied by a ceremony or not. The law takes no cognizance of the matter. But if a marriage is celebrated according to traditional ritual, and there is no personal registration according to law, and no issue of a certificate, then it cannot be considered to have the effect of marriage. The parties do not establish between themselves the rights and duties of a husband and wife, neither can they enjoy the protection of the Marriage Law. This

[1] Huang Chia-yin, edit: *Mi-kung*, pp. 97–9, Shanghai, 1948.

is a point to which all men and women henceforward contracting marriage must pay attention.'[1]

Nothing could be clearer than this. Yet it soon appeared that the peasants did not change their ways so readily as had been imagined, and in particular found it hard to believe that when a bride had been carried in triumph to her new home with all the time-honoured pomp of the red sedan-chair, she was not legally a married woman until she had received a piece of paper from a Communist official. Furthermore, the new régime, then in the midst of Land Reform, saw no profit to itself in a rigid application of the law which might, by the trouble it would cause in the countryside, offset the popularity being won by the elimination of the landlords. Accordingly, in a set of 'Answers to questions about marriage', published by the Legislative Committee of the Central People's Government in March 1953, we read: 'It is wrong not to go and register marriage. But in the case of marriages which have in fact come into existence, but lack merely the procedural requirement of registration, then we recognize the relationship of husband and wife, even without supplementary registration: though if the parties are willing to go and register, this can be done and a certificate issued accordingly.'[2]

The late Professor Niida from an examination of the material available came to the conclusion that, to be legally recognized, such *de facto* marriages should fulfil all the following three conditions. First, both the parties must believe that they are legally husband and wife. Secondly, there must be a sharing of connubial life together. Thirdly, their union must be acknowledged as valid by the community. It seems, too, that the recognition granted to a *de facto* marriage means that if during its existence either of the parties to it should purport to conclude a registered marriage with a third person the action would be treated as bigamy.[3]

There is no doubt that this concession was made with reluctance by the People's Government, and that it was intended to be no more than a temporary measure. Unregistered marriages do not reveal themselves to makers of statistics, but it would be safe to say that every year that passes brings nearer the victory of universal registration.

Divorce

Nothing has illustrated the development of Communist thinking before and after their victory more than their attitude towards divorce. In traditional Chinese society, the absence of any religious ingredient

[1] Niida: op. cit., p. 52. [2] ibid., p. 53. [3] ibid., p. 39.

in marriage meant that, as a purely civil contract, it could be terminated at the desire of both parties. In other words, from the earliest times divorce by consent was always permissible. Unilateral repudiation was allowed only to the husband and then only for a number of specified causes when it was a matter of divorcing a wife. A concubine could be dismissed without cause, and this was a fundamental inferiority of status between her and a wife. In fact, however, divorce was in all classes of society exceedingly rare. Among the poor, a wife was an economic asset whom it would be improvident to get rid of. Among the rich, she was protected by the general prejudice against divorce and by the fear of giving offence to her family. Even if a wife's conduct gave grounds for repudiation by her husband and he was unwilling to waive his rights altogether, it was usual, to spare the family embarrassment, for the wife to connive in a divorce ostensibly by consent.

The Nationalist Civil Code in Article 1050 retained divorce by consent, which could be achieved without any intervention by a court if both the parties signed a declaration of their intention to terminate their marriage and had it countersigned by two witnesses; but an application for divorce by either the husband or the wife required the decree of a court, which was granted for certain specific causes. Nevertheless, throughout the Republican period, the ancient prejudice against exposing domestic quarrels to the public view induced many people, especially women, to go against their own inclinations and agree to a divorce rather than contest their spouse's application in a court of law.[1] Then again, the influx of Western ideas from the beginning of the twentieth century led most young Chinese of what were called 'progressive' tendencies to revolt against the old doctrine that society was founded upon the notion of duty, and to demand instead that they should be permitted to enjoy their right to personal liberty. That a marriage contracted early in life should later on prove an impediment to a man's full development, whether social, intellectual or even sexual, was thought to be a sin against nature. Accordingly, the annals of the time contain numerous examples of what would seem to a detached observer to be remarkably unsentimental repudiations of spouses. Both Sun Yat-sen and Chiang Kai-shek prevailed on the rustic wives of their earlier days to make way for younger and more sophisticated women.

Communist intellectuals were if anything even more forward than other 'progressives' in asserting this marital freedom, and it was widely

[1] Tai Yen-hui: *Chūka Mingoku konin-hō*, p. 143 (in K. Miyazaki, edit: *Shin hikaku konin-hō*, Tokyo, 1960).

believed that the new Marriage Law would apply the saying of Marx: 'When a court grants a decree of divorce it is doing no more than putting on record that a marriage has already broken down.'[1] True, the Law, for the first time, made the intervention of the State necessary even for divorce by consent, but this aroused no apprehension. Article 17 provided that when both parties agree to divorce, they must attend in person at the local government office, where, as soon as it has been satisfactorily proved that the consent is genuine and that equitable arrangements have been made regarding children and property, a certificate of divorce must be issued. A unilateral application must also in the first instance be addressed to the local government office, which then summons both parties and tries to effect a reconciliation. If this fails, the matter is referred to the County or Municipal Court, which in its turn begins by trying to reconcile the parties. If here, too, all efforts are of no avail, the Court will proceed to give judgment. Unilateral petitions for divorce are not restricted to specific grounds, as in the Nationalist Civil Code.

A commentary on the Marriage Law, published as early as August 1950, contained some directives from the Peking People's Court on the treatment of matrimonial problems. The first of these referred to the case where one partner persisted in demanding a divorce, and the Peking Court declared: 'The principle of free marriage, by repudiating forced marriage, naturally produces a tendency towards free divorce. For divorce resembles marriage insofar as it is based on the consent of man and woman. Just as a party who does not consent cannot be forced into marriage, so when one spouse persists in demanding divorce while the other persists in refusing it, the couple cannot be compelled to continue to live as husband and wife. In such circumstances, the court must first of all inquire whether the marriage was at the free will of the parties, and whether the grounds of the party demanding divorce are true and proper, and congruent with the marriage policy of the People's Government. Generally speaking, when divorce is persistently demanded by one party it should be allowed. For divorce removes suffering, and causes a person to have more time and energy to devote to production. But any party who treats marriage lightly and irresponsibly, ought to be subjected to stern criticism.'[2]

After reading these words, one cannot feel much surprise that in the text of Article 17, reprinted in the same book, we find the words 'the

---

[1] Quoted in *Li-hun wen-t'i lun-wen hsüan-chi*, p. 9, Peking, 1958.

[2] P'ang Tun-chih: *Hsin hun-yin-fa chi-pen jen-shih*, pp. 38–9, Hong Kong, 1950.

Court will proceed to give judgment' changed by some extraordinary blunder into 'the Court will proceed to grant a divorce'.[1]

Before many months had gone by, there was great deception in certain quarters. The Hong Kong newspaper *Ta Kung Pao* on May 10, 1951, carried a report of a very significant case. A man of Tsinan in Shantung province had married a neighbour's daughter and lived with her for ten years, in the course of which they produced two children. The husband then went on his own to work in Shanghai, where he fell in love with another woman. He now applied to the Court for a divorce, alleging that his first marriage had been contracted at his parents' orders. His application was denied, and on appeal the East China branch of the People's Supreme Court upheld the refusal, and severely reprehended him for his errors. The view of the judges is summed up by Professor Niida as follows: 'If there is a reason why husband and wife cannot live together then the Court will grant a divorce. However, a divorce will not be granted at the request of the party responsible for creating the cause (of the failure of the marriage).'[2]

This doctrine was followed during the 1950s with such strictness that on April 13, 1957, during the so-called 'Hundred Flowers' enthusiasm, the Peking *People's Daily* carried a protest from somebody who obviously regretted a past, not so long since, when there had not been all this stifling concern for respectability. 'Surely,' he said, 'the Courts cannot refuse to grant a divorce because the parties' ideology is unsound, or because they have committed errors in their sexual relations? A surgeon cannot refuse to operate for appendicitis just because the patient has caused the trouble by eating too much or too quickly!'[3]

The protest was quickly howled down, and in the chorus of recrimination one theme emerged with particular vehemence. It was to the effect that the controversy itself had shown the extent to which bourgeois ideas regarding love and marriage had made their way among Chinese intellectuals, and especially among many of the cadres. A real Communist knows that a marriage has several aspects: political, economic, sexual, and that the determining factor should always be the political one.[4] It is particularly odious to find people so corrupted by bourgeois notions that they allege 'parental coercion', 'incompati-

---

[1] P'ang Tun-chih: *Hsin hun-yin-fa chi-pen jen-shih*, p. 29.

[2] Niida: op. cit., p. 93.

[3] Quoted in *Li-hun wen-t'i lun-wen hsüan-chi*, p. 10, Peking, 1958.

[4] ibid., p. 45, Peking, 1958.

bility of temperament', and 'lack of love' as reasons for seeking divorce.[1]

It may well seem odd that men and women should be blamed for pleading that they are victims of the system of arranged marriages against which the Communists have for most of their history inveighed so violently. The fact is that the really objectionable side of traditional marriage—or at any rate what the Communists considered as such—was to all intents and purposes laid low by the joint action of the Marriage Law and the Agrarian Law in the first three or four years after 1950, and that from then on the most insidious enemy was the presence throughout intellectual circles of liberal bourgeois ideology. True, in 1958 it could still be said that a sizeable proportion of marriages were 'semi-voluntary'—an expression which was taken to mean that the parties were introduced as potential spouses by go-betweens acting for their parents, and then agreed, without any real period of courtship, to settle down as husband and wife.[2] But the structure of Chinese society ensured that this pattern of match-making would endure for some time to come, and with all its imperfections it was redolent of the Chinese earth. Couples who met in this way would lead laborious uncomplicated lives. They would have their quarrels, of course, and sometimes would even come to blows, for it is characteristic of working people to be hot-blooded and direct in all they do.[3] But as for talk of incompatibility and the rest, such luxuries were strictly for the bourgeoisie.

Today this tendency is reinforced, and a campaign of unexampled vindictiveness is in full swing to extirpate from the Chinese scene all traces of 'bourgeois liberalism'. It is conveniently forgotten how deeply many of the Communist heroes in their private lives thirty years ago showed the influence of ideas which are now condemned. Certainly Mao Tse-tung's matrimonial career would have been markedly different if it had been governed by the Marriage Law of People's China as at present administered.

[1] Quoted in *Li-hun wen-t'i lun-wen hsüan-chi*, p. 31, Peking, 1958.

[2] ibid., p. 28, Peking, 1958. 'If the marriage, although at the start having the nature of an arranged union, was with the consent of the parties, and after the marriage a certain degree of affection has been established, the parties should not lightly seek a divorce': *Hun-yin-fa wen-ta*, p. 41, Hofei, 1964. The same work says that sons and daughters should ask their parents' views when thinking of marriage, as the latter have more experience of life.

[3] ibid., p. 46, Peking, 1958.

5

THE THEORY OF MATRIMONIAL CAUSES ACCORDING TO THE *DHARMAŚĀSTRA*

LUDO ROCHER

Professor of Philology, Free University of Brussels

Introduction

Before dealing with the subject of matrimonial causes according to the *dharmaśāstra* a few comments on the title of this paper may not be out of place. These comments will be mainly of a methodological nature.

A first comment is that the *dharmaśāstra* does not have a *Matrimonial Causes Act*, as is the case in England since 1857. In other words, in the whole of ancient Hindu law one would look in vain for a treatise, or even for a separate chapter, dealing exhaustively with what we call matrimonial causes. The result is that the data which I shall present to you as a more or less coherent whole are really drawn from various unrelated chapters of *dharmaśāstra* literature.

This first comment leads me on to my second preliminary remark. The fact that no Sanskrit text deals with matrimonial causes as such should not make you think that the data upon which I shall have to work are few in number. In reality they are numerous, far too numerous to be dealt with at all completely in a short paper. Moreover, they are not only numerous; as is the case with most other topics of ancient Hindu law, here, too, the various sources often seem to contradict or even to be repugnant to each other.

It is true that in Roman law, too, the law of marriage and matrimonial causes is far from being uniform. However, in Rome we are usually able to ascribe a date to the various changes, and we are well equipped to place them in their historical perspective. We know, for instance, that from being very strict in olden days, marriage gradually developed into a *liberum matrimonium* at the time of the Republic, to become much more strict again with Justinian who, here as elsewhere, made a conscious effort to return to ancient purity.[1] The problem is

---

[1] W. W. Buckland: *A Manual of Roman Private Law*, Cambridge University Press, 2nd ed., 1939, p. 70–1.

that in India this broad historical background is missing. Here we find the varying legal prescriptions simply juxtaposed; and if we consider that Indian history is much longer than that of Rome, and that the territory catered for by ancient Hindu law is much vaster than that of Roman law, it will be evident that the number of varying situations in India must have been immensely greater than was the case in Rome.

If I mention all this as a preliminary remark, it is mainly to tell you that, in this state of affairs, various attitudes are possible, and to explain to you the attitude which I have myself adopted while preparing this paper.

It is, of course, possible for the historian of ancient Hindu law to try to emulate the historian of Roman law, and to search for the historical background of the changes in Hindu law too. But I have two objections against such a procedure. In the first place, I cannot regard the efforts which have been made in that direction so far particularly convincing: far too often they lead to a vicious circle, in which the *dharmaśāstra* texts are used to reconstruct historical situations which are, then, in their turn employed to explain the changing data in the *smrtis*. And my second objection is that such historical reconstructions go straight against the very spirit of the ancient Hindu law texts. Differently from us—and this includes a number of modern Indian authors—the ancient *dharmaśāstrīs* firmly believed in a single and unchangeable *dharma*. If their works display differences, it is not because they wanted them to do so. On the contrary, whenever possible they tried very hard harmoniously to integrate the variants into one single system. To give only one example: the various forms of marriage existing in ancient India have not only been integrated into the classical *dharmaśāstras*, but have been worked out into a wonderful system of eight forms methodically arranged in a series proceeding from the most respectable to the most detestable.

If I, therefore, reject the approach of those who try to explain the rules of *dharmaśāstra* against their historical background, this does not imply that I want to be blind to the changes which undoubtedly manifested themselves in the long history of Hindu law generally and Hindu matrimonial causes in particular. This, then, is the reason why you will hear me quote far more often from the old *śāstras* than from the more recent commentaries. The commentaries are characteristic of one period of ancient Hindu law, no doubt: namely, of the later period. And, once Sir William Jones had stated that 'nothing could be more obviously just than to determine private contests according to those laws which the parties themselves had ever considered as the rules of their conduct and engagments in civil life',[1] it was completely justified, at the end of the eighteenth century, to have Jagannātha Tarkapañcānana compile a digest based on the *commentaries*. On the other hand, the commentators are not representative of the whole history of *dharmaśāstra*. Their reconstruction of the theory of matrimonial causes is based on the axiom of a perfectly static corpus of *dharmasūtras* and *dharmaśāstras*, a concept which is as unacceptable as the steady search for the historical background which I referred to before. Like the commentators, we, too, shall have to reconstruct the theory of matrimonial causes on the basis of the several *dharmasūtras* and *dharmaśāstras*—not to speak of the *arthaśāstra*—which, although theoretically uniform, in reality display a wide range of variety. I can only hope that my precautions, some of which I have just mentioned, will allow me to reach a certain degree of historic precision. I apologize for these theoretical speculations. But I thought that, in a series of papers touching upon different legal systems, it was my duty to indicate briefly the difficulties and the restrictions which research on matrimonial causes in ancient Hindu law is confronted with. But I shall now come to the study of matrimonial causes themselves.

Since the treatises on *dharmaśāstra* do not provide us with an intrinsically binding scheme, I had to establish one myself. I propose to divide this paper into three parts. In the first place I should like to examine the *dharmaśāstra* theories on matrimonial rights. Next, I shall try to answer the question whether and, if so, how far ancient Hindu law recognizes the dissolution of marriage. And, finally, I shall venture to give you my opinion on the vexed problem as to how the theory of matrimonial causes worked out in practice.

Matrimonial Rights

There is no doubt that the *dharmaśāstra* pays much attention to the mutual rights of husband and wife, at least indirectly. I shall immediately explain my restriction: 'at least indirectly'. As is well known, the *dharmaśāstra* primarily establishes sets not of 'rights' but of 'duties', duties to be performed by human beings in all situations of life. Hence, as far as married persons are concerned, too, the ancient Indian law texts enumerate their various duties, not their rights. However, inasmuch as a duty of one spouse coincides with a right of the other, I shall conform to modern usage, and speak of matrimonial 'rights' in ancient Hindu law.

The mutual rights of husband and wife in a Hindu marriage cannot,

[1] Colebrooke's Preface to his *Digest*.

I think, be fully appreciated without a short reference to one aspect of the Hindu marriage itself.

Far be it from me to desire to open the file of Hindu marriage as such; although I must confess that, when trying to understand the Hindu theory of matrimonial causes, I often had a feeling that a clearer insight to the nature of the Hindu marriage itself would have been extremely useful. Unfortunately here, too, the data are not such as easily to allow a clear and neat picture.

Whether we agree with Westermarck or not when he holds that among the Indo-European peoples generally there has been a stage when, as a rule, the woman was sold to the man,[1] it cannot be denied that the element of 'sale' is not completely absent from the Hindu marriage.[2] I am the more inclined to say so because the authors of the lawbooks vigorously react against this conception. And this is no paradox on my part: my impression is that the non-legal texts represent a widely spread 'popular' view which was unacceptable to the *dharmaśāstrīs* who not only had a more technical notion of sale but also, as we shall see, a more idealistic view of marriage.[3]

On the other hand, if the *dharmaśāstra* thus rejects the identification of marriage and sale, it definitely discloses another characteristic which for our purpose is no less interesting. One has only to read the definitions of at least four of the eight forms of marriage—the most respectable ones—to be convinced of the constant presence in the minds of the authors of the idea of a gift, a gift of the maiden by the father to the husband.[4]

[1] Westermarck's *History of Human Marriage*, chapter 23, as quoted, e.g. by P. E. Corbett: *The Roman Law of Marriage*, Oxford, Clarendon Press, 1930, p. 1.

[2] e.g. Maitrāyaṇīyasaṃhitā 1.10.11: 'she indeed commits falsehood (or sin) who being purchased [*kr̄tā*] by her husband roams about with other males'. Cf. P. V. Kane: *History of Dharmaśāstra* II, pp. 503–7.

[3] e.g., Manu 3.51: 'No father who knows (the law) must take even the smallest gratuity for his daughter; for a man who, through avarice, takes a gratuity, is a seller of his offspring.' For other references, cf. Kane, ubi cit.

[4] Thus Manu 3.27–30: '*The gift of a daughter* after decking her (with costly garments) and honouring (her by presents of jewels), to a man learned in the Veda and of good conduct, whom (the father) himself invites, is called the Brâhma rite.

'*The gift of a daughter* who has been decked with ornaments, to a priest who duly officiates at a sacrifice, during the course of its performance, they call the Daiva rite.

'When (the father) *gives away his daughter* according to the rule, after receiving from the bridegroom, for (the fulfilment of) the sacred law, a cow and a bull or two pairs, this is named the Ârsha rite.

However, as I said before, I do not want to discuss here the nature of the Hindu marriage. My only purpose was to point out the existence —consciously or unconsciously—of the view according to which the future husband participated to some extent in the characteristics of a buyer or a donee. In other words, through marriage the husband acquired *some* kind of ownership over his wife.

If, after all this, I say that according to the *dharmaśāstra* both spouses had a right to each other's affection and society, it will be clear from the outset that, if such a right existed on both sides, it was given a completely different content when applied to the husband and wife, respectively.

As far as the wife is concerned, not only does she have to share her husband's life, but she has to do so under any circumstances, even if the husband is wholly vicious. Manu [5.154] holds:

> Though destitute of virtue, or seeking pleasure (elsewhere), or devoid of good qualities, (yet) a husband must be constantly worshipped as a god by a faithful wife.[1]

The same idea has been expressed again and again in the *dharmaśāstra* texts, and equally numerous are the other literary sources illustrating in practice the theoretical rule of the *smṛti*. When, in the Śatapatha-brāhmaṇa, the young princess Sukanyā has been given in marriage to the old sage Cyavana who had been wronged by her brothers, the Aśvins come by, and they desire to win the young wife's favour:

> They said, 'Sukanyā, what a decrepit, ghostlike man is that whom thou liest with; come and follow us!' She said, 'To whom my father has given me, him will I not abandon, as long as he lives!' But the *Ri*shi was aware of this [4.1.5.9.].

The highest rewards have been promised to a wife who thus behaves as a *pativratā*, 'one faithful to her husband':

> She, who, controlling her thoughts, speech, and acts, violates not her duty towards her lord, dwells with him (after death) in heaven,

---

'*The gift of a daughter* (by her father) after he has addressed (the couple) with the text, "May both of you perform together your duties", and has shown honour (to the bridegroom), is called in the *Smṛiti* the Prâjâpatya rite.'

[1] Here as elsewhere, rather than translating ourselves—which would involve repeated discussions and justifications—we quote from the existing classical translations of the ancient Hindu lawbooks.

and in this world is called by the virtuous a faithful (wife, *sādhvī*) [Manu 5.165 =9.29].

But if a wife does not appreciate the society of her vicious husband, a sanction follows automatically:

> She who shows disrespect to (a husband) who is addicted to (some evil) passion, is a drunkard, or diseased, shall be deserted for three months (and be) deprived of her ornaments and furniture [Manu 9.80].

Whereas the husband thus has a quasi-absolute right to the wife's society, the same can hardly be said about the wife's right to the husband's company. For instance:

> She who drinks spirituous liquor, is of bad conduct, rebellious, diseased, mischievous, or wasteful, may at any time be superseded (by another wife) [Manu 8.90].

It is true that supersession by another women did not leave the superseded wife without means of existence—I shall come to that later— nevertheless it could be a severe punishment from which the husband in similar circumstances remained exempt.

Another eloquent example opposing the husband's absolute and the wife's relative rights to the other's society may be quoted from Kauṭilya [3.2.46–47]. It refers to the case in which either spouse is suffering from an incurable disease:

> And the man, if unwilling, need not approach a (wife) who is leprous or insane.
> A woman, however, shall approach a (husband) even of this type, for bearing a son.

Here the element 'for bearing a son' is fundamental; I shall have to mention it again very soon.

In connection with the purely sexual aspect of the spouses' right to each other's society, too, the difference between the rights—or the duties—of husband and wife is considerable. About the wife who shuns this type of marital duty Baudhāyana [4.1.20] has the following *sūtra*:

> Let him [i.e. the husband] proclaim in the village a wife who, being obdurate against her husband, makes herself sterile, as one who destroys embryos, and drive her from his house.

The husband, under the same circumstances, is, of course, guilty of the same offence:

He who does not approach, during three years, a wife who is marriageable, incurs, without doubt, a guilt equal to that of destroying an embryo [4.1.17],

but the sanction could hardly have been more different:

But for the transgression of that husband who does not approach a wife who bathed after temporary uncleanness, (the performance of) one hundred suppressions of breath is prescribed (as a penance) [4.1.21].

A right which undoubtedly belonged to the wife is that of maintenance by the husband. One of the basic principles of *dharmaśāstra* in connection with women is that they must be constantly protected. Manu [9.3] says:

Her father protects her in childhood, her husband protects (her) in youth, and her sons protect (her) in old age; a woman is never fit for independence.

Even though this protection has in a number of cases been interpreted as a kind of custody—'Woman must particularly be guarded against evil inclinations'—the fact remains that it also implied that, as far as married life is concerned, the wife has a right to be maintained by her husband.

Moreover, even if some texts seem to suggest that the husband's duty to maintain his wife applies only as long as she is faithful to him:

The husband receives his wife from the gods, (he does not wed her) according to his own will; doing what is agreeable to the gods, he must always support her (while she is) faithful [Manu 9.95],

there are other texts which suggest that maintenance should be continued even after the wife has, for some reason or other, been superseded.[1]

A factor which must have profoundly influenced the matrimonial rights—especially as enjoyed by the wife—was the birth of a son. When reading the texts I often wondered whether the procreation of a son was one of the main results of marriage, or whether it was the

[1] Yajñavalkya 1.74; cf. below. The texts about maintenance have been discussed in detail *per* Chandavarkar, J., in *Parami* v. *Mahadevi* (1909), I.L.R. 34 Bom. 282–5.

very purpose of marriage for a man.[1] But even if I am unable clearly to answer the question—it is one of those questions about the nature of marriage about which I feel I should like to come to a better under-standing—the very fact that the question can be raised whether marriage was not contracted with a view to the husband's having a son is a sufficient indication that everything in marriage, i.e. also the matrimonial rights of the wife, depend to a large extent upon whether she gives birth to a son or not.

I cannot refer here to all the rules in which the matrimonial rights of the wife are influenced by her having a son or not, but I must at least mention the most spectacular one, namely that a wife who fails to give birth to a son may be superseded by another woman. Thus Kauṭilya [3.2.38-9]:

> The (husband) shall wait for eight years if the wife does not bear offspring or does not bear a son or is barren, for ten if she bears dead offspring, for twelve if she bears only daughters. After that he may marry a second wife with the object of getting a son.[2]

I shall come back to the legal consequences of supersession later, but it is clear that the status of a sonless woman changed considerably when superseded by another woman who was capable of giving her husband a son.

The high esteem which the ancient Indian sources display for the mother of a son—as against women generally—is well known. For our subject today it might, however, be not without interest first to quote a rule from the Vāsiṣṭhadharmaśāstra [13.47] dealing with the relations between a son and his parents:

> A father who has committed a crime causing loss of caste must be cast off. But a mother does not become an outcast for her son.

Indeed, this *sūtra* helps us to understand another rule, from Śaṅkha-Likhita's *dharmaśāstra*,[3] concerning the attitude to be taken by the son in a dispute—the text is so vague that we must assume it includes matrimonial causes—between his parents:

> The son should not take sides between his father and mother: indeed he may, if he so chooses, speak in favour of his mother alone, since the mother bore him (in her womb) and nourished him.

[1] Kauṭilya (3.2.42), when treating the possibility for a man to supersede his wife by one or more others if she does not give birth to a son, adds: 'For wives are (necessary) for having sons.'
[2] Cf. Manu 9.81.
[3] Quoted by Kane, op. cit. II, p. 580.

Dissolution of Marriage

It is a well-known fact that the peoples of ancient India had a very high conception of marriage as such. Says Dr Kane: 'This is the most important of all saṃskāras. Throughout the ages for which literary tradition is available in India marriage has been highly thought of.'[1]

The aura of sanctity with which the Hindu marriage has ever been surrounded is so real that it has even influenced the recent developments of Indian marriage law. To quote Professor Derrett: 'In fact, in no other respect are the feelings of Hindus so acutely sensitive as when their concept of and beliefs in the importance of marriage as an institution are questioned or attacked. This is largely the work of the *dharamaśāstra*, which, after more than two millennia of relentless propaganda, has produced an effect which the West would unhesitatingly label "puritanical". Nor is there any trace of conscious hypocrisy in the attitude which is characteristic of caste Hindus: profession and practice keep good company with each other. Such a fact is not to be ignored when considering the proposed alterations in the law.'[2]

In principle the Hindu marriage is indissoluble; the basis for this principle has been found in passages like this, from the *Nāradasmṛti* [12.27–8]:

Therefore a father must give his daughter in marriage once (for all), as soon as the signs of maturity become apparent. (By acting) otherwise he would commit a heavy crime. Such is the rule settled among the virtuous.

Once is the (family) property divided, once is a maiden given in marriage, and once does a man say, 'I will give'; each of these three acts is done a single time only among the virtuous.

Add to this that one of the traditional duties of husband and wife has been the common performance of religious acts:

... from the time of marriage, they are united in religious ceremonies.
Likewise also as regards the rewards for works by which spiritual merit is acquired . . . [Āpastamba 2.6.14.16–17],

and it will be clear that as far as its sanctity and indissolubility are concerned, the ideal Hindu marriage corresponds to the old view of Roman law as expressed in the definition given at the end of the classical period by Modestinus—and accepted by Justinian: *nuptiae*

[1] op. cit., II, p. 427.
[2] *Hindu Law Past and Present*, Calcutta, Mukherjee, 1957, p. 82.

sunt coniunctio maris et feminae et consortium omnis vitae divini et humani iuris communicatio.[1]

However, even though marriage in ancient India—in theory and in practice—was so highly thought of, we may state without hesitation that marriage has never been completely indissoluble. I promised to speak about matrimonial causes 'according to the *dharmaśāstra*'; so I should not go beyond this restriction. Otherwise it would not be difficult at all to produce evidence of the fact that the ideal of the *dharmaśāstra* has not been adhered to by the whole population of India.

I shall restrict myself to quoting one single example from a report on the customary law of the Punjab: 'It is well known that according to the strict principles of Hindu law, which in this respect is entirely different to the Muhammadan, marriage is regarded as a sacrament, which, when once solemnized, becomes indissoluble. . . . But amongst the Jat population of the province these sacerdotal notions of marriage have obtained but little if any countenance; and thus nothing is more common than to find a deserted wife, or one who has been set aside by her husband, marrying another man in the lifetime of the first husband, and succeeding to his property as a wife.'[2]

But I shall come back to the *dharmaśāstra*, and quote two stanzas from Manu [9.101–2]:

'Let mutual fidelity continue until death', this may be considered as the summary of the highest law for husband and wife.
Let man and woman, united in marriage, constantly exert themselves, that (they may not be) disunited (and) may not violate their mutual fidelity.

It is clear from these very verses that, although in the ideal situation marriage should be for life, this ideal was not always fulfilled. The fact that husband and wife are encouraged to make an effort in order to avoid separation implies that separation was not always avoidable.

We shall now try to establish how far separation of spouses existed in the *dharmaśāstra*, and which were the forms it assumed.

A first question which I shall try to answer is whether or not ancient Hindu law draws a distinction between what we call void and voidable marriages.

Remarkably enough the distinction has not only been made, but

[1] Cf. Buckland, op. cit., p. 70.
[2] Ch. Boulnois and W. H. Rattigan: *Notes on Customary Law as Administered in the Courts of the Punjab*, Lahore, Albert Press, 1876, pp. 95–6.

marriages have been declared null and void for a reason which today, in English law and elsewhere, continues to be a ground for nullity: namely, relationship within the prohibited degrees.

This is not the place to examine the exact extent of the prohibited degree in ancient Hindu law—which would mean to define the terms *gotra*, *pravara*, and *sapiṇḍa*; the main point is that such prohibited degrees exist from the *dharmaśāstra* onward. Medhātithi, when commenting on Manu 3.11, appeals to a basic principle of Mīmāṃsā to say that when a rule forbidding some action has a 'visible', worldly purpose (*dṛṣṭārtha*), it is meant only to express a recommendation; but when such a rule has an 'invisible', transcendental purpose, it is a mandatory injunction. The practical difference is that in the former case the act committed is valid and remains so; in the latter case, on the contrary, the act itself is to be considered as not having taken place. When applied to marriage, this means that the purpose of rules forbidding a man to marry, e.g. a diseased girl, is patent, with the result that he who does marry such a girl commits an offence but the marriage as such remains valid; the rules forbidding him to marry a girl who is a *sagotra*, *sapravara*, or a *sapiṇḍa*, on the other hand, have no immediately patent purpose, so that those who marry such girls not only commit an offence but such marriages are also null and void.

Whatever the practical value of these Mīmāsṃā speculations may have been, and even if another commentator on Manu, Nārāyaṇa, rejects the distinction established by Medhātithi, the fact remains that the ancient Hindu commentators, too, have at least conceived the distinction between void and voidable marriages.[1]

It seems to me that the concept of a void marriage as against a voidable one also found expression in another way; namely, through the channel of the well-known distinction between two stages in marriage. It is true that the later one goes in the history of *dharmaśāstra*, the more it is the second stage only which has been considered as marriage *stricto sensu*; the first stage more and more becomes a preparatory one which finally—I suspect, under Western influence—is spoken of as 'betrothal'.[2]

Personally, however, I am convinced that this is a later evolution only, and that, according to the *dharmaśāstra*, both the so-called betrothal and the actual marriage were but two successive stages of the

[1] cf. R. M. Das: *Women in Manu and His Seven Commentators*, Varanasi, Kanchana Publications, 1962, pp. 144-5.

[2] e.g. Mayne's *Hindu Law*, 11th ed., p. 136: 'Marriage is not to be confounded with betrothal. The one is a completed transaction; the other is only a contract.'

same *saṃskāra*, 'sacrament', marriage. Let me quote the following *śloka* from Nārada [12.2]:

> When a woman and man are to unite (as wife and husband), the choice of the bride must take place first of all. The choice of the bride is succeeded by the (ceremony of) joining the bride and bridegroom's hand. Thus the ceremony (of marriage) is twofold (*saṃskāro dvilakṣaṇaḥ*).

But Nārada [12.3] goes on:

> Of these two parts (of the marriage ceremony) the choice of the bride is declared to lose its binding force, when a blemish is (subsequently) discovered (in either of the two parties). The Mantra (prayer), which is recited during the ceremony of joining the bride and bridegroom's hands, is the permanent token of marriage.

In other words: although the *saṃskāra* did actually start with the so-called betrothal, even after this the marriage can be considered null and void; but it can no longer be so once the second stage of the ceremony has taken place. At that moment marriage becomes, in principle, indissoluble, provided that in a number of cases, which we shall come to immediately, it can become voidable.

To be complete I must add that, in the lower forms of marriage especially, nullity during the period separating the two stages of the ceremony seems to have been easily accepted. In connection with the uniqueness of the father's giving his daughter in marriage, Nārada [12.29–39] adds:

> This rule applies to the five (first) marriage forms only, beginning with the Brâhma (form of marriage). In the three (others), beginning with the Âsura form, the (irrevocable) gift (of a maiden to a particular suitor) depends on the qualities (of the suitor).
>
> Should a more respectable suitor (who appears), eligible in point of religious merit, fortune, and amiability, present himself, when the nuptial gift has already been presented (to the parents by the first suitor), the verbal engagement (previously made) shall be annulled.

One of the reasons which most surely render marriage insecure is the husband's prolonged absence from the house. What is meant by absence from the house is clear from a stanza in the *Manusmṛti* [9.76]; differently from Roman law, where absence includes such situations as

captivity and military enlistment,[1] ancient Hindu law conceives mainly
of three forms of absence:

> If the husband went abroad for some sacred duty (she) must wait
> for him eight years, if (he went) to (acquire) learning or fame six
> (years), if (he went) for pleasure three years.

Nārada [12.98–100], without mentioning other forms of absence,
takes into account several other factors in order to determine the length
of the period during which the wife has to wait for her husband: caste,
the fact whether or not there are children, and the fact whether or not
any news is received from the absent husband:

> Eight years shall a Brahman woman wait for the return of her
> absent husband; or four years if she has no issue: . . . A Kshatriya
> woman shall wait six years: or three years if she has no issue; a
> Vaiśya woman shall wait four (years) if she has issue; any other
> Vaiśya woman (i.e. one who has no issue), two years.
>
> No such (definite) period is prescribed for a Śûdra woman, whose
> husband is gone on a journey. Twice the above period is ordained,
> when the (absent) husband is alive and tidings are received from
> him.

Manu [9.74–5] seems to see no ground for dissolution of the
marriage in case where the husband duly provided for maintenance for
his abandoned wife:

> A man who has business (abroad) may depart after securing a
> maintenance for his wife; for a wife, even though virtuous, may be
> corrupted if she be distressed by want of subsistence. If (the hus-
> band) went on a journey after providing (for her) the wife shall
> subject herself to restraints in her daily life; but if he departed
> without providing (for her), she may subsist by blameless manual
> work.

As a matter of fact, Manu never states what the wife shall or may do
after having waited for the said periods of eight years, six years, etc.
Nārada [12.101], however, leaves no doubt:

> The above series of rules has been laid down by the Creator of the
> world for those cases where a man has disappeared. No offence is
> imputed to a woman if she goes to live with another man after (the
> fixed period has elapsed).

[1] Corbett, op. cit., p. 211.

In connection with the absent husband I found one interesting case in which the marriage is capable of termination because of the husband's connivance. Kauṭilya, who of course does not profess to lay down the requirements of righteousness (*dharma*), states [4.12.30–2]:

> The husband's kinsmen or his servant should keep under guard the wife who misbehaves when the husband is away on a journey. Kept under guard, she should wait for the husband. If the husband were to tolerate, both should be set free (*nisṛjyetobhayam*).

The same *śloka* of Nārada [12.97] which allows the wife to take another husband when her first husband has been absent for a long time, also allows her to do so 'when he has been expelled from caste'. According to Kauṭilya [3.2.48], too:

> A husband who . . . is . . . an outcast . . . may be abandoned (*tyājyaḥ*).

The fact that a husband may thus be abandoned because he has been excluded from his caste is, in my opinion, extremely important. I shall not insist upon it here, but I shall not omit using it as an argument in discussion later in this lecture.

In order to exhaust the *śloka* of Nārada [12.97] I must add that a wife is also entitled to take another husband if the first husband proves to be impotent.[1]

At a first glance impotence is just another ground which makes a marriage voidable. The question of impotence is, however, complicated by another stanza of Nārada [12.8]:

> The man must undergo an examination with regard to his virility, when the fact of his virility has been placed beyond doubt, he shall obtain the maiden (but not otherwise).

This prescribed physical examination of the husband must have taken place after the girl had been verbally promised to him but before their hands had been ceremoniously joined together, i.e. between the so-called betrothal and marriage proper. Thus impotence fits in with the whole theory of blemishes attaching to either spouse; compare Manu [9.72–3]:

> Though (a man) may have accepted a damsel in due form, he may abandon her (if she be) blemished, diseased, or deflowered, and (if she have been) given with fraud. If anybody gives away a maiden possessing blemishes without declaring them, (the bridegroom) may annul that (contract) with the evil-minded giver.

[1] cf. also Kauṭilya 3.2.48. For further details, see Nārada 12.15–18.

Although the texts are not very clear on this point, my impression is that all blemishes,[1] whether detected before or after the final marriage ceremony—most of these blemishes could hardly have been detected before—having a bearing not upon the 'marriage' but upon the 'betrothal'. The result is that, if my reasoning is correct, impotence and the other blemishes, instead of being grounds for dissolution of marriage, actually rendered the ancient Hindu marriage null and void from the beginning, or at least voidable.

A number of passages from the *dharmaśāstras* deal with situations which we would normally qualify as cases of cruelty. After what I said before, I need no longer insist that cruelty is to be understood as cruelty committed by the wife; for we saw that the wife has to endure her husband, however mischievous he may be.

I shall merely remind you of the verse of Manu [9.80] quoted above:

She who drinks spirituous liquor, is of bad conduct, rebellious, diseased, mischievous, or wasteful, may at any time be superseded (by another wife).

to which is added in the next verse that she who is quarrelsome may be superseded without delay.

Nārada [12.93] has a slightly different sanction:

One who shows malice to him, or who makes unkind speeches, or eats before her husband, he shall quickly expel from his house.

According to whether the commentators are more or less favourably disposed towards such wives, Nārada's 'banishment from the house' has been extended to 'banishment from the village' in the *Nāradabhāṣya* or reduced to 'banishing her from the principal habitation, let him assign to her a *separate* dwelling within his close' in Colebrooke's *Digest* [4.1.63].

Kauṭilya's *Arthaśāstra* has still another ground for dissolution of marriage, a ground which, I think, we may interpret as mutual agree-

---

[1] For an enumeration of such blemishes, see Nārada 12.36–37: 'Affliction with a chronic or hateful disease, deformity, the loss of her virginity, a blemish, and proved intercourse with another man: these are declared to be the faults of a maiden.

'Madness, loss of caste, impotency, misery, to have forsaken his relatives, and the two first faults of a maiden (in the above text): these are the faults of a suitor.'

ment. In the section on *dveṣa* 'hatred, disaffection' the following passage occurs [3.3.15.16]:

A dissaffected wife is not to be granted divorce from the husband who is unwilling, nor the husband from the wife. But mutual disaffection (*parasparaṃ dveṣāt*) (alone) a divorce shall be granted.

The only restriction would be that such a dissolution of marriage would be possible in the four lower forms of marriage only.[1]

I suppose you must have been struck by the fact that, in a discussion about terminating marriages, I have not so far mentioned adultery. Adultery, which even in the Ecclesiastical Courts in England before 1857 was a ground for a divorce *a mensa et thoro*, is certainly not unknown to the authors of the *dharmaśāstra*. On the contrary, the ancient Hindu lawbooks contain numerous rules about adultery; even more so, adultery with other similar offences appeared as one of the eighteen *vivādapadas* 'titles of law' into which ancient Hindu substantive law has been traditionally divided.

In the *Manusmṛti* alone about thirty-five stanzas have been devoted to the subject of adultery. As far as the details of the prescriptions are concerned I admit that it is extremely difficult to detect a system underlying these rules. If it is true that the laws of Manu as we have them are the result of several revisions, revisions which severely undermined its unity, this certainly is the case in the portion dealing with adultery. For the later commentators such portions were a special treat: on them they could display all their skill in harmonizing rules which at first sight were not very harmonious. However, these details are of less importance to us today. I shall rather stress a few basic characteristics of adultery as far as its place within the theory of matrimonial causes is concerned.

A first remark must be that adultery, according to Nārada [14.2] and others [Bṛhaspati 22.1, Jolly] is one of the four types of 'heinous offences' (sāhasa):

Manslaughter, robbery, an indecent assault on another man's wife, and the two species of insult, such are the four kinds of Heinous Offences (*sâhasa*).

This is extremely important, as it locates adultery within the framework of ancient Hindu substantive law, with far-reaching consequences upon adjective law as well—but I shall come to that later.

[1] Nārada 12.90, on the contrary, states: 'When husband and wife leave one another, from mutual dislike, it is a sin, . . .'

Moreover, not only is adultery a *sāhasa*, but, *sāhasa* being divided in the usual way into *sāhasa* of the first degree, the middlemost degree, and the highest degree, Nārada [14.6] adds:

> Taking human life through poison, weapons or other (means of destruction), indecent assault on another man's wife, and whatever other (offences) encompassing life (may be imagined), is called Sāhasa of the highest degree.

With the result that he who commits adultery is liable to the punishment normally prescribed for this highest degree of *sāhasa*:

> For Sâhasa of the highest degree, a fine amounting to no less than 1,000 (Paṇas) is ordained. (Moreover) corporal punishment, confiscation of the entire property, banishment from the town and branding, as well as amputation of that limb (with which the crime has been committed), is declared to be the punishment for Sâhasa of the highest degree [Nārada 14.8].

To be complete I must add that, according to a general rule of ancient Hindu criminal law, in the case of a *brāhmaṇa* offender, corporal punishment is replaced by some other type of punishment. Thus Nārada [14.9.10] continues:

> This gradation of punishments is ordained for every (caste) indiscriminately, excepting only corporal punishment in the case of a Brahman. A Brahman must not be subjected to corporal punishment.
>
> Shaving his head, banishing him from the town, branding him on the forehead with a mark of the crime of which he has been convicted, and parading him on an ass, shall be his punishment.

Much more important, however, and far more characteristic of the degree to which the adulterer was resented, is his actual exclusion from society:

> Those who have committed Sâhasa of either of the two first degrees are allowed to mix in society, after having been punished, but if a man has committed Sâhasa of the highest degree, no one is allowed to speak to him, even if he has received punishment [Nārada 14.11].

It only rarely—too rarely—happens that the ancient Hindu lawbooks explicitly inform us about the justification for their rules. With regard to the extremely severe treatment of adultery, however, we are lucky to possess the following passage in Manu [8.352-3]:

Men who commit adultery with the wives of others, the king shall cause to be marked by punishments which cause terror, and afterwards banish.

For by (adultery) is caused a mixture of the castes (*varna*) among men; thence (follows) sin, which cuts up even the roots and causes the destruction of everything.

My next remark in connection with adultery is that adultery is a very comprehensive term, I mean that it includes acts which, in our opinion, are still relatively innocent. In Halhed's *Code*[1] it has been described as follows:

First Species is, when, in a Place where there are no Men, a Person, with intent to commit Adultery, holds any Conversation with a Woman, and Winks, and Gallantries, and Smiles pass on both Sides; or the Man and Woman hold Conversation together in the Morning, or in the Evening, or at Night, or any such improper Times; or the Man dallies with the Womans's Cloaths, or sends a Pimp to her; or the Man and Woman are together in a Garden, or an unfrequented Spot, or such other secret Place, and bathe together in the same Pool, or other Water; or the Man and Woman meet together in One visiting Place: This is called the First or most trifling Species.
Second Species is, when a Man sends Sandal Wood, or a String of Beads, or Victuals and Drinks, or Cloaths, or Gold, or Jewels to a Woman: This is called the Second, or middle Species.
Third Species is, when the Man and Woman Sleep and Dally upon the same Carpet, or in some retired Place kiss and embrace, and play with each others Hair; or when the Man carries the Woman into a retired Place, and the Woman says Nothing: This is called the Third, or worst Species of Adultery.

But not only does adultery cover a large range of acts, it even applies to intercourse with women who are not really married to another man. Nārada [12.7], after having enumerated the women with whom intercourse is allowed—prostitutes, female slaves, etc.—adds:

When, however, such a woman is the kept mistress (of another man), intercourse with her is as criminal as (intercourse) with another man's wife. Such women, though intercourse with them is not (in

[1] Chapter XIX (*Of Adultery*), Sect. I (*Of the several Species of Adultery, which are of Three Sorts*). The work as printed is an English translation of a Persian version of the Sanskrit original.

general) forbidden, must not be approached because they belong to another man.

Finally there is a last remark about adultery which, I think, is also the most important one as far as this paper is concerned. What I have so far briefly called 'adultery' really corresponds to a much longer term in Sanskrit which may be translated literally as 'connection with another man's wife'. That means that the whole chapter on adultery deals with the crimes committed by and the punishments prescribed for the man who has intercourse with the wife of another person. In other words: if in the *dharmaśāstra* texts the king is called upon to inflict punishment for adultery upon a male, he never does so because the said male committed adultery *as a husband*.

As to the adulteress, a number of texts are very severe with her too. The punishment which in the *Gautamasmṛti* [23.14] is still reserved to the woman who commits adultery with a man of lower caste, seems to have been generalized with Viṣṇu [5.9] and Manu [8.371]:

If a wife, proud of the greatness of her relatives or (her own) excellence, violates the duty which she owes to her lord, the king shall cause her to be devoured by dogs in a place frequented by many.

But there is another text which propounds a completely different view:

When a married woman commits adultery, her hair shall be shaved, she shall have to lie on a low couch, receive bad food and bad clothing, and the removal of the sweepings shall be assigned to her as her occupation [Nārada 12.91].

This is the text which has been quoted repeatedly by later commentators, such as Mitramiśra in his *Vīramitrodaya*, in order to show the humane character of ancient Hindu law which, even for such a serious offence as adultery, far from casting off the adulteress, upholds her claim to maintenance. And the framers of the Indian Penal Code could not have been more in agreement with Nārada than they were when they declared, in regard to section 497 where the other man's wife is said not to be punishable as an abettor in case of adultery: 'There are some pecularities in the state of society in this country which may well lead a humane man to pause before he determines to punish the infidelity of wives. They are married while still children: they are often neglected. They share the attention of a husband with several rivals.'[1]

[1] V. B. Raju: *Commentary on the Penal Code*, Bombay, the author, 1957, p. 1335.

After this long discussion about dissolution of marriage, you must have noticed that I have avoided using the term divorce. And I have done so on purpose: instead of asking the question immediately whether or not ancient Hindu law knew the concept of divorce, I have preferred to deal with the various aspects of the problem first, and only then to introduce the word divorce.

I suppose that the answer to the question whether or not ancient Hindu Law knew divorce depends on what one exactly understands by 'divorce'. I consulted the *Oxford English Dictionary* in order to compare the Indian situation with what I hoped would be the standard definition but nothing could be more vague than:

Legal dissolution of marriage by a court or other competent body, or according to forms recognized in the country, nation or tribe.
[In small type]: Formerly and still often (e.g. historically or anthropologically) used in the widest sense; hence, including the formal putting away of, or separation from, a spouse by a heathen or a barbarian; . . .

Certainly the situation in which the wife is superseded by another woman can hardly be identified with divorce. Although the husband actually contracts another marriage during the lifetime of his first wife,[1] the superseded woman is supposed to stay on in the house, as may be inferred from Manu [9.83]:

A wife who, being superseded, in anger departs from (her husband's) house, must either be instantly confined or cast off in the presence of the family.

A verse from Yājñavalkya [1.74] even suggests that the husband should maintain his wife in the same way before and after the supersession.[2]

Moreover, as I said before, according to certain authors at least, it seems as if even adultery was not a sufficient reason to expel the wife from the house; and although some older *dharmaśāstras* do prescribe expulsion from the house for apparently minor offences, the later commentators are found prepared to interpret these passages in such a way that they merely refer to expulsion from the main body of the house.

[1] Colebrooke: *Digest* IV.1.67: 'A *second* marriage, *or one* subsequent to her's, contracted by the husband, is supersession.'
[2] Even then her situation cannot have been a highly appreciated one; she seems to have become a symbol with Nārada (1.203): 'A perjured witness shall spend his nights in the same manner as a wife who has been superseded (by another) . . .'

It has been said by a modern Indian author that '*Tyāga* in Kauṭilya is a technical term denoting "separation from conjugal intercourse" as opposed to *moksha* ("freedom"), the technical divorce'.[1] Even *a priori* I feel suspicious about such applications of modern Western concepts to the ancient Indian situation, moreover, I am unable to find confirmation for this distinction in the texts.

My own impression is that a husband could not obtain a decree of divorce against his wife according to any rule of *dharmaśāstra*. But the *dharmaśāstra* alludes to and actually permits a situation which, in practice, came very close to divorce, for the husband at least. And even though the *dharmaśāstra* does not say so, custom seems to have recognized what we would call the rights of a divorced wife. However, if complete dissolution of marriage—let us call it divorce—was not explicitly sanctioned by the *dharmaśāstra* and by the public authorities recognized therein, the question remains to be answered, which authority did sanction the situation which so closely corresponded to divorce? In order to answer this question, I must now turn towards the last point which I wanted to treat here.

Procedure

As I said in my introduction, the last question I should like to pose is that of procedure: how were matrimonial causes dealt with in practice? Here my task becomes perhaps even more difficult than it has been so far. The point is that we do possess whole chapters and, later, complete treatises on the subject of ancient Hindu adjectival law. In the *dharmaśāstras* these rules have been expounded in the context of the first 'title of law', namely, recovery of debts; later they become more or less independent. But in both cases they are cast in such general language that they do not teach us anything about matrimonial causes in particular.

The prima facie view would, then, be that we shall assume that matrimonial causes were treated along the same lines as the general theory of ancient Hindu procedure, which I shall outline briefly. However, from the very circumspection with which I introduce the topic it will be understood that this would not be completely correct.

Indeed, all our rules concerning procedure refer exclusively to the procedure as applied in the royal courts. Either *suo motu* or after a plaint has been introduced—that depends upon the nature of the offence—the king hears the plaintiffs and the defendant, examines the various

[1] K. P. Jayaswal: *Manu and Yājñavalya—A Comparison and a Contrast: A Treatise on the Basic Hindu Law*, Calcutta, Butterworth, 1930, p. 230.

kinds of evidence, and pronounces a judgment. As far as matrimonial causes are concerned, however, we have good reason to believe that they mainly lay outside the king's jurisdiction.

The case of adultery is clear enough. Adultery being a species of *sāhasa*, not only did it belong to the royal jurisdiction, but the king had a right to intervene of his own motion. The perpetrator of adultery is brought into court not through a plaint introduced by a plaintiff, but by the action of the king's spies whose duty it is to find him out and arrest him.[1]

So much for adultery; but this is, as we saw before, not a regular matrimonial cause. In regard to the real matrimonial causes the situation is much more complex.

Both Nārada [Quotations 1.6] and Bṛhaspati as quoted in the *Vyavahāramātṛkā* [p. 285] have a most embarrassing *śloka*:

A lawsuit cannot be instituted between a teacher and his pupil, or between father and son, or man and wife, or master and servant.

It is true that such a *śloka* should not *a priori* surprise us: other legal systems too have forbidden spouses to bring actions against each other.[2] However, against the *śloka* of Nārada and Bṛhaspati stands the undeniable fact that 'duties of husband and wife' do form one of the eighteen classical 'titles of law' or 'grounds of judicial procedure'. The result is that one would be entitled to infer with Dr Kane: 'As it was the husband's duty to provide residence and maintenance for his wife and as the wife was bound to stay with the husband, it follows that either party could after marriage enforce his or her rights in a court of law if the other party refused to perform his or her duties.'[3]

---

[1] Cf. the author: 'Ancient Hindu Criminal Law', *Journal of Oriental Research*, 24 (1955), pp. 31–2.

[2] Corbett, op. cit., p. 125: 'Husband and wife owe to each other a respect and a kindness which cannot indeed be directly enforced by action, but which have important legal consequences. . . . So long as the marriage lasts, they may not institute penal or defaming actions against one another, and even after separation the *actio furti* for things appropriated in contemplation of divorce is replaced *in honorem matrimonii* by the less drastic *actio rerum amotarum*.'

[3] It is certainly true that the modern courts often use ancient remedies, as Kane himself rightly points out: 'where the courts make the husband pay maintenance, they are in principle following Yāj. I.76 and Nārada' (op. cit., p. 569); but the fact that modern courts do use these ancient remedies in no way justifies the conclusion that the ancient courts did so too. The Anglo-Indian courts may well have started to do so without there being any precedent. The situation is far more correctly presented by Professor Derrett: 'Each spouse has a right to the affection and society of the other, unless forfeited. The current law has developed

The principle put forward by Kane has actually been applied in the Anglo-Indian Courts. Says the headnote of a leading case in which an exhaustive judgment was delivered by the celebrated Mr Justice Mahmood: 'The texts of Hindu law relating to conjugal cohabitation and imposing restrictions upon the liberty of the wife, and placing her under the control of her husband, are not merely moral precepts, but rules of law. The rights and duties which they create may be enforced by either party against the other and not exclusively by the husband against the wife. The Civil Courts of British India, as occupying the position in respect of judicial functions formerly occupied in the system of Hindu law by the king, have undoubtedly jurisdiction in respect of the enforcement of such rights and duties. The Civil Courts of British India can therefore properly entertain a suit between Hindoos for the restitution of conjugal rights, or for the recovery of a wife who has deserted her husband.'[1]

Various solutions have been proposed in order to reconcile both points of view, none of them, however, being such as to satisfy me completely.

In the typical commentator-like fashion Jīmūtavāhana in his *Vyavahāramātṛkā* [p. 285] refers the texts of Nārada and Bṛhaspati to minor matrimonial matters; only when they are more important do they constitute 'titles of law'.

A little more sophisticated but equally unsatisfactory is Caṇḍeśvara's explanation in the *Vivādaratnākara* [p. 409]:

Though the appearance of Husband and Wife as Plaintiff and Respondent at the Royal Court has been forbidden—yet it is quite possible that the King may have to hear indirectly of their dereliction of duty towards each other; and in that case it becomes his duty to bring them to the path of righteousness; or otherwise, to punish them. This is the reason why this subject has been brought in as a *Head of Dispute.*[2]

Much more helpful is a modern proposal by Nares Chandra Sen-

---

various remedies which may be used to protect the interests of one spouse when they are threatened by the misconduct, neglect or spite of the other. Though the remedies are foreign in nomenclature they are in reality founded upon a *shastric* basis, and not upon justice, equity and good conscience, which would otherwise have supplied them' (op. cit., p. 100).

[1] *Binda v. Kaunsilia* (1891), I.L.R. 13 All. 126–7.
[2] According to G. N. Jha, in his translation of the *Vivādacintāmaṇi*, p. 165.

MATRIMONIAL CAUSES ACCORDING TO THE 'DHARMAŚĀSTRA'

Gupta. According to Sen-Gupta disputes between husband and wife are not *vyavahāra* because 'vyavahāra means litigation before the King's Court while these disputes were matters for domestic tribunals'.[1] In his opinion matrimonial causes only gradually came within the range of royal justice; thus a number of topics which do not appear in such old *dharmasūtras* as Gautama's do appear later with Manu, Nārada and Bṛhaspati.[2]

I cannot agree with the latter part of Sen-Gupta's theory, viz. the suggestion that matrimonial causes gradually passed from the jurisdiction of inferior courts to the royal court. If his reasoning were correct, the evolution should have come to an end by the time of Manu, when matrimonial causes have been dealt with in detail. I fail to see, then, how still later authors like Nārada and Bṛhaspati, who also have a detailed treatment of matrimonial causes, would again declare them not to belong to the royal jurisdiction.

But I do agree with Sen-Gupta that matrimonial causes normally were dealt with by lower courts. My only contention is that this has always been the case, irrespective of whether rules about matrimonial causes are found in the contemporary *dharmaśāstras* or not. In short, I think that we have a right to say that caste and, therefore, the caste council, was very important in matters of matrimonial disputes.

Here I should like to come back to the fact that a husband may be abandoned by his wife when he is excluded from his caste. If such could be the case—whereas normally a wife must bear any vice, physical as well as moral, of her husband—or, in other words, if caste could prevail over marriage, it seems to me that marriage must primarily have been a caste affair.

Moreover, not only are there indications of the importance of caste in matrimonial causes in the *dharmaśāstras*; the same conclusion is also borne out by the evidence provided by customary law. There are

[1] *Evolution of Ancient Indian Law*, London, Probsthain, 1953, p. 46.
[2] ibid., p. 46–7: 'This indicates a course of development of King's justice not dissimilar to developments elsewhere. As we shall find more fully later, originally people's tribunals were the authorities for deciding all disputes. The King's justice was first confined to punishment of crimes and more serious social offences. Gradually the King began to deal with a few matters of a civil nature not involving punishment. For some reason or other, administration of justice by the King became popular and people began to flock to King's Courts for redress of their grievances which were previously adjudicated by popular tribunals, with the result that topics of law which, being matters for domestic tribunals, were kept by early law outside the King's justice were absorbed under Vyavahāra step by step.'

numerous cases, in early Anglo-Indian law, where the judges intervened in matrimonial causes which had already been dealt with by the
caste panchayat according to the customs prevailing in that particular
caste.[1]

In *Reg. v. Sambhu Raghu*, e.g. it has been held that 'Courts of law
will not recognize the authority of a caste to declare a marriage void,
or to give permission to a woman to remarry. Bona fide belief that the
consent of the caste made the second marriage valid does not constitute
a defence to a charge.' The point which interests us most in all this is,
in the words of H. Batty, Assistant Sessions Judge of Khandesh:
'Among the lower classes of the Hindus it was a widespread, if not a
correct, belief, that where a *pharkhut, sod chitty* or letter of divorce has
been given by the husband, and a *Panchayat* has decided that the
marriage has been dissolved, the party so divorced is at liberty to marry
again on repayment of the marriage expenses incurred by the first
husband.'[2]

However, even if caste has been very important, to say simply that
matrimonial causes were a matter of caste is not sufficient. The king
does in certain cases have to intervene, as, for example in this case
cited by Nārada [12.95]:

> If a man leaves a wife who is obedient, pleasant-spoken, skilful,
> virtuous, and the mother of (male) issue, the king shall make him
> mindful of his duty by (inflicting) severe punishment (on him).

Even more instructive is a passage from Viṣṇu [5.9.18]:

> Let the king put to death ... a woman who violates the duty which
> she owes to her lord, the latter being unable to restrain her.

This passage says in so many words that the king does not intervene as
long as the husband himself is capable of restraining his wife; he
merely does so when the husband fails. And this notwithstanding the
means at his disposal, which go as far as permission to beat his wife with
a rope or a split bamboo.[3]

My general impression about the *dharmaśāstra* theory of matri-

[1] *Reg. v. Karsan Goja* and *Reg. v. Bai Rupa* (1864), 2 Bom. H.C.R. 124;
Uji v. Hathi Lalu (1870), 7 Bom. H.C.R. 133; *Rahi v. Govinda* (1875), I.L.R. 1
Bom. 97; *Reg. v. Sambhu Raghu* (1876), I.L.R. 1 Bom. 347; *Narayan Bharthi v.
Laving Bharthi* (1877), I.L.R. 2 Bom. 140; *Jukni v. Queen Empress* (1892),
I.L.R. 19 Cal. 627; *Sankaralingam Chetti v. Subhan Chetti* (1894), I.L.R. 17 Mad.
479; etc. See also Derrett, 'Divorce by caste custom, *Bombay Law Reporter,
Journal*, Vol. 65 (1963), 161ff.

[2] (1876) I.L.R. 1 Bom. 350.

[3] Thus Manu 8.299–300: 'A wife, a son, a slave, a pupil, and a (younger)

monial causes would be this. Ancient Hindu law, whatever be its fluctuations in detail, is, as far as marriage and matrimonial causes are concerned, subject to two tendencies which, if taken strictly, point in opposite directions.

The first of these two tendencies is the idea that marriage is something more than a contract between the two persons directly concerned. The ancient Hindu lawyers understood, as well as Mr Justice Scrutton in *Hyman v. Hyman,* that 'the stability of the marriage tie, and the terms in which it should be dissolved, involve far wider considerations than the will or consent of the parties to the marriage'.[1] Marriage also concerns the family; perhaps we might even say that it concerns the Hindu joint family far more than it normally concerns any other family. It also concerns the caste, and here Manu was explicit: if matrimonial causes are not properly dealt with, the order and the purity of the castes will be upset. Finally marriage also concerns the State: in ancient Hindu law, too, it would be true to say that 'the State is too deeply concerned with the sanctity of family life . . . to leave marriage to the caprice of the individual spouses, to be made a mere temporary union and relaxed or dissolved at will'.[2]

At the same time, however, there was also a secondary tendency at work. Section 199 of the Criminal Procedure Code (Act V of 1898) says that 'no court shall take cognizance of an offence under section 497 [i.e. adultery] or section 498 [i.e. the offence of enticing or taking away or detaining with a criminal intent a married woman] of the Indian Penal Code, except upon a complaint made by the husband of the woman, or in his absence, made with the leave of the Court by some person who had care of such woman on his behalf at the time when such offence was committed'. More than the section of the Criminal Procedure Code itself I want to quote a comment made on it by Mr Justice Pigot and Mr Justice Hill: 'The intention of the law is to prevent Magistrates inquiring, of their own motion, into cases connected with marriage unless the husband or other person authorized moves them to do so.'[3]

---

brother of the full blood, who have committed faults, may be beaten with a rope or a split bamboo.

'But on the back part of the body (only), never on a nobler part; he who strikes them otherwise will incur the same guilt as a thief.'

[1] *Per* Scrutton L. J., in *Hyman v. Hyman* (1929), P.1,30, quoted in *Latey on Divorce,* 11th ed., p. 135.

[2] *Nachimson v. Nachimson* (1930), P.85, 217 C.A.

[3] *Jatra Shekh v. Reaẓat Shekh* (1892), I.L.R. 20 Cal. 483 (headnote).

In other words, marriage also is—perhaps, essentially is—a private
affair, where, as far as possible, disputes must be settled *intra muros*
without any public authority intervening. I am convinced that this
second general principle, too, is strongly present in ancient Hindu
law. And here I should like to come back to the text of Nārada and
Bṛhaspati according to which, in Jolly's translation, 'a lawsuit cannot
be instituted between man and wife'. In reality this text does not mean
that a lawsuit must not or may not be instituted between husband and
wife; the Sanskrit expression *vyavahāro na sidhyati* simply means that a
lawsuit between spouses is 'not accepted', i.e. 'not acceptable', i.e. 'not
to be recommended'. In other words, the stanza of Nārada and
Bṛhaspati implies that such lawsuits could exist, that they did exist,
but that they should be avoided as much as possible.

Moreover, the interpretation which I propose here is not only in
agreement with the Sanskrit text; it is also confirmed by legal practice.
In his book, *Hindu Law of Marriage and Stridhan*, Sir Gooroodass
Banerjee says that, although his subject is a difficult one, at least 'it is
free from one source of complication which often perplexes the student
of law. It has not to be disentangled out of a mass of unconnected
precedents.' And, after this statement, he offers an explanation which,
I think; is a most interesting one: 'One cause of this scantiness of case-
law is, I believe, the sacramental character of marriage in Hindu law.
Owing to this, the Hindus are so careful to observe the rules concerning marriage and to avoid error, unless it be on the safe side, and
so strong is their disinclination to question the validity of marriage in
any case, that disputes concerning this topic seldom arise for judicial
determination.'[1]

Indeed, marriage and matrimonial causes being considered highly
private affairs, it is but natural that, rather than the royal court, caste
and caste customs were allowed to play an important part. These
customs were very much closer to the spouses than the general rules of
dharmaśāstra.

I gladly confess that my understanding of this difficult problem of
legal procedure in ancient Hindu law has been helped very much by
another modern judgment. It is by Mr Justice Sankaran Nair of
Madras who, when having to decide about the validity of a particular
marriage, said: 'Where . . . the religious and legal consciousness of a
community recognizes the validity of a certain marriage, it follows
that it cannot be discarded on account of its repugnance to that system
of law [i.e. the *dharmaśāstra*]. Whether the marriage is valid or not,

[1] 5th ed., 1923, pp. 33-4.

according to the caste rules, it is for the caste itself to decide. So far as ancient history and modern usages go, marriage questions have always been settled by the caste itself and the validity of a marriage between members of a caste who recognize it as binding has not been questioned by outsiders though the caste itself may be lowered in their estimation when such marriages are repugnant to their notion of morality. When, therefore, a caste accept a marriage as valid and treat the parties as members of the caste, it would be, it appears to me, an unjustifiable interference for the courts to declare those marriages null and void.'[1]

The ancient Hindu law texts have perhaps less eloquently worded these principles than the modern authors and judges. However, the principles are there, be it with variations and fluctuations. On the one hand, marriage and matrimonial causes are private affairs, to be dealt with, if not by the spouses themselves, by their family and their caste, according to the caste customs. Only if and when this is insufficient do the public authorities intervene, and then in so far as possible according to local customs, and otherwise according to the general principles of *dharmaśāstra*. Either tendency may prevail with a particular author, or even in different parts of the works of the same author, but I think that these variations are of less importance than the general principles underlying them.

[1] *Mushusami Mudaliar v. Masilamani* (1910), I.L.R. 33 Mad. 342, 355.

PART TWO

FAMILY PROPERTY AND SUCCESSION

6

FAMILY PROPERTY IN WEST AFRICA: ITS JURISTIC BASIS, CONTROL AND ENJOYMENT

A. N. ALLOTT

Professor of African Law in the University of London

The legal scene in former British West Africa is reminiscent—if you will permit the fancy—of a wide beach from which the tide has receded. The eye notices, stranded upon the shore, deposits of extraneous material left behind on the ebb of colonial overrule. Here one sees substantial portions of the English law (such as the law of crimes) torn away from the main body of our legal system; battered and chipped on their journey, it is true, but still recognizably English. There are less substantial fragments, half-buried in the enveloping sand—the law of monogamous marriage, for instance. Scattered everywhere is the detritus of English legal terminology; often strangely out of fit with the beds upon which it rests. Underneath all is the broad, variegated, primeval beach, solid in some places, in others contorted by the waves —the traditional social and legal institutions of the peoples of West Africa.

No doubt in time the ceaseless internal activity of a million micro-organisms, as well as the more majestic and sudden impact of external forces such as wind and wave, will wear all these elements down into a common and stable uniformity; but that time is not yet, and the legal anomalies remain visible to the eye. It is about some of these anomalies that I wish to concern myself in this paper. At the same time I hope that it may be possible to predict the way in which legal disintegration and re-integration will proceed. To illustrate these processes at work I have chosen what I believe to be the central institution of African private law: the institution of family property. This is a branch of law (or a kind of legal institution, one should perhaps say) which is un-familiar in modern England. The English law which was exported to West Africa was that prevailing in England at the end of the nine-teenth century. This was the period of the most pronounced individual-ism in our native legal system, when the recognition of the power of unrestricted testation and of freedom of contract, and the entrenchment of the rule against perpetuities, had all but destroyed the possibility of building up permanent family holdings in property. The terminological inadequacies of the English law for the description of West African property systems constitute one of my themes for analysis here.

A second task will be to expose the traditional rules which governed, and still largely govern, family property in West Africa. It will be necessary to see how far these traditional institutions continue to function in modern West Africa, and how far they have been modified or displaced by the law-making of judges, legislatures or populations.

This exposé naturally involves, first, the elaboration of a mode of analysis or categorization which fits the complexities of the indigenous systems; and, secondly, an appreciation of the extent to which these systems have been affected by social and legal change.

Lastly, I must try to predict the way in which the reduction of legal pluralism, the promotion of economic development, and the social evolution of the peoples, will affect the existence and expression of family property systems in West Africa during the remainder of the century.

A VOCABULARY OF DESCRIPTION FOR PROPERTY SYSTEMS

Before I begin to describe and analyse traditional property systems in West Africa, it is necessary to agree on a vocabulary of description. If I were a Continental lawyer trained in the Romanist tradition, I would be tempted to analyse these systems in terms of rights of *dominium* or ownership, and rights less than ownership. I should then have to look for 'ownership' and for 'owners' in West Africa. I might or might not find such owners and such ownership: some writers argue that ownership in the 'real' or 'true' sense was unknown in traditional African law either because there was no *jus abutendi* (signifying the rights to alienate as well as to abuse), or because of the fragmentation of rights in the hands of a number of holders. Other writers disagree: they say that there was 'ownership', but that this was vested in groups and communities, never in individuals. A third group would disagree with both camps, and say that there was ownership, and that this was typically vested in individual users, rather than in groups. For myself, I would refuse to adhere to any of these schools of thought, by opting out of all discussions of what is 'ownership' and whether one category of person or another possesses it is African law. I know what these different schools of jurists are trying to say; in a sense, they are all right simultaneously; but I find that juristic analysis and description are much facilitated if the words 'ownership' and 'owner'—which, I need hardly remark, have no real or true sense—are omitted from one's vocabulary.

There are vernacular terms which are often rendered as 'owner', usually owner of something or another, be it village, country or house; but these could with equal precision be translated as 'master' or 'controller', which would enable one to leave discussions about owners on one side. To my mind, no term is meaningful unless its context and possible modes of use are specified. Thus, such a specification requires one to investigate and list the actions which the potential owner under consideration may or may not perform in connection with the property he is alleged to 'own'. It is this specification, and not the employment of one English word or another, which is the important task.

An English lawyer would feel much less need to specify who had or did not have 'ownership' in a given property system. After all, he has been brought up in a system which finds it unnecessary to employ the word—at least as far as real property is concerned. More important to the English lawyer is the idea of a hierarchy of estates which may concurrently subsist in the same subject-matter, an idea which is also frequently present, though in a disguised form, in African real property systems. On the other hand, modern English conveyancing practice requires that the law should be able to point to the individual who is competent to 'make title' for the purposes of a particular legal transaction; and this has caused difficulties for the lawyer in West Africa who wishes to register title to land, or accommodate the interest of customary law to the framework demanded by the imported conveyancing systems.

Any analysis of a given property system should, in my view, conform to the following principles:

1. It should answer the questions (a) Who/whom?; (b) How?; and (c) What? In other words, one must specify (a) Who are the *interest-holders*, and the persons towards whom the rights and powers comprised in such interests are exercised; (b) what is the content of each *interest*, i.e. what rights, powers, responsibilities, and liabilities are comprised in the interest, and how these may be exercised under the law; and (c) what is the *subject-matter* of the interest, i.e. what is the property or thing affected by it.

2. A distinction should be made between rights and powers, the former relating to the enjoyment of privileges in connection with the

subject-matter of the right, the latter relating to the power that the holder has to affect legal relationships in connection with it. This distinction may also be made in terms of a division between *control* or management on the one hand, and *benefit* on the other.

3. An interest in property may be conceived of as a cluster of associated rights, powers, responsibilities[1] and liabilities[2] held by a single holder or group of holders in relation to a given thing. A description of the interest implies a listing of these rights, etc.

4. A given interest, or a given constituent right or power, may be absolute or qualified. If qualified, it is implied that there exists a superior right or power from which the inferior right or power depends.

5. Concurrent interests in property arise in two modes: (i) the mode of *subordination*, where of two concurrent interests in the same subject-matter one is superior and the other is dependent; and (ii) the parallel or *co-ordinate* mode, where one interest does not prevail over the other.

6. Interests may be classified according to the number of co-holders. I describe an interest as (i) *corporate* or *community*, where it is conceived of as attaching to a group of persons who for this purpose are deemed to constitute an entity detached from its constituents; in such an instance the corporate body must be able to act through representatives duly mandated, it must have a defined structure and membership, and so on; (ii) *joint*, where the interest is held by a group of persons by a single inseparable title, but who are not thought of as constituting a separable entity; (iii) *common*, where the interest is held by a group of persons, each with his own separate or separable title; and (iv) *individual*, where the holder is a single person on a single title.

I must apologize for boring you with this recitation from the dictionary, but it would be quite impossible to achieve a satisfactory description of the different family property systems if we do not have a sufficient vocabulary available for use. So far as possible this vocabulary steers clear of the technicalities and technical expressions of English and Roman law—thus fee simple, usufruct, estate (as a synonym for interest) find no place within it.

THE TRADITIONAL SYSTEMS OF FAMILY PROPERTY

Perhaps I had better insert a hasty explanation here, before we go any farther, so as to satisfy our sociological friends. The English word 'family' is by now almost a term of art in modern West African law.

[1] i.e., the duty to do something.
[2] i.e., the duty to allow something to be done.

It figures constantly in the law reports. Anthropologists doubtless find this usage imprecise; but it is not necessarily so. It can, however, be seriously misleading if an attempt is made to equate all kinds of kinship grouping together under the single label of 'family'; lawyers and judges in West Africa have not been entirely free from this temptation.

Let us therefore remind ourselves that there is no such thing as the standard or typical West African 'family', whether we judge this matter on sociological or legal grounds. Instead, there is a variety of groupings which tend to fall into one of two main categories (though a grouping may be both at the same time): (a) unilineal descent groups—clans and lineages; (b) residential family units—households, etc. The lineage groupings are in some areas organized patrilineally, in other areas matrilineally; and some communities recognize both patrilineal and matrilineal groupings simultaneously for different purposes. The difference between patrilineal and matrilineal is more than a mere choice of line of descent. In the matrilineal case there is the contrapuntal connection between father and child which cuts across the matrilineal one; this tension is largely absent from the patrilineal societies. A matrilineal grouping is thus *a priori* likely to function differently in the legal sense from the patrilineal one.

The kinds of household recognized in each society also vary widely. Even in a given society there may be more than one kind of household; e.g. parental, fraternal, localized, lineage. The extent of a lineage its structure and government, and its functions in regard to control over and benefit from property, also vary.

Our conclusion must be that there is no single description of the law of family property in West Africa that will be valid even for one country with a multiplicity of customary laws, let alone for the entire region. We must accordingly reject judicial or other dicta which assert that there is essentially a single system of family property law in Ghana, say, or in Nigeria, and that decisions affecting one system are necessarily applicable to others. At the same time we must recognize the tremendous judicial pressure towards uniformity of family laws, which arises from their administration by a single set of courts using a standard vocabulary and relying indiscriminately on precedents from any community as guides to the law.

On the other hand, there are certain common factors. The factor of family intervention in the process of succession to property on death is one of them; the system by which control and/or exploitation are shared amongst a number of relatives, or managed by one or more of them on behalf of the rest, is also common.

It is not just a question of variations in the make-up of the family or other kinship groups which are somehow involved in the joint exploitation of property; the title upon which such exploitation takes place can be quite different in different areas. In some communities ultimate title to the so-called family property is retained within the group as a whole, for whom it is managed by the head or leading members—in these systems there may be a periodic allocation and re-allocation of holdings amongst the members, none of whom acquires a durable, exclusive, indefeasible interest as against the family. In other groups the situation is quite different: there is still overall family control, but right to benefit from particular portions of the family land is attributed, whether by operation of law through the processes of succession, or by act of the family head through allocation, to specific members who acquire exclusive and durable, though subordinated, interests. In still other socieities, family control is merely a transitional stage in the partitioning of members' property; once so partitioned, the erstwhile family property becomes individual property in which the family as such retains no legal claim or interest.

Let me give some specific illustrations, drawn from the extensive literature. Among the patrilineal IBO, as described by Obi, kinship groups recognized as controlling the use of land include the *umunna*, or localized patrilineage headed by an *okpala* and council; major sublineages, frequently called 'compounds' or extended families, *obi* or *oluama*, each with its *okpala* again; and parental or grandparental households typically consisting of a man, his wives and dependants. Obi says:[1]

> 'The *umunna* has practically the same rights and interests in all unallocated land within its territory as has the village in village land. Thus the *umunna* can sell or lease its land at will. . . . In addition to the right to sell, lease or pledge, the *umunna* has a reversionary interest in family or individual holdings. Thus, should a family die out, its land reverts to the *umunna*.'

Obi then goes on to point out that in some parts of Iboland the individual member can exploit *umunna* unallocated (I prefer to say unappropriated) land without prior permission or control, by mere occupation only. But such use only vests in the exploiter an exclusive right whilst the crops stand, and it then lapses. In other parts of Iboland, says Obi, there is a seasonal allocation of community-controlled land by the land authority to individual members, though again the plots are only held for one farming season at a time.

[1] p. 48.

As for the collection of wild fruits from *umunna* land, in some areas members enjoy common rights to collect palm nuts and other wild fruit at will; in other places collection is controlled, or is made jointly by the young men and women, though with a division of the fruits collected at the end of the day amongst all the members. Ultimately therefore in each instance the right to benefit is individual, even if the preliminary mode of collection is communal.

The extended family may also have some land within its control, i.e. that which has not been subjected to allocation or appropriation. It also possesses land control powers over land held individually by members, e.g. by forbidding planting of particular kinds of trees, and the reversion to land abandoned for one reason or another by a constituent nuclear family.

Within the nuclear family (parental household) the head as husband must allocate plots to his wives, and as father must similarly allocate farming plots to his sons as they grow up. When the sons grow up, the father must (says Obi) share his farmland with them, or provide them with land acquired from third parties, subject to their rendering him periodic tributes.

If we now look at the matter from the point of view of the individual, we see that he can either acquire interests in land free from family interests, through succession, purchase, first clearing of unappropriated land, gift or prescription; or he can acquire a dependent interest through allocation of community land. The position in regard to succession is particularly interesting. If a successor belongs to a society where singular succession by a sole heir is the rule, then he takes immediately the same interest as the deceased. If the society recognizes plural succession, then the individual successor (e.g. one of a dead man's sons) finds himself a joint holder with his co-successors until such time as the land is partitioned; whereupon the successor acquires as full a title as his ancestor (though obviously to a smaller tract of land).

So-called 'family farm land' (attaching to a parental family in the first instance) therefore subsists in two distinct modes. When the individual holder of an absolute interest in farming land dies, if he was a polygynist and left several 'houses' each consisting of a wife and at least one son, then typically the successors are the eldest sons in each house, who take jointly in the first instance. If they decide to postpone partition, then all the unapportioned land of deceased is available for use by the individual family members severally. Partition may be postponed for generations, in which case no member gets a permanent transmissible title to any distinct portion of the expanded family's land. When at last partition is agreed upon, the principle of partition is by houses (or *per stirpes*) left by the original acquirer, provided each house is represented by a living male descendant. A secondary partitioning within each house or line, but on a *per capita* basis, may then be made. After partitioning, the original family farm land has ceased to exist as such.

Obi would argue that it is wrong to talk about succession at all as far as a member's claims in connection with group-controlled land are concerned, since the individual occupier of a portion of such land has no heritable interest.

The pattern with the Afikpo branch of the Eastern Ibo, who recognize double unilineal descent groups, is naturally rather different. The localized patrilineages control certain rights in land, though matri-lineages control most farmland. Movables are typically inherited patri-lineally on a divisory system, but interests in land are generally transmitted matrilineally; but this· statement grossly simplifies the extremely complex situation described by S. Ottenberg. A man could formerly acquire an absolute interest in unappropriated bush land through clearing it. Today an individual may have numerous small plots acquired from different sources, situated in his own and other villages. 'A man's own matrilineal land, generally his largest holdings, is acquired for him by his father through the head of the latter's matri-lineage, when the man is young.'[1] Then a son can use land which his father acquired from his (the father's) matrilineage, even after the father's death. Thirdly, a newly married man may acquire land from his wife's matrilineage. Fourthly, an agnatic half-brother may give him some land. Lastly, a man may receive some land from his own patri-lineage.

Land to be used by a lineage is divided after clearing. Although re-allocation is apparently in theory seasonal, in practice a person receives the same plot each time. Once land has been so acquired, the user can allow anyone else to use it without reference to the group for consent. When the holder dies, the land of his matrilineage reverts to the lineage, though the sons, as already noted, continue to farm their plots on their father's land. Rights in trees planted by an individual tend to pass patrilineally. A deceased's house falls within the control of the minor patrilineage, but its use passes to his eldest son.

The YORUBA system, as described by Lloyd, has some resem-blances to that of the patrilineal Ibo. Among the differences are the

[1] p. 56.

general recognition of corporate patrilineages controlling much, if not most, of residential and farming land; the existence of large 'family houses', within which each lineage member has a right to be allocated a room or rooms according to need and availability; the rareness of total partition between segments (though family farm land is frequently divided between segments, so that the right to use and benefit, though not the power of alienation or ultimate control, inheres in the segment and its members). Property acquired by a man absolutely, through his own efforts, is inherited by his children. Either the children retain the property jointly, or it is divided *per stirpes* (by houses). Cash is typically divided, the family house is not. There may be a secondary division within the inheriting sub-group, at least as far as movables are concerned.

Under Yoruba law an individual has a much more precise claim to family land in which he has acquired an individual subordinate interest. Infringement of his claim by other family members is a legal wrong. Particularly so far as rights in houses are concerned, the member's interest is not periodic but generally for life, subject to the power of the family to reallocate rooms and farms. Where the individual holder creates an improvement, e.g. builds a house or plants a farm, then he acquires the right to possession during his lifetime, and has an absolute interest in the improvement, though a subordinate interest in the land.

When we turn to the HAUSA, we find from M. G. Smith's description that the commonest rural exploitation unit is the *gandu*, or set of agnatically linked nuclear households, typically consisting either of a man, his wives and children, together with his married sons and their dependants, or of two or more brothers and their families (which may come into existence when the father dies). The *gandu* is described by Smith as a joint family with a common holding of land, controlled by the head, *mai-gida*, who allocates plots to male members and controls the production and consumption of food. The *gandu* is necessarily co-residential; but as the size of the family increases and pressure on land grows, so fission takes place, and the eldest son is established as an independent household head with his own land. At the death of the father, the household may split and the land of the compound be divided amongst the sons (but *per stirpes*, by groups of full brothers, rather than *per capita*). Eventually the entire land is allocated, and each allocation may form the eventual portion of the son who received it, when he is emancipated and separated (often on marriage, apparently).

If we move over to Northern Ghana, and to the KONKOMBA as described by Tait, we find many similarities between the Konkomba household and the Hausa household; but there is superimposed upon the immediate control and enjoyment which the household head exercises over the land of the household, both compound land and bush farms, the control of the lineage of which the household forms part. On the one hand, sons not yet advanced may receive from the lineage elder an allocation of their dead father's compound lands, but, on the other hand, any man can occupy and cultivate land freely in the bush, and this land is not closely controlled by the lineage elders. Superimposed upon the lineage structure is the clan, of which the lineages form part. (Essentially each clan consists of persons believed to be agnatically related, occupying a defined district, subjected to a single elder, and having a common land shrine.)

In southern Ghana the various systems of law collectively described as AKAN, which include the FANTE, ASANTE and AKIM, have a clearly defined institution of 'family property'. This institution rests upon the matrilineal family system, or *abusua*. The matrilineage, in these systems, consists of a number, often quite large, of persons all of whom are descended exclusively in the female line from a known ancestress, who recognize the authority of a common *abusuapanin*, or elder of the family (usually called 'head of the family'), who share a common family burial ground, acknowledge their mutual duty to contribute to each other's funeral expenses, and in many areas have a principal family house. The lineage, as found among the Akan, differs from some of those in other parts of West Africa in having a precise membership and structure and of acting together habitually as a corporate entity in major legal matters, especially those which concern the acquisition, enjoyment or disposal of rights in immovable property.

Under Akan law it is possible for an individual to acquire interests in property, either by his own efforts (self-acquired property), or by allocation of, or succession to, family-controlled property. It is only in the case of the latter that family control is imposed; though formerly, I was informed, the sale even of a man's self-acquired land required notice to, and the consent of, his family. As elsewhere, the lineage or family is segmented into a number of branches or houses, which I refer to as sections; and there is further segmentation until one comes to the immediate matrilineal sub-lineage of a person, typically consisting of his or her mother, siblings (and children, in the case of a female member only). The residential unit is much smaller than the whole lineage, households tending to be organized either on the matrilineal sub-lineage or parental family basis. On the death of an individual male family member, all his property, self-acquired or inherited, immediately vests in his lineage. The lineage has the power to appoint a successor to the deceased, who takes all or most of deceased's rights and responsibilities; but the successor does not, and cannot, acquire the absolute title to the property which he has inherited, which remains vested in the family, and of which he may be dispossessed for good reason. Cash and movables tend to be divided up and become the absolute individual property of the recipients.

NATURE OF THE FAMILY'S INTEREST IN FAMILY PROPERTY AND MEMBERS' PROPERTY

The first juristic problem to which these legal arrangements give rise is how to describe the family's interest in the so-called family property, and also in other property in which members of the family enjoy an interest.

It is my primary contention that the description must distinguish adequately between powers of control and rights to benefit. It is also essential to distinguish hierarchies of rights and powers. If we may use the AKAN system as a starting point, a family (lineage) may acquire rights in property originally or by way of succession. In the former instance, as where the lineage as such purchases property, control vests immediately in the family (and may be exercised by the head as advised by the elders of the family and the family members in general meeting); the right to benefit also vests jointly or in common in the family members. If the property is exploited jointly in the name of the family, then the proceeds may be divided up among the members; on the other hand, it is possible for the family to allocate the right to use and benefit from the property to individual members or sub-groups within the family, retaining ultimate family control over the property.

But most family property in the AKAN system is not acquired in this way, but by way of succession to the self-acquired property of individual members. When a member dies, his self-acquired property vests in his lineage; but the lineage is under a duty to appoint a successor to him. This successor is normally drawn from the immediate sub-lineage of deceased (i.e. his uterine brother or sister's son), and this sub-lineage has a preferential claim in the matter of succession. Often also the deceased's immediate relatives and dependants may retain the right to continue to live in his house or to work land which they have been permitted to work by him in his lifetime. When the successor himself dies, the body within which the successor is normally to be found has expanded; and in course of time may attain the status of a

section or major segment of an autonomous lineage. In time, the
section itself will separate and will become a separate lineage.

For property to which the family has succeeded in this way, the
legal position may be described as follows: (1) the ultimate title to the
property (which means the power to control its use, to alienate it, and
to take its benefit in the case of a lapse in the chain of succession) is in
the whole lineage; (2) a subordinate or dependent interest vests in the
smallest sub-lineage which includes both the original acquirer's mother
and her living descendants in the female line; this interest usually
comprises a power to control minor transactions affecting the property
(e.g. pledging and letting), and a preferential claim by its members to
be designated as holder or successor of the property, and rights of
use (e.g. residence in a house) where relevant; (3) a still further subordinated interest of indefinite duration, deriving in part from the
immediate sub-lineage's claim, but also from appointment or recognition by the family, is held by the successor (or other members to
whom the use is apportioned)—this interest is exclusive, or largely
exclusive, as against other members, and gives right both to use and
to take the proceeds from the property so held.

A surprising re-interpretation of AKAN family law has been made in
certain recent decisions of the superior courts in Ghana. In *In re
Eburahim* (1958), 3 W.A.L.R. 317, Adumua-Bossman, J., said that the
self-acquired property of a person dying intestate became the property
of his so-called 'immediate family' only (i.e. his minimal matrilineage),
and not of the whole of the family (lineage), and further that it was the
principal members of the immediate family alone that were competent
to appoint the successor, to the exclusion of the wider family. Ollennu,
in his *Principles of customary land law in Ghana*,[1] dissents from this
view; Bentsi-Enchill would support it.[2] A judgment of the Ghana High
Court in 1961, *Kwakye v. Tuba*, goes even further in saying that 'head
of family' and 'successor' are terms which mean one and the same thing,
and are interchangeable.

Now although it is true that the preferential claim to benefit from
the self-acquired property left by a deceased vests in his immediate
sub-lineage, this claim depends on the superior title of the lineage as a
whole; the lineage has not merely the reversion to the property, but a
right to control its alienation. To deny the title of the family (meaning
lineage), and to equate successor and head of family, would contradict all the previous authorities on Akan family law and make nonsense
of the texts which have previously expounded it. It may well be, and

[1] p. 152.   [2] p. 141.

indeed is probable, that Ga succession in Accra differs from Akan succession in respect of the group in whom the property is vested, so that the dicta quoted might be acceptable if confined to this geographical area. It is also perhaps desirable to amend the previous Akan law of succession in the interests of greater certainty; but such amendment should be by statute and not by alteration in the definition of well-accepted legal terms.

Family property, both in the sense of property exploited jointly or in common and in the sense of family-controlled but individually exploited property, is mainly limited to land; movables are generally distributed free of family claims, except for heirlooms and perhaps large furniture or other assets.

The family's claims, as a corporate unit, and the claims of other members of the family individually, do not extend to the self-acquired property of members, in which the family has no present interest, and no right to benefit therefrom, nor power to control its use. A problem arises with assets created by the individual efforts of a family member on land controlled by the family. Such self-made farms and houses are usually treated separately from the land upon which they stand, and are the exclusive property while he lives of the member who created them. The land remains subject to family control, however, and the holder cannot deal with his farm or house without the family's consent in such a way as to challenge or destroy the family's interest.

Various English-law analogies have been used to represent this sort of proprietary structure. The commonest has been that of trustee and beneficiary. Noting the considerable powers of the lineage-head to manage and deal with family property, subject only to his duty to consult the family members and to look after their interests in the property, some judges concluded that the head could be said to be a trustee for the other members of the family. There could be no better example of the perils of importing a technical word from a foreign legal language. Reliance on the trust concept would imply, under the ordinary principles of English law, that the head of the family was the legal owner of the family property, and that the other members merely had equitable interests in the property. Fortunately, the view— which corresponds most closely to the thinking of the customary law —has now become established that title to family property is with the family as a whole as a corporate entity; title must be made by the family, and the head is no more than a manager and agent for the family. In so acting, he holds, it is true, a fiduciary position, but this implies only that he should be as careful of the family's property and interests as he is of his own. The impact of English equity on customary property law is still uncertainly defined, and is worthy of detailed study. It is clear that a head would be a trustee in the formal sense of property or money which has come into his possession in his capacity as head, for instance.

Another institution widely relied on to describe the Akan property system is that of joint tenancy. There is a sense in which it is appropriate to call the holding by the family members a joint holding, in that there is a single inseparable title to the family's property, and there automatically accrues to the survivors the right of any member who dies. But as new members of the family are born, so they are automatically added to the list of those who share in the property, as joint controllers and users in common.

The analogy with unincorporated associations such as clubs in English law has also been made. It is true that customary families are unincorporated as far as English law is concerned, and it is also true that the customary law knows no formal process of incorporation; nevertheless the Akan family at least has sufficient of the characteristics of a corporation to make it not inept to refer to its members as corporately associated. What is more, the differences between the Akan family and the English club are more striking than the similarities: the family, both in the customary and statutory systems, is accorded legal personality and is permitted to take part in acts in the law, to sue and be sued in its own name, and to hold property, none of which is true of the English member's club.

The English law of agency is also relevant and some of its principles have infiltrated into the modern analysis of the powers and responsibilities of the head of the family. One of the most interesting questions is how far the head is capable of binding the family in his dealings with the family property. If, for instance, the head purports to alienate family property, without previously consulting the family and obtaining its authority, the modern law as interpreted by the courts is uncertain whether the transactions is (i) absolutely void, but validable if either the family adopts the transaction or by its failure to act to set aside the alienation impliedly approves it; or (ii) voidable, in that it is prima facie valid as far as the purchaser is concerned, provided he was bona fide and lacked actual or constructive notice of the defect in title, but capable of being set aside if the family acts in good time.

Another analogy which is attractive is that between the family and the limited liability company. In both instances, it is argued, the property of the corporate entity is vested in the entity as such; management of the property and of the entity itself is vested in a board of directors, who in the case of a customary family would comprise the head and senior members of the family, with the head himself as a sort of chairman and managing director. But one of the most important facts about the family system is that family members do not have, and are not felt to have, distinct shares in the family property; and it is clearly understood that although on one level family property vests in the hypothetical entity, the family, on another, more realistic, level the property belongs to the members of the family collectively.

There have been judicial dicta in Ghana which have attempted to equate the position of the Akan individual holding self-acquired property with that of the holder of a life estate in English law; this equation being based on the principle that self-acquired property of which the holder has not disposed during his lifetime becomes family property on his decease. This view is, in my opinion, quite untenable. A man may, in the modern customary law, freely alienate such property during his lifetime, and his family has no vested interest in it, but merely a *spes successionis*. There are stronger arguments for equating the position of the family member who has created self-made property on a family-controlled site with a life tenant in English law, in that permanent alienation of the improvement outside the family is not allowed without the consent of the family; in such an instance, therefore, the family can effectively ensure that the improvement descends to it.

I conclude that all these analogies have some relevance in the attempt to understand the institution of family property; indeed, principles drawn from these different branches of English law have been used and will increasingly be used by the superior courts to develop and control the operation of the institution. But family property, so far as English law is concerned, is still a novelty for which no comprehensive rules exist (though doubtless if one looks at the modern law of India one will find rules aplenty).

I have been speaking so far about the family property system among the AKAN of Ghana, as it has been interpreted by the courts; to what extent is the distribution of rights, the corporate character of the so-called family, and the judicial interpretation placed upon the institution, similar in other West African property systems? According to Fortes, among the TALLENSI of Northern Ghana the farming unit is the group of male agnates who constitute a single household and belong to what he terms a nuclear lineage. He says that farmland is mostly vested in such nuclear lineages. 'To say that land is owned by a lineage is equivalent to saying that it is generally acquired by right of inheritance. All males of the lineage have the right to inherit lineage land, but at any given time control over it is vested in the head of the lineage, by right of seniority. He inherits (*vaa*) what amounts to full usufructuary rights within the limits of the co-existing rights of the other members of the lineage. The utilization of the land is at his discretion; he disposes of the crops; and in some settlements he is nominally free to pledge or to sell the land.'[1] In other words, the Tallensi follow a system much closer to that of the southern Bantu, and attribute absolute rights, both of benefit and control, to the titular head of the group. In practice these rights are fettered by the head's social obligations to his dependants, but these are not expressed as legal responsibilities. This is quite a different situation from the Akan, where the head is no more than manager for those absolutely and collectively entitled to exercise control. Furthermore, the scale of the unit is quite different. Among the Tallensi the primary land-controlling and exploiting unit is the household, and there is no superior lineage authority (except for some parcels of land controlled by higher-order lineages); among the Akan the exploiting unit is the individual or household, but their rights and powers are fettered by the superior interests of section and lineage.

As we have seen from Obi's description of IBO property systems, much of the land held by individuals is not affected by patrilineage or extended family claims; it is only the unallocated portion of lands under the control of such groups that could be described as 'family property'.

Even the household occupied by a parental or nuclear family, reminiscent of the household systems found elsewhere, will fragment in time, and on partition the emancipated male members will acquire their own separate holdings. Whereas in the Akan system the amount of land which a lineage claims to control will tend to expand over time, in these other systems there is a continual reduction in each generation of the amount of directly controlled family or household land. The persistence or non-persistence of the identifiable group from generation to generation is also involved in any assessment of the meaning of 'family property'.

The YORUBA system as described by Lloyd has many points of similarity with that of the AKAN. This may in part be due to their both being interpreted over the years by the same sort of judges or courts. One difference, however, is that the Yoruba family or descent

[1] p. 178.

group, *ebi*, is a group of very varying size, from 'a dozen members descended from a common father to one of a thousand or more members descended from an ancestor through many generations'.[1] It is not enough, therefore, to find out whether property is family property or not; the appropriate group must also be specified. Thus on the one hand land acquired by a remote ancestor on his first arrival in a locality may fall within the control of a group of many members, and a house built in a father's compound by collective contribution of the sons will be termed the 'family house' of the father, in which all his sons will have an interest. Although Lloyd uses the term 'corporate' to describe such groups of variable size, one wonders whether the term 'joint' would not be more appropriate, at least in the first or second generations away from the founder. The possibility of partition also marks out the Yoruba system from the Akan.

Let me close this brief analysis of the appropriate modes of description of West African family property systems by saying that any mode of description which lumps together large precisely defined lineages with a corporate structure, lineages of varying spans and with no defined structure, households and extended families of various kinds; patrilineal, matrilineal, double unilineal and cognatic modes of defining relationship; systems where the head of the unit, of whatever size, is considered to be the holder of the absolute interest in the property exploited by the unit, and systems where such a head is no more than a manager for those who hold the absolute interest; land collectively exploited by the group and land individually exploited by members of the group on a separate, exclusive title—I repeat, a mode of description which lumps together so many variable arrangements and relationships cannot be said to be a satisfactory one.

JURISTIC PROBLEMS AFFECTING FAMILY PROPERTY IN MODERN WEST AFRICAN LAW

There are many practical problems to which such family property systems give rise. Two quite characteristic problems are those of decision-making within the family, and the head's accountability.

Decision-making within the family

In systems, such as that of the TALLENSI, where control of household property is deemed to be vested in the household head, no legal problem arises; decisions affecting the property are taken by the head.

[1] p. 77.

But even then, as we have seen, he is under a moral duty to consult his dependants before taking such decisions; and there are fetters on the legal acceptability of such decisions, e.g. the head must ensure that he has provided fairly and equitably for the wants of his dependants.

In other systems in which (a) the power to take decisions affecting the disposal of family-controlled interests is vested in the responsible members of the group generally, and (b) the group by custom or express or tacit authority delegates some of its powers of management to the head or controlling members of the group, serious difficulties can arise. Often it is a rule in such societies that a sale of family-controlled land is not valid unless the family members agree; does this mean that there must be unanimity, or need there be no more than a majority decision? If unanimity is essential, what happens if a member is absent or not notified? If a majority, of whom should the majority consist—of all the members, of the sections or houses into which the family is divided, or of the senior members of the family? Can the will of the head prevail against that of the other members?

The unanimity rule seems to have been widespread in West African systems, provided only that the view of a minor member might be disregarded. Unanimity is sometimes stated to be that of all responsible (i.e. adult) members, sometimes unanimity of family sections. Today in modern YORUBA law unanimity is rare, and according to Lloyd alienation of family land is valid if the consent is obtained of the elders of each segment of the group.[1] The head cannot alienate without such authority.

For Ghana (especially southern Ghana) Ollennu expresses it as the accepted principle that no valid alienation can be made of family lands except by the occupant of the stool (i.e. family head) with the consent and concurrence of the principal members of the family. Bentsi-Enchill[2] accepts this proposition as generally stating the current law, though he goes on to say: 'It is not possible to assert that unanimity is absolutely insisted on' (sc. of the principal members each representing a branch of the family). My own information from various parts of southern Ghana indicated that in AKAN law as observed today a majority decision may be acceptable, provided that there is general agreement.

The accountability of the head of the family
How far is the head accountable to family members for his use and management of the family property?

[1] p. 340.   [2] p. 59.

Among the TALLENSI, and other systems where the law deems control of the property to vest in the household or lineage head, the head is apparently not accountable for his management.

Rather surprisingly, a similar principle has been accepted for a long period as applying also to the lineage heads of southern Ghana. This alleged principle traces back to a dictum of Sarbah in his *Fanti customary laws* to the effect that though a family can remove a family head who has been misappropriating or squandering the family's possessions, 'no junior member can claim an account from the head of the family'. Later decisions of the Gold Coast and Ghana courts have taken this principle even further. Bentsi-Enchill has very strongly and cogently criticized both the basis and effect of the alleged non-accountability of a family head in his book on *Ghana land law*;[1] I entirely endorse his arguments, and might add one or two points thereto. (1) In the traditional pre-colonial law it was unthinkable that a junior member of a family, acting by himself, could challenge the authority of the head of the family, still less ask for an account, which one would assume to be a remedy introduced by British law. (2) On the other hand, the *senior* members of the family, say the elders of each branch or section, could go collectively into the question of the head's management, where this had given cause for serious complaint, and this would include reckoning what the head had received on the family's account. Sarbah's dictum should therefore be read in this sense. (3) Subsequent judicial decisions have misunderstood and misapplied this principle, and should now be reversed. In any event, the pre-1960 decisions are no longer of binding authority in Ghana courts. (4) A caretaker of family property, e.g. one looking after a house belonging to the family, can definitely be called to account by the family. (5) A successor, i.e. one holding inherited property apportioned to him and in which he has the exclusive claim to use and benefit, cannot be called upon to account for the proceeds of the property; but he can be called to account and if necessary dismissed if he is committing waste which is causing the asset to suffer permanent deterioration (6) One must be extremely cautious about applying AKAN dicta or principles, if they exist, to other customary laws, especially to GA-ADANGME and northern Ghana laws, where the group of relatives jointly interested in property is differently defined, and the relationship of the manager of such property to his co-beneficiaries is of a different order.

[1] p. 95ff.

THE FUTURE OF THE FAMILY PROPERTY SYSTEM IN
WEST AFRICA

Despite my earlier cautionary remarks about the dangers of generalization, there are certain characteristics of West African family property systems which are both conspicuous and general, though in each instance there are exceptions to the generalizations!

(1) The family property system, in the sense of a system of management and benefiting from property by a group of relatives, is mainly limited to immovables. Movables on the whole do not fall into a common kin-group-controlled fund (though note the exception among the TALLENSI, for instance, where crops from the land form a common household fund; and family herds where these exist).

(2) Movables in this context refers not only to things obviously transportable, such as animals, clothes, food, money, utensils, but also to houses and farms in some areas—hence the possibility of a person's enjoying the exclusive use of property which he has created himself on land controlled by his family.

(3) The exploiting unit, which jointly works and benefits from the property, is usually much smaller in extent than the controlling unit. Family property systems thus tend to rest on a dialogue between group maintenance and control of the fixed assets, and individual, or small unit, entitlement to benefit.

(4) Divisory and joint or corporate systems of succession will produce quite different patterns of family property control.

(5) The family property systems not only ensure a building up of capital for present members of the group, but also provide security for future members.

Because of the durability of many lineage groupings over time, a sort of perpetuity is thus created. No one has as yet, so far as I am aware, discussed the legal and social implications of these customary perpetuities. Is there going to be, or perhaps has there already occurred, a conscious or unconscious attempt to 'break the entail', to prevent the formation of family property or to facilitate its alienation? Those systems where partition is possible already possess the legal facility for dissolving the corporation, or at least for breaking it down into smaller fragments. The modern recognition of customary and statutory wills also assists with the postponement of the conversion of property into family property; though, certainly in the AKAN system, a failure in any generation to keep the individualist ball in the air, as where the holder for the time being fails to dispose of self-acquired or transmitted property during his lifetime or by will, means that the particular property falls into the pool of family property thenceforward.

It is often picturesquely stated that there are three groups of relatives interested in family property; the deceased members of the family, the ancestors; the living; and those who are yet to be born. As for the ancestors, no one should underestimate the power of sentiment; but equally no one can allow the past to tie up the present for too long ahead. Contrariwise, to allow individual appropriation or alienation of family property against the wishes of the family is to defeat, not the rights of the ancestors, but those of the living members of the family, and would clearly be unjust. As for those who are yet to come, the notion of laying up a store for future generations is an admirable one; but again one cannot allow the future to dictate to the present.

In the customary systems provision was made for capital accumulation; the capital thus accumulated often could not be dissipated by the foolish act of one man. This had the effect of protecting both the individual and his dependants, thus offering them a sort of social security. How can capital formation, security for an individual and his dependants, and a proper respect for the labours of one's ancestors, be secured in the modern world? The answers of twentieth-century Britain to these demands are the welfare state and its social security services, and statutory family provision from a deceased's estate. No one could possibly claim that these measures are adequate, nor that the sort of atomized self-regarding society which they both provoke, and are caused by, is attractive, even if it *is* better than the horrors of nineteenth century *laissez faire*. The judges in England, aided by the legislator, are trying to rebuild a legally-structured integrated family system after the ravages of individualism have done their worst. A new family property system, according shares or claims to wife and children over the property of the main wage-earner, may well result—something like this is already roughly achieved through various presumptions of law and the contributions of employed married women to the household resources. It would be a tragedy if, as so often seems to be the case, the laws in England and in West Africa move in opposite directions, the West African law towards nineteenth-century English individualism whilst the English law moves towards an 'African' concept of the integrated family or household production or property-controlling unit. In the field of tort, as in the law of the family and succession, a similar process may be at work.

On the other hand, the traditional African lineages, especially in those areas where economic development and educational advance have already moved far, may well be too large units for the future. What some judges and writers in Ghana apparently want to achieve by a re-definition of the law, cutting down the 'family' to the immediate sub-lineage of a given person, may well be the right answer, though it should perhaps be achieved in a more elegant and effective way. Is our recognition test going to be whether the members of a proposed group share a common residence, or habitually co-operate together in production, or acknowledge a single supreme and central family authority? If a group of persons wish to be associated in this way, there is presumably little harm in permitting them to do so—after all they might in any event form a partnership, or incorporate themselves as a family company, or establish a trust, to achieve the same end.

But some aspects of such associations may need to be more precisely regulated in future, if they are to be effective. (1) It must be clearly defined, for instance by a restatement of law, what sort of family groupings are recognized in a particular legal system, and what their functions are in regard to property. (2) Membership of a given family grouping must be precisely defined. This is an obvious requirement once an attempt is made to register family-controlled land; but would be invaluable in any event so as to cut down uncertainty in legal dealings. (3) The authority in a given family must be unambiguously indicated; i.e. the persons competent to make decisions, to manage the property, or to alienate it. This would clarify such questions as whether unanimous or majority approval was required before a family decision could be validly made. A register of family units, perhaps coupled with a property register, would seem to be called for. To prepare such a register is not an impossible administrative task. The alternative will be to leave the evolution of the family property system to the uncertain flux of individual decisions, judicial opinions, and economic pressures. The need for security both economic and psychological, and for the accumulation and wise disposition of capital, remain; and the institution of family property (though probably in an altered form) is likely to prove, for the foreseeable future, the most generally acceptable method of satisfying these needs in the circumstances of a rapidly developing West Africa.

(Instead of giving footnote references in this article to published works, a list of those on which I have relied may be found on p. 301.)

7

THE MATRIMONIAL RÉGIMES OF SOUTH AFRICA[1]

H. R. HAHLO

Dean of the Faculty of Law, University of Witwatersrand, Johannesburg

To the psychologist and sociologist South Africa is a race laboratory—
a land in which peoples of different race and nationality meet and
commingle, striving with and against each other, seeking the road to
peaceful co-existence. The diversity of their *mores* is reflected in South
Africa's legal institutions, which provide an essay in living comparative law. The basic common law system is the Roman-Dutch law
—the law of Holland during the seventeenth and eighteenth centuries,
which came to South Africa with the first Dutch settlers in 1652. Made
up of indigenous Dutch law and Roman law, as received in the
Reception, Roman-Dutch law was a branch of the flourishing common
law tree which spread its foliage over Northern France, the Netherlands and North Western Germany in the pre-codification age. From
1652 until the end of the eighteenth century South Africa was a
colonial possession of the Republic of the Netherlands, and the law of
Holland was the law of the Cape.

A new era commenced with the occupation of the Cape by the
British early in the nineteenth century. There was no attempt to
replace Roman-Dutch law with English law; on the contrary, Roman-
Dutch law was expressly recognized as the common law of South
Africa. Inevitably, however, the laws and institutions of the new
rulers began to make their influence felt. South African law today is
one of the family of hybrid systems of law which combine in varying
proportions civil and English common law elements.

If Roman-Dutch law, modified to some extent by English law, is the
private law of European South Africa, governing the legal position
of whites, Indians and coloured persons, the customary laws of the
African peoples of South Africa continue to lead a somewhat shadowy

[1] For a detailed exposition, see Hahlo, *The South African Law of Husband and
Wife*, 2nd ed., 1963, p. 139. A more condensed statement will be found in
Hahlo and Kahn, *The Union of South Africa*, 1960, p. 409.

existence as 'native law and custom'. Concerned mainly with family law and the law of succession, 'native law and custom' is the personal law of the tribal African, especially in the native reserves and territories.

The multi-coloured splendours of its laws and customs, which make South African law such a delight for the comparative lawyer, are mirrored in its matrimonial régimes. There are three of them, widely apart in parentage. First and foremost, there is the common law régime of universal community of property and profit and loss, in which all the assets and liabilities of the spouses are merged into a single estate, administered by the husband by virtue of the marital power. Community of property and profit and loss, which came to South Africa as part of the law of Holland in 1652, is established whenever a couple enter upon the state of matrimony under South African law without having concluded an antenuptial contract.

Second in rank comes a conventional system of total separation of goods: approximately 35 per cent of all marriages in South Africa are contracted in this way. If it is borne in mind that not many couples of the poorer classes enter into antenuptial contracts, it will be realized that separation of goods is the normal matrimonial régime of the well-to-do.

Already in Roman-Dutch law community of property and of profit and loss could be modified or excluded by antenuptial contract. Several standard forms were in use, with the accent on partial community systems, from community of movables to community of acquests. A form of antenuptial contract, which seems to have enjoyed considerable popularity, gave the wife or her heirs the option on dissolution of the marriage either to reclaim intact whatever she had brought into the marriage or to share in her and her husband's combined estates on a community basis—truly a case of permitting the wife to have her cake and eat it.[1] Marriage settlements and succession clauses were also widely used.

There is no reason why an equal variety of antenuptial contracts should not be used today, cutting the matrimonial property suit to the needs of each couple. In practice, however, the tailor-made marriage covenant has disappeared. There is, to all purposes and effect, only one form of antenuptial contract in South Africa today: one by which all the variable common law consequences of marriage, viz. community of property and community of profit and loss and the marital power, are excluded. Succession clauses have practically disappeared. The individual needs of each couple are met by marriage

[1] cf. art. 1338 of the Quebec Code.

settlements, which usually take the form of a settlement by the husband on the wife, immediately on marriage or within a fixed time thereafter, of a life insurance policy, money, shares or a residence. Not infrequently, wedding presents and furniture are also settled on the wife.

Spouses married with the standard antenuptial contract are to all intents in the same position as if they were married under English law, indeed there can be little doubt that the adoption of complete separation of goods as the favoured conventional régime owes much to the influence of English *mores*. Each spouse owns and administers his or her separate estate, which cannot be attached by the creditors of the other spouse. The wife has full legal capacity and does not require her husband's consent for contracts and other legal transactions. The spouses can freely contract with each other. They can appoint each other as agents, and can sue each other, in contract[1] as well as in delict.[2] There is, however, one important exception to the rule that the spouses are (except, of course, for the duty of reciprocal support) in the same position as if they were unmarried: donations between spouses are prohibited.[3] The purpose of this prohibition, which South African law has inherited from Roman law,[4] is to prevent connubial affection from being bought and sold—'lest she be kissed or cursed out of her money', as it used to be put in England. This prohibition, which cannot be excluded by antenuptial contract, is of little practical importance where the spouses are married in community of property. It is of the greatest importance where they are married out of community. If a man who is married to his wife by antenuptial contract makes a substantial donation to her, he can revoke it at any time. Similarly, the wife can revoke at any time a donation made by her *stante matrimonio* to her husband. A prohibited donation becomes validated if the donor spouse dies before the donee spouse without having revoked it, expressly or by implication.

To be effective as against third parties, antenuptial contracts must be executed notarially, and registered within a certain time after execution —normally, three months. Postnuptial contracts are not permitted. The doctrine of the immutability of the matrimonial régime established at the time of marriage applies: once the marriage has been con-

[1] See, e.g., *Ex parte Smith*, 1940 O.P.D. 120; *Hamman v. Hamman*, 1949 (1) S.A. 1191 (W).

[2] *Rohloff v. Ocean Accident and Guarantee Corporation Ltd*, 1960 (2) S.A. 291 (A.D.).

[3] Voet, 24.1.1.

[4] D. 24.1. 1, 2, 3 pr.

tracted it is not possible to change from community to separation, or vice versa.[1] The court may, however, grant leave for the postnuptial execution and registration of an antenuptial contract,[2] provided the spouses are able to satisfy it (1) that they have actually, though informally, agreed upon the terms of the contract before the marriage; (2) that there was some good reason why they did not execute the contract in proper form before the marriage, e.g. they received wrong legal advice, or were unable to find a notary on the day of the wedding;[3] and (3) that they acted with reasonable promptitude after discovering the need for recourse to court.

A statutory variant of marriage out of community applies in respect of legal marriages contracted by natives (Africans). Unless they opt in prescribed form for community of property (which they may not do if there is a subsisting customary union between the man and another woman) the marriage is out of community, but the husband has the marital power.[4]

The 'lobola' marriage of the African is the typical form of matrimoney of the indigenous tribes of Africa south of the Sahara. It corresponds closely to the marriage of the early Germanic peoples at the time when Caesar came to Gaul. Known in modern South African law as 'native customary union', the *lobola* marriage does not, strictly speaking, qualify for inclusion among South Africa's systems of matrimony. Being potentially polygamous, it is not recognized as a legal marriage. The fact remains that it is the traditional 'marriage' of the Bantu; that even today millions of Bantu couples in South Africa are joined in this form of matrimonial relationship; and that South African law, though it does not accept the union as a legal marriage, grants recognition to it in important respects. Section 11(1) of the Native Administration Act,[5] after providing that native law is not to be applied where it is opposed to the principles of public policy or natural justice, expressly states that 'it shall not be lawful for any court to declare that the custom of lobola or bogadi or other similar custom is repugnant to public policy or natural justice'.

Generally speaking, a native customary union is given effect to in accordance with native law and custom. The contract of 'lobola', a

[1] *Union Government v. Larkan*, 1916 A.D. 212, esp. at 214.

[2] Deeds Registries Act, No. 47 of 1937, section 88.

[3] *Ex parte Siebert*, 1936 O.P.D. 120. Mere lack of money is no excuse: *Ex parte van der Merwe*, 1938 O.P.D. 62.

[4] Native Administration Act, No. 38 of 1927, section 22 (6) and (7). Cf. below, p. 9.

[5] No. 38 of 1927.

consideration which the bridegroom pays to the father of the bride, traditionally in cattle, is enforceable.[1] So is a 'husband's' claim for a fine for adultery. Polygamy is permitted.[2] Ranking among 'wives' is fixed by tribal custom. Women have no proprietary capacity. Each 'wife' is equipped by the Kraalhead with a hut, a piece of land and a few beasts. Together with her children, she constitutes a separate 'house' within the Kraal.

After her 'husband's' death the 'wife' continues to live in her 'house', now under the tutelage of her late 'husband's' heirs. With the consent of the new Kraalhead she may enter into a union with a brother or other paternal relative of her late husband in order to 'raise seed' to her 'house'.[3] Children born of such a union rank as issue of her late 'husband' (the 'levirate' of the Old Testament). Succession to 'Kraal' and 'house' property is regulated by tribal custom.

A subsisting native customary union does not preclude either the man or the woman from contracting a legal marriage with another person. If this is done, any subsisting native customary union is automatically dissolved, and no new one may be concluded whilst the legal marriage lasts. The 'material rights' of the 'wife' and children of the customary union are, however, protected. If at the time of the legal marriage a customary union subsists between the man and a woman other than the one he is marrying, the spouses cannot contract to be married in community of property, and the 'wife' and children of the customary union retain the property and succession rights to which they are entitled according to native law and custom.[4]

Several general statutes recognize native customary unions, e.g. the Workmen's Compensation Act[5] so defines the widow of a native workman as to include a woman associated with him in a conjugal relationship according to native law and custom, provided that neither the man nor the woman is a party to a subsisting legal marriage. At common law the female partner to a native customary union had no claim for loss of support if her man was killed as a result of the delictual

[1] Variously interpreted by anthropologists as 'brideprice', 'childprice' or security for good behaviour, the 'lobola' of the African corresponds closely to the *pretium nuptiale* of early Germanic law.

[2] Not many natives, other than chiefs, can afford to pay lobola for more than one 'wife'. Tacitus said the same about the early Germanic peoples.

[3] Needless to say, she can no longer be forced to do so, as this would be repugnant to public policy.

[4] For details, see Hahlo, *The South African Law of Husband and Wife*, 2nd ed., p. 29.

[5] No. 30 of 1941, section 2.

act of a third party,[1] but this has recently been remedied by statute.[2]

Community of property and profit and loss (*communio bonorum*), the common law régime of the Roman-Dutch law, is one of the mutlitude of community systems, from community of movables and acquests to universal community of property, which developed on the Continent between the tenth and the twelfth centuries. The first Dutch source to mention it is the Zeelandsche Keur of 1256,[3] which succinctly states its principles: all the assets and liabilities of the spouses are merged into a joint estate, which is administered by the husband by virtue of his marital power. The wife cannot enter into legally binding contracts without her husband's consent. To the last rule there are two exceptions: first, a married woman can bind her husband and the community in respect of expenses incurred for the common household; secondly, if she is carrying on some public trade with his consent, she can validly enter into contracts connected with such trade.

Subject to minor modifications and refinements, this all-inclusive community system is South Africa's common law régime. Important inroads have been made into the marital power by legislation; more especially, the Matrimonial Affairs Act of 1953.[4]

Community comes into being as soon as the marriage is solemnized. Without any acts of delivery, transfer or cession being required, all assets brought into the marriage by either spouse are merged in a joint estate, in which the spouses hold equal, undivided shares. In the same way, any property or right which either spouse acquires during the marriage falls automatically into the joint estate, no matter whether it is acquired by onerous or gratuitous title, by legal or by illegal activities. The shares which the husband purchases and the mink coat which the wife buys; the husband's salary and his winnings at poker; the diamond bracelet and the farm which the wife inherits from her grandmother: all automatically become part of the joint estate. In *Strydom v. Saayman*[5] the husband had committed adultery. His wife forgave him but, duly assisted by her now repentant husband, sued his former girlfriend for damages for adultery. The court held that she was entitled to recover, despite the fact that the damages fell into the joint estate, with the result that the husband benefited financially from his own infidelity.

[1] *Suid-Afrikaanse Nasionale Trust en Assuransie Maatskappy, Bpk v. Fondo*, 1960(2) S.A. 467 (A.D.).

[2] The Bantu Laws Amendment Act, No. 76 of 1963, section 31.

[3] De Blécourt, *Bewijsstukken*, II, pp. 454–5. See also Fockema Andreae, *Bijdragen*, II, p. 110.

[4] No. 37 of 1953, as variously amended.

[5] 1949(2) S.A. 736(T).

Excluded from the joint estate are rights and property in which a spouse holds a limited or determinable interest only, e.g. a usufructuary or fiduciary right.[1] Moreover, a third party who gives or bequeaths property to one of the spouses can effectively provide that it shall be excluded from the joint estate and, where the wife is the beneficiary, from her husband's administration.[2] Excluded from the community are further life insurance policies which the wife has effected upon her own life or that of her husband, or which the husband has effected upon his own life or that of his wife and ceded to her.[3]

The corollary of community of assets is community of debts. '*Die de man ofte wijf trouwt, die trouwt oock de schulden.*'[4] Antenuptial as well as postnuptial debts of the spouses, whatever their source, are charges on the joint estate and have to be paid by the husband as its administrator. This includes contractual debts incurred by either spouse before the marriage, as well as contractual debts incurred by the husband during the marriage. It also includes debts validly contracted by the wife during the marriage, e.g. with her husband's consent or as a *publica mercatrix*. Maintenance claims of the divorced wife, an illegitimate child of the husband's or of the child of a previous marriage of the wife, have also to be met out of the joint estate.

The position as regards delictual liabilities incurred by one of the spouses during the marriage is controversial. The problem is how to reconcile the principle that no one should be held liable for another's wrongdoing (*culpa tenet auctores suos*) with the existence of a single estate. There is support in South African case law for the view both that the joint estate is liable in full (possibly with a right of recourse by the innocent against the guilty spouse on dissolution of the marriage)[5] and that it is liable only up to the guilty spouse's half-share.[6] The former view seems to be at present in the ascendancy.

Community comes to an end when the marriage is dissolved by death or divorce. It also comes to an end when an order of separation of goods (*boedelscheiding*) is made by the court *stante matrimonio*, e.g. in connection with a *separatio a mensa et thoro*.

On dissolution of the marriage by death the net estate, after pay-

---

[1] Gr. 2.11.10; Voet, 23.2.77; *Barnett v. Rudman*, 1934 A.D. 203.

[2] Voet, 23.2.77; *Erasmus v. Erasmus*, 1942 A.D. 265.

[3] Insurance Act, No. 27 of 1943, secs. 39–46. For details, see Hahlo, op. cit., pp. 303–7.

[4] Mattheaeus, *Paroemiae*, II, 22.

[5] *Erikson Motors (Welkom) Ltd v. Scholtz N.O.*, 1960(4) S.A. 791(o); *Opperman v. Opperman*, 1962(3) S.A. 40(N).

[6] e.g. *Levy v. Fleming*, 1931 T.P.D. 62, esp. at 67.

ment of all debts which are charges on the community, is divided equally between the surviving spouse and the heirs of the first-dying spouse. Continued community, not uncommon in the old law, has ceased to be a living institution in South Africa.

On dissolution of the marriage by divorce, the innocent spouse is entitled to an order of forfeiture of benefits. Failing such an order the estate is divided equally between the spouses, irrespective of who has contributed more to the marriage, the innocent or the guilty spouse. If an order of forfeiture is made, on the other hand, the guilty spouse forfeits any financial benefits which he would derive from the marriage if equal division were to take place. In the result, there will be equal division if the guilty spouse has contributed more to the marriage than the innocent spouse, but if the innocent spouse has contributed more to the marriage, he (or she) will get his (or her) own contributions back. The idea, of course, is that a spouse should not benefit financially from a marriage which he or she has wrecked, an application of the wider principle that no one should be allowed to benefit from his own wrong.

To ascertain how much of the joint estate has been contributed by each spouse is frequently a matter of practical difficulty. No distinction is made between assets which the spouses have brought into the marriage and those which they have acquired during the marriage, and acquisitions from any source—employment, investment, inheritance and gift—are included. In at least one case, *Gates v. Gates*,[1] the court took the services of the wife in looking after the household and caring for the children into account.

The court granting a divorce may make an order against the guilty spouse for the payment of maintenance until death or remarriage (whichever occurs first). What the wife, if she happens to be the innocent party, receives out of the joint estate will, of course, be taken into account in assessing her needs.

The universal community of Roman-Dutch law goes together with the husband's marital power. At common law this power is all-comprehensive. The husband administers the joint estate. He may, without his wife's knowledge or consent, and without being in any way accountable to her, enter into contracts and other legal transactions that will be binding on the joint estate and his wife personally, not only during the subsistence of the marriage, but after its dissolution.[2] The wife, on the other hand, is reduced to a status of legal incompe-

[1] 1940 N.P.D. 361.
[2] e.g. *Oliver v. Matzner and Matzner*, 1942 T.P.D. 324 esp. at 329.

tence. She has no *locus standi in judicio*. She cannot, without her husband's consent, bind herself or her husband by contract; alienate or hypothecate property; release a debtor from liability; accept office as guardian of a minor, executrix in a deceased estate or director of a company. In theory, she may not, without her husband's consent, take up employment or engage in a trade or profession, but in practice there is little he can do to stop her. The wife does not require her husband's consent to make a will of her half-share in the joint estate or any property separately owned by her (e.g. property left to her by her father with the proviso that it shall not fall into the community).

As manageress of the joint household the wife can bind her husband and herself by contracts for household necessaries (*in re oeconomica*). If she openly carries on a public trade, business or profession in her own name, with the consent, express or implied, of her husband, she may, as a *publica mercatrix*, validly enter into contracts and other transactions connected with such trade, business or profession. Liabilities so contracted by her bind both herself and her husband.

Wide as the marital power is, even at common law the wife is not without protection against an abuse by her husband of his powers. If he makes out of the joint estate a donation in deliberate fraud of his wife (or her heirs)—e.g. to a mistress or to his children by a previous marriage—the wife (or her heirs) may recover it from him, and if necessary, from the donee.[1] And if the husband wastes or maladministers the joint estate, threatening to reduce his family to destitution, the wife can apply to court for an order of separation of goods (*boedel-scheiding*). In modern practice, little use is being made of court orders of separation of goods, except in connection with decrees of separation from bed and table.

Important statutory inroads on the marital power were made by the Matrimonial Affairs Act of 1953.

As regards immovable property, Section 1 of the Act provides that upon application in writing of the husband or the wife a special entry may be made in the deeds registry in respect of property which

    (a) the wife brought into the community at marriage;

    (b) was acquired with moneys or other means which the wife brought into the community at marriage;

    (c) was inherited by or donated to the wife during the marriage;

    (d) was acquired with money or other means inherited by or donated to the wife during the marriage;

[1] *Davis v. Trustee of Minors Brisley* (1901) 18 S.C. 407; *Pickles v. Pickles*, 1947(3) S.A. 175(W).

(e) was acquired with the wife's earnings, whether made before or during the marriage;

(f) was acquired with the proceeds of any of the aforestated categories of immovable property.

Once the fact that the property falls within one of the protected categories has been noted in the register and endorsed upon the title deeds, the husband can no longer alienate, hypothecate or otherwise burden it, unless he obtains his wife's written consent (which, in an appropriate case, may be replaced by the court). If, because no one applies for it, no such entry is made, the common law position obtains and the husband may dispose of the property as he pleases, without requiring his wife's consent.

Section 2 of the Act deals with movable property. It prescribes that no husband may, without his wife's written consent,

i receive or take possession of any remuneration due to her from her employers;

ii receive or take possession of any compensation awarded to her in respect of personal injuries sustained by her;

iii withdraw any deposit standing in her name in the Post Office Savings Bank, a building society, or any account in a banking institution, or take possession of any moneys withdrawn by her from such an account;

iv alienate or pledge any shares held by her in a building society, or receive or take possession of any dividends on or the proceeds of such shares;

v receive or take possession of any amount payable in terms of an education policy taken out by her for a child of hers, the premiums of which have been paid by her;

vi alienate of pledge any tool or implement of trade with which his wife is earning any remuneration.

Correspondingly enhanced powers are conferred upon the wife. She may, without her husband's assistance, receive and sue for her salary or wages and any other of the aforementioned items, and may be a depositor in any account in a banking institution, but may not without her husband's consent overdraw on a current account. Save with her written consent, her husband is not entitled to demand from her bank particulars concerning her deposits.[1]

---

[1] Until recently a wife who was married to her husband in community of property could open and operate without his consent on a savings account in a banking institution, but not a current account. This was changed by section 1 of Act No. 13 of 1966, amending section 2 of the Matrimonial Affairs Act, No. 37 of 1953.

Property protected in terms of sections 1 and 2 forms a kind of *peculium* within the community. Though withdrawn from the husband's sole control, it remains part of the joint estate and can be attached for community debts incurred by either spouse.[1]

Special provision is made in the Matrimonial Affairs Act for the protection of movable property acquired by a deserted wife.[2] The wife may apply to court for an order declaring such property to be free from her husband's control and prohibiting him from dealing with it. Once such an order is made, the property cannot be attached or sold in execution for community debts, except liabilities in respect of necessaries for the joint household and orders of costs awarded against the wife in legal proceedings under Section 2 of the Act.

It remains to assess South Africa's community system in terms of its 'functional adequacy in terms of contemporary values'.[3]

The great merit of universal community of property is that it projects the partnership which a good marriage should be into the economic field. It gives each spouse a stake in the other's success and ensures that the wife of a wealthy man cannot find herself destitute if he decides to disinherit her.[4] It is in conformity with one's sense of justice and fairness that the wife should share as of right in an estate which has been built up 'by the industry of the husband and the thrift of the wife'.[5]

Though the most satisfactory system from the wife's point of view if the marriage is financially a success, universal community does not work out well for her if it is financially a failure. If the husband goes insolvent, the wife, too, is involved. A delict committed by the husband may spell ruin for the wife, and vice versa.[6] Finally, even though the Matrimonial Affairs Act of 1953 has given her the control of her own earnings, savings and banking account, it still remains true that during the marriage the wife is largely dependent on her husband's generosity. As far as she is concerned, participation in the joint estate does not become a reality until the marriage is dissolved. Community is a partnership which for the wife, in the words of Mr Justice Holmes, 'begins only at its end'.

But all these are risks which the average wife might be prepared to

[1] There is a minor exception: movable property falling within the terms of section 2 may not be attached for bottle store debts incurred by the husband.

[2] Section 3.

[3] John G. Fleming, *Law of Torts*, 3rd ed., 1965, Preface, p.v.

[4] cf. *Glazer v. Glazer N.O.*, 1963(4) S.A. 694 (A.D.).

[5] *Ex parte Podlas*, 1935 W.L.D. 13 at 16, per De Wet, J.

[6] I assume here that *Erikson's* and *Opperman's* cases have been correctly decided, which, with respect, is not certain. Cf. above, p. 13.

face, were it not for the fact that the common law marriage reduces her to a position of legal inferiority. The gradual whittling away of the husband's powers, in which the Matrimonial Affairs Act of 1953 constituted the first step, is far too slow and hesitant a process to reconcile the women of our day to a matrimonial régime which groups them together with minors and lunatics as persons of diminished capacity.

No wonder, then, that there is a widespread disinclination to accept the common law system of universal community. The rush into ante-nuptial contracts excluding community and the marital power is more than a passing fashion: it is clear evidence that the common law régime is out of harmony with modern notions.

But total separation is not satisfactory either. For her legal independence the wife has to pay a high price. She does not participate in any way, as of right, in her husband's earnings and acquisitions. 'The deceased could not successfully have conducted his . . . business if his wife had not cooked the dinner and minded the children,' said one of South Africa's great judges, the late Mr Justice Van den Heever, in *Edelstein v. Edelstein N.O.*[1] However successful the husband may be in his business or profession, under a system of total separation of goods the wife does not share in the fruits of his victories. 'She may have sacrificed her own career on the altar of matrimonial life; she may have helped him with her own earnings . . . over the early years of the marriage; yet unless she can show an express or implied agreement of partnership she has no share in his gains and acquisitions.'[2] And if, after twenty or thirty years of marriage, her husband, for an old man's reasons or no reason whatsoever, sees fit to disinherit her, she may find herself a beggar. There is no legitimate portion in South African law, nor is a destitute widow entitled to maintenance out of her late husband's estate.[3]

The following, it is suggested, are the minimum requirements with which a matrimonial property régime must comply, if it is to be acceptable to the men and, more important, to the women of our time:

(1) There must be no *capitis deminutio* as far as the wife is concerned. She must enjoy full and unrestricted legal capacity, in no way inferior to that of her husband.

[1] 1952(3) S.A. 1 (A.D.) at 14.
[2] Hahlo, *The South African Law of Husband and Wife*, 2nd ed., p. 93.
[3] *Glazer v. Glazer, N.O.*, 1963(4) S.A. 694 (A.D.).

(2) During the marriage, save for matters such as the reciprocal duty of support and the payment of household expenses, the estate of the spouses must remain separate and independent. Each spouse must have the free disposition of his or her estate. This does not exclude rules (a) requiring the consent of both spouses for the alienation and hypothecation of immovable property, for dispositions concerning the matrimonial home, and for donations; and (b) providing for the avoidance of dispositions in fraud of the other spouse or his or her heirs.

(3) On dissolution of the marriage by death, the surviving spouse must be ensured of an adequate share in the estate or acquisitions of the first-dying, of which he cannot be deprived, except for good cause. The formula for the calculation of this share should be simple and straightforward, so as to obviate the need for complicated and protracted liquidation procedures.

(4) On dissolution of the marriage by divorce, the wife, at any rate where she is the innocent party, and perhaps even if she is the guilty one, should be entitled to a share in her husband's acquisitions during the marriage, apart from any alimony that may be awarded to her.

There are several ways in which the apparently contradictory aims of independence and partnership, of separateness and sharing, may be achieved. The legitimate portion of Continental systems is one, the *jus relicti(ae)* and *terce* or *courtesy* of Scottish law another, the 'widow's share' of American jurisdictions a third. Of special interest are the participation systems of modern Continental laws where, in the previously quoted words of Mr Justice Holmes, 'community begins when the marriage ends'. Of this kind are the universal community of property of the present law of the Netherlands; the conventional *'régime de participation aux acquets'* of French law, as introduced by *Loi No 65–570 du 13 juillet 1965 portant réforme des régimes matrimoniaux*, and put into effect on February 1, 1966; and the *Zugewinngemeinschaft*, which is the statutory régime of modern German law.

In South Africa wholesale reform is not to be expected in the foreseeable future. Change is likely to continue along the lines of piecemeal legislation, chipping bits out of the solid block of the marital power until it will eventually be reduced to a hollow shell.

8

FAMILY ARRANGEMENTS IN DEVELOPING COUNTRIES

J. DUNCAN M. DERRETT

Professor of Oriental Laws in the University of London

Family arrangements, favoured by equity,[1] may have several roles to play in developing countries which have inherited common law and equity. Before they can be used with confidence they must be understood. Their origin is, in a sense, against them, in that the peculiar conditions of English land tenure and society which surround the early days of the concept have tended to colour the manner in which the law is expounded as well as the authorities themselves. The special feature of the family arrangement is the right it may create in those who are not parties to it. In developing countries beneficiaries under a family arrangement may often not have any personal knowledge of the questions in discussion between the principal parties, and there may also be minors whose consent would be immaterial, or persons under various disabilities preventing them from playing a major part in any discussion concerning their future. The English assumption that it is right and proper for every person whose legal rights are debated to take a share in all negotiations affecting them, either personally or through his agent, by no means operated in all developing societies. There are many contexts in which it is not good etiquette to obtrude one's own views, and no good outcome can be expected from negotiations one has oneself pressed forward. Unlike normal contracts, therefore, it is interesting to note that where a contract is intended to secure a benefit to a third party as a beneficiary under a family arrangement he may sue in his own name to enforce it.[2] This is another example of

[1] Story, *Equity Jurisprudence*, S 132. *Kerr on Fraud and Mistake*, 7th edn. (1952), 168–9.2.

[2] *Nawab Khwaja Muhammad Khan v. Nawab Husaini Begam* (1910) L.R. 37 I.A. 152, 158–9 (familiarly known as the '*Kharch-i-pandan* case'); *Dan Kuer v. Sarla Devi* (1946) 73 I.A. 208, 221; *Shangmugan v. Annamalai* A.I.R. 1935 Mad. 141, 143–4. *Tweddle v. Atkinson* (1861) 1 B. & S. 393, 121 E.R. 762 (now to be read in the light of *Beswick v. B.* (1967) 2 All E.R. 1197 (H.L.), is not applicable. The case of *Tweddle v. Atkinson* itself divides the Indian High Courts. Madras in

156

Equity at work in a non-common-law environment.[1] A further advantage is that in a genuine family arrangement the consideration may be partly valuable and partly good consideration, i.e. love and affection, and the court does not concern itself with the proportion between these.[2] In any event, if the requirements of the bona fide family arrangement are met, the court will not scrutinize the consideration at all closely. Many may benefit, for example minors or others to whom no share of a disputed estate has already fallen, who contribute no valuable consideration at all: but to provide for their needs may be a consideration of another kind, and this the court allows.

The occasion for this review of what can be a puzzling subject is, to put it distinctly, the effect of the Hindu Succession Act, 1956, in India. This is only symptomatic of other legislative interference with the lives of the people. The Shariat Act, 1937, of pre-Partition India caused similar upheavals. Elsewhere the introduction, or extension, of the capacity to leave property by will, and indeed any other clash between the immemorial usages of the people and the law as developed in the courts (sometimes under misapprehensions as to the true customary law), or in the legislatures, produces situations which only family arrangements can cure. Not only cure: prophylaxis as well may be sought in this valuable instrument. The family arrangement enables parties to dispose in advance of such estate as would fall to them or to any of them upon the death of a person now living. This is an extremely valuable power which is again a peculiarity of the family arrangement because the courts favour the instrument whereby the peace, happiness, and welfare of families is secured and litigation is avoided.

To take a specific situation: in the State of Kerala many families are governed by *marumakkattayam*, i.e. matrilineal descent of undivided family property. If a member dies undivided his share passes, nevertheless, as separate property to heirs who are selected according to a method incompatible with matriliny. If these do not at once demand

---

Subbu Chetti v. Arunachalam (1929) 53 Mad. 270, F.B., adheres to the principle. Calcutta emphatically dissents from it in *Kshirodebihari v. Mangobinda* (1933) 61 Cal. 841. There it was asserted that the rule was repugnant to 'justice, equity and good conscience', while in India complete justice might be sought in a single suit.

[1] For others see Derrett, 'Fiduciary principles, the African family, and Hindu law', 15 *International and Comparative Law Quarterly* (1966), pp. 1205–16.

[2] *Persse v. Persse* (1840) 7 Cl. & Fin. 279.

their fractions, and especially if the only joint property is not readily partible, and some sharers die, the process is repeated, until persons related by various relationships, belonging to various families, perhaps having nothing else in common except the burden of maintaining relatives about whom some care very little, find themselves in a financial tangle which baffles all but the experts. But not every household can afford the necessary legal advice. And even if it can afford this advice, are the members of the family sufficiently aware of the need for it? To take another example: the right to be a manager of the property of a Hindu idol passes under the codified law of India to relations who can be very remote and share neither the same locality nor, sometimes, the same cult. How will such management, which coincides with ownership in respect of the surplus of considerable endowed funds,[1] be provided for?

The family arrangement is the obvious answer, so that it appears that all we need to do is to acquaint ourselves with its requirements. However, we are at once in a difficulty. England has always coupled with large properties the desire and also the capacity to obtain legal advice. The rule very naturally developed that if the parties were not actually compromising doubtful rights they must be aware of their legal position, otherwise relief against the arrangement could be obtained by the party whose consent was obtained upon a false premise as to his legal entitlement.[2] Thus although mistakes of fact or even of law might not *ipso facto* vitiate a family arrangement, provided that neither party misled the other, the distinction between a true compromise and any other arrangement was a real one and stands boldly out in our reference books.[3] Translate this into terms of life in a Nigerian village, or a remote area in south-western India, and the virtue of the institution is removed. The great value of the family arrangement in such an environment would be precisely that it could settle finally property rights and expectations between people who cannot know, as well as those who do know, their legal rights. If a family arrangement were to be upset merely because at some remote

[1] G.-D. Sontheimer, 'Religious endowments in India: the Juristic personality of Hindu deities', 67 *Zeits. f. vergl. Rechtsw.*, pt. 1 (1964), 45ff.

[2] *Halsbury's Laws of England*, Vol. 17, S 384 (cited and relied on in *Maturi Pullaiah v. M. Narasimham* A.I.R. 1966 S.C. 1836). Relief may be given where there was ignorance or mistake on the parts of both parties: *Reynell v. Sprye* (1849) 8 Hare 222. If the parties proceed on a false notion of the law and claims were not compromised the deed will be set aside: *Lawton v. Campion* (1854) 18 Beav. 87.

[3] It is equally evident in Story, Kerr, and Halsbury.

date, a party or even third-party beneficiary, were to prove to a court's satisfaction that the legal rights at that time were not merely distinct and capable of being known but were known in such a sense that prejudice was suffered by him, the institution would be worse than useless. Naturally in the Indian case-law this requirement has manifested itself in various ways. The Privy Council and courts subordinate to it in India have never acknowledged openly that the family arrangement in Asia differed from that in England: and the rules which emerge bear a close resemblance to those to be found in Halsbury's *Laws of England*. But we still seek the intellectual clarity which is required if one would introduce the institution to those who remain at present hardly aware of it.

Meanwhile, Indian cases reveal a supposition that if ignorance of legal rights is to be fatal to the permanence of a family arrangement, the *other* alternative, namely that it must be a compromise of a doubtful claim by people entertaining genuine doubts, must develop so as to be able to carry the entire weight which the institution is designed to bear. This has led to curious situations in which there were evidently no real doubts, the family was not about to be upset by internal conflicts, and such uncertainty as there was related merely to the degree of discomfort which *would be experienced in the future* if the arrangement were not entered into *now*.

It is the contention of the present writer that this was a natural, but misconceived, approach, due to a mistaken notion of the history of the institution. It is submitted that the family arrangement exists in principle as much to rearrange property rights about which the parties may have no clear notion, as to compromise a doubtful claim. The supposition that parties will all have adequate legal advice has naturally led to the rule that if they are deceived as to what each gains and what each loses by the arrangement their agreement is founded on a premise which is false, and therefore must be voidable. If we remove that supposition, and substitute for it the proposition that the parties would seek legal advice if they could, but are satisfied with their own apprehensions of what might ensue should any legal position be explored and should any legal answer be obtained, being equally indifferent to the result, or equally disinclined to any solution but the one of their own choice (as must very often be the case in developing countries), we are better placed. If we suppose that the parties will not take legal advice, but will rather proceed on the footing that it is within their competence to provide for their collective future irrespective of what any testamentary disposition may have provided or any intestate law may have prescribed, the arrangement is not founded on any premise as to facts or law, and cannot be upset if it afterwards turns out that, had the matter been taken to law, one party, for example, would have come off much better financially than he did by reason of the arrangement into which he entered in happy ignorance. There is no need to posit a compromise of a doubtful claim. In the light of this submission we may investigate the law relating to family arrangements as it has developed in South Asia, where it has had more scope than anywhere outside the parent common-law jurisdictions.

Courses in equity jurisprudence seldom include a discussion of the family arrangement.[1] Courses in family laws, whether personal laws or customary laws, naturally tend to ignore the family arrangement since this seems to be the enemy of the customary or the personal law, which it can readily undermine if the public so wish.[2] Yet cases in family arrangements have come before supreme tribunals. The Supreme Court of India has frequently made pronouncements on them, especially in recent years;[3] and we may take this as a sign that at prior stages in the litigation insufficient certainty must have been manifested as to the main features of the institution. This would not be surprising, since, as now used in developing countries, the family arrangement may evidently be the means whereby Equity is called upon to endorse a fraud.

[1] The writer finds no reference to it in Hanbury's *Modern Equity* (8th edn.), Nathan's *Equity through the Cases* (4th edn.), or Funiak's *Handbook of Modern Equity* (2nd edn.). Professor G. W. Keeton, *An Introduction to Equity* (4th edn.), 355, deals with one aspect, shortly. Professor P. M. Bromley's excellent *Family Law* (3rd edn.) handles family arrangements very summarily at pp. 466–7.

[2] It is of no consequence whether the dispute (if any) relates to book law or custom: *Jagannath Singh v. Tirloki Singh* A.I.R. (All India Reporter) 1954 All. 769. See also the writer's comment at Derrett, ed., *Studies in the Laws of Succession in Nigeria* (O.U.P., London, 1965), at p. 281: the deviation from the Islamic law of inheritance on the part of inhabitants of Northern Nigeria cannot be attributed to custom (which the Islamic law itself will not admit for the purpose) but the recurrent instances of *ṣulḥ* (family arrangement in this context), no doubt imputed. In *Rao Kishore v. Mst. Gahenabai* (1919) 24 C.W.N. 601, 22 Bom. L.R. 507, the Privy Council thought a custom of impartibility could have originated in successive family arrangements.

[3] *Sahu Madho Das v. Pandit Mukand Ram* (1955); *Potti Lakshmi Perumallu v. P. Krishnavenamma* (1965); *Ram Charan Das v. Girja Nandini Devi* (1966): *Tek Bahadur Bhujil v. Debi Singh Bhujil* and *Maturi Pullaiah v. M. Narasimham* (1966): all referred to below.

ADVANTAGES OF THE INSTITUTION

The period when the family arrangement, or family settlement as it is often called, was most in vogue in England was while the law of property and succession was still unreformed. The multiplicity of tenures, the conflicting rights of members of the family (some of whom were underprivileged by any standard), the occurrence in wealthy families of members or quasi-members whose legitimacy was in doubt or who, though admittedly illegitimate, claimed by virtue of a will or other disposition, and finally the frequency of long, complicated, and difficult testaments, provisions of which might become inoperative due to events (including construction) outside the testator's contemplation—all these factors made the period prior to 1925, or even prior to the Family Provision statutes, fecund in family settlements. The main object was in every case to vary the title to property, including expectancies, in a manner conducive to the best interests of the family, and to put an end to any actual disputes between the members. Whether these disputes had advanced so far as litigation did not matter. The waste of the family's estate by improvident and avoidable litigation was to be obviated, and Equity favoured that object. In course of time it became evident that a family arrangement was not merely a class of compromise, but a larger institution in as much as it might, if not improperly entered into, bind parties (including minors[1] and persons yet to be born[2]) who have not actually become involved in litigation, and between whom no actual dispute has broken out, provided that a dispute might develop unless such a step were taken by responsible members of the family.[3] The court may well be astute, as it was in the case of *Sahu Madho Das*, to find evidence of a situation fraught with the makings of a dispute. This writer has already submitted that, though understandable, this course was not inevitable.

The widow of the last male holder of the estate, who had died intestate, gave certain of the properties (over which she had a power of disposal limited to cases of necessity or of evident benefit to the estate itself) to each of her three daughters, who were then next in the line of succession though for an equally limited estate.

---

[1] *Keramatulla v. Keamatulla Meah* (1915) 23 I.C. (Indian Cases) 118; *Dwarka Das v. Krishnan Kishore* (1921) I.L.R. 2 Lahore 114.

[2] *Re New* (1901) 2 Ch. 534 C.A. *Chabildas Lallubhai v. Ramdas Chabildas* (1909) 11 Bom. L.R. 606, cf. *Ramdas v. Chabildas* (1910) 12 Bom. L.R. 621.

[3] *Rameswar Rai v. Sheopal Rai* (1929) 117 I.C. 822 (All.).

She gave the properties to them absolutely. She also gave other properties from the same estate to each of her four grandsons, likewise absolutely. It was urged when the actual reversioner—the male holder's next heir—sued for recovery of the properties that there had never been any dispute and that the gifts were not part of a family settlement. The Supreme Court of India held otherwise. The widow, though she took as heiress subject to a restricted estate, claimed to be able to dispose of the property by her will prior to the impugned distribution. This claim would give all the reversioners a right of suit to prevent her alienation. The donees themselves tried to persuade others, including the persons to whom they ultimately sold their shares, that they had taken the properties absolutely. Thus from a long course of dealing the arrangement (which alone could account for this) could be imputed.[1]

Such an imputing will be valuable, whether or not traces of doubtful claims can be found, especially in those jurisdictions where the same or similar complexities of tenure remain or difficulties regarding testaments and/or alienations *inter vivos*.[2]

P. left a will by which he purported to dispose of property belonging to the family of which he was a member. Under his personal law he had no power of testamentary disposition in respect of such an interest. The will was invalid. But the invalid alienation was acted upon by the testator's relatives, including those entitled under the personal law by survivorship from the deceased, as if it were valid. This was held by their Lordships of the Privy Council as good evidence of a family arrangement contemporaneously made and acted upon by all parties.[3]

Particularly where families are ignorant of the new law and successive deaths occur the only way to avert desperate chaos may be to impute to the parties a family arrangement. Yet we must note that a family arrangement may not set up for the family any private law of succession in conflict with the general law, that is to say by attempting to provide for the future devolution of the properties once they have

[1] *Sahu Madho Das v. Pandit Mukand Ram* (1955) 18 S.C.J. 417, 419, following *Clifton v. Cockburn* (1835) 3 My. & K. 76 and *Williams v. Williams* (1867) L.R. 2 Ch. App. 294.
[2] Numerous examples of such difficulties appear in the book referred to above, p. 160, n. 2. See in particular the introductory chapter.
[3] *Lakshmi Chand v. Mst. Anandi* (1926) L.R. 53 I.A. 123. See also *Brijraj Singh v. Sheodan Singh* (1913) L.R. 40 I.A. 161, I.L.R. 35 All. 337 (P.C.).

vested absolutely.[1] No doubt some intestate laws seek to obviate the need for this manoeuvre. But a statutory right to demand mainten-ance, for example, out of the estate of a deceased person, whether or not he dies intestate, is in practice no substitute for a good settlement, envisaging all likely needs and coping in advance with the problems which a well-to-do person's death always brings with it. If this regular imputing of an arrangement between heirs of owners of property is to be envisaged, the requirements of a family arrangement must be known, even where the details of the intestate law may not be!

For developing countries the family arrangement has other useful features. Firstly, no conveyance is needed. The agreement need not be in writing, and if intended to be oral need not be registered.[2] It may be proved by oral evidence, and especially from a long course of dealing, even if the actual terms of the agreement (and its date)[3] have been for-gotten, and have to be inferred from the conduct of the original parties, or even their successors. The validity of the agreement by no means depends on an ability to prove whether it was fair in the circum-stances.[4] This is especially helpful in the case of illiterate parties or those who cannot afford regular legal advice, or would otherwise be hit by statute or by court-determined customary law, of which they have no actual knowledge. An imputed arrangement, as we have sug-gested, may be essential for their welfare. Secondly, since the court will not scrutinize minutely the quantum of consideration passing from one party to another, there is no requirement that the parties should emerge in approximate parity so far as the benefits are concerned. An indirect result of the equitable requirements is that females and children who are frequently unaware of their legal rights—and are to that extent normally a hazard to those who deal with them—will be bound by the arrangement if, in general terms, they have been fairly treated and their ignorance has not been exploited.[5] If the whole estate

[1] *Purna Shashi Bhattacharji v. Kalidhan Rai Chowdhuri* (1911) I.L.R. 38 Cal. 603 (P.C.).

[2] See *Tek Bahadur* (below); also *Mst. Jaleba v. Mst. Parmeshra* I.L.R. (1952) 2 All. 703, 721.

[3] *Krishnan Nayar v. Krishnakutty Menon* (1949) 40 Cochin L.R. 386 (F.B.), following *Gopal Chandra Adale v. Harimohan* (1935) 62 Cal. L.J. 380.

[4] Where no record of valuation was kept, the circumstances may still raise a presumption that the member who entered into the agreement knew what he was about: *Bishambhar Nath v. Amar Nath* A.I.R. 1937 P.C. 105, 167 I.C. 561.

[5] In *Brijraj Singh v. Sheodan Singh* (1913) L.R. 40 I.A. 161, I.L.R. 35 All. 337 (P.C.), the heads of branches fully represented their branches: the arrangement had been acted upon for ten years without dispute.

is preserved by a judicious arrangement Equity sees this advantage as a consideration in itself. For example, if a man, his wife and his widowed sister are involved in a family quarrel which can be solved by distributing the property, and if under the arrangement the man keeps the title to the estate, but the two females have fixed rights of maintenance out of it, this may well be entirely equitable in the light of local customs, and it would be wrong to disapprove of anything less than a distribution into thirds between the parties. In other words, the family arrangement travels well, is at home in any climate, and shows great elasticity—as well it may, seeing that it is merely a manifestation of the working of Equity, which favours agreements entered into fairly and reasonably for the benefit of all those who have any sort of claim to the estate in question, and particularly favours agreements which settle or prevent litigation which would diminish the total available for all parties. A further advantage, easily overlooked, is that such an arrangement may well bind transferees who have or ought to have notice of it, whether they are voluntary alienees or have taken under a compulsory transfer from the parties or from any of them.[1]

But, in order that the family arrangements may be valid and binding upon all parties and their representatives or successors, certain requirements must be met. These have been tested repeatedly in a multitude of cases in South Asia. It will be observed in passing that the arrangements arose amongst Muslims, Hindus, or Christians: the most intricate family problems arose (as usual) amongst the Hindus, but the requirements of a valid family arrangement are not related to religion as such, and the factor of religion can be neglected for our purposes.

Before commencing to review those requirements one warning must be given. It may well be advantageous to overcome the difficulties created by an invalid disposition (as in *Lakshmi Chand's* case, which we have noticed above) by recourse to an actual or imputed family arrangement. But the court may neither accept nor impute such an arrangement if in fact a member of the family remains capable of impugning the disposition and insisting upon having his share on the ground that at the so-called settlement his guardian or other representative did not, on his behalf, acknowledge the title of others in property to which he had a claim, in exchange for their acknowledgement of his title to property in respect of which they might have had a claim. Participation in this mutual adjustment of rights is essential or else the family arrangement which might have been expected to compose all differences turns out to have a flaw and to be no family arrange-

[1] *Raya Shenoi v. Kesava Mallan* (1943) 34 Cochin L.R. 465 (F.B.).

ment at all.[1] This is, of course, confined to cases where the arrangement purports to comprise all the property rights of the members of the group, in which case an exchange of considerations must figure throughout.

The first requirement: The parties must be 'interested' in the property concerned

The basic proposition asserted is that there must be an antecedent title of 'some sort' in the parties (even an expectancy),[2] while the agreement acknowledges and defines what that title is, each party relinquishing all claims other than that falling to his share and recognizing the right of the others to the parts allotted to them.[3] Even on this basis, it is submitted, it would not be correct to insist that the parties must have *competing titles* in respect of the properties in dispute, as the Madras High Court has recently held.[4] Such a formulation, as we shall see, conflicts with a well-considered judgment in Allahabad. But it insists on the reality of a dispute, and to that extent is satisfactory if it is hostile to a fraud. Yet, as we have surmised already, the requirement of an antecedent interest is a conveniently wide requirement. In reality only in cases where the arrangement stands on the footing of a compromise need the search be made for an antecedent title. As we have seen, the search for a compromise behind every family arrangement, real or imputed, is an error. Granted that compromise is a prominent class of family arrangement we should not assume that the arrangement is not binding if it is not a compromise. Therefore the search for an 'interest, or even a title, may be misdirected. We must remember that 'title of "some sort",' or 'interest', actually covers such situations as a moral claim upon the estate in the hands of others, which will afford consideration enough to support a family arrangement. Yet we see that the Supreme Court of India has recently shown a desire to trace out if possible signs of a title even if evidence will not support this—and such a tendency would indicate that the desire to find an antecedent title to support a family arrangement is still in vigour.

---

[1] *Ghulam Mohammad v. Ghulam Husain* (1931) L.R. 59 I.A. 74, 87.

[2] *Ram Pratap v. Indrajit* A.I.R. 1950 All. 320. An instance of relinquishment of a right to inherit is declared valid in *K. Sitamahalakshmi v. K. Ramachandrarao* A.I.R. 1957 A.P. 572.

[3] *Rani Mewa Kuwar v. Rani Hulas Kuwar* (1874) L.R. 1 I.A. 157, 166; *Khunni Lal v. Gobind Krishna Narain* (1911) L.R. 38 I.A. 87, 21 Mad. L.J. 645, I.L.R. 33 All. 356 (P.C.); *Sahu Madho Das* (above).

[4] *Syed Sulaiman Sahib v. Kader Ibrahim Meerah Bivi* [1952] 2 Mad L.J. 104.

A woman who had earned money and bought property had two sons by different fathers. One sued the other for division of what he called joint family property (it remained uncertain under what customary law, if any, it could claim such a description). In 1942 the brothers decided with their mother's consent to enjoy the properties and businesses in a certain manner. In 1946 one brother denied that any of the properties were joint family property or that there had been a division as alleged. Their Lordships held that there must have been a dispute at the time of the arrangement as the parties did not agree later as to the source of some items. One brother claimed that some items were his own self-acquired property. The agreement, though incompletely consigned to writing, was valid and binding, notwithstanding that no written evidence could be produced for the mother's consent. Their Lordships added, 'How they (the brothers) got some antecedent title in the property is not for us to determine.'[1]

A dispute may thus arise or be apprehended between a family and a stranger. We have inferred that an illegitimate child is not a stranger for this purpose, correctly.[2] But we can imagine a stranger, having no relationship with the family, claiming an interest by gift, lease, mortgage, etc. If a compromise is reached between the major members and this stranger, will it bind the minors if such an act would be beyond a legal guardian's powers, or if there is no legal guardian? The answer would seem, prima facie, to be no. The major members might bind themselves, but cannot claim to have bound the minors, because this is not a family arrangement. But an exception may arise where membership of the family is itself one of the issues in controversy, inimical to the harmony of the family.

P. died leaving a mother, a daughter, and a widow. The mother then adopted a son, S., to her own deceased husband. She did not have the power to do this under the personal law. The daughter and S. disputed possession of the property originally belonging to P.'s father. The dispute was resolved by an agreement whereby the daughter admitted S.'s status as adopted son in exchange for a gift from S. of part of the properties to her. Later the daughter sued S. for possession of the properties he had retained. The Bombay High

[1] *Tek Bahadur Bhujil v. Debi Singh Bhujil* A.I.R. 1966 S.C. 292, 294, 295.
[2] *Stapilton v. Stapilton* (1739) 1 Atk. 2, 5. *Gopal Das Hassanand v. Dhanraj Mal* (see below, p. 178, n. 3).

166

Court held that the agreement was a valid family arrangement though S. had no antecedent title as his adoption was void, and though he was therefore a stranger to the family. Where no antecedent title is present, however, registration of a document of transfer was essential and failure to register it would, as in this case, render evidence of the terms inadmissible.[1]

The following instance, which came before the Privy Council, illustrates the latitude with which membership of the family is construed and also the need for consideration.

P. bequeathed all his property to an idol to secure its worship, directing each of his two widows to adopt a son, both of which he appointed managers of the idol's estate subject to the control of the widows during their minority, with a monthly allowance from the surplus income, the residue being undisposed of. The widows purported to act under this direction, adopting simultaneously two minor boys. Without admitting that their act might be invalid or suggesting that differences existed or might exist between them, they entered into an arrangement (*ikrar*) whereby each bound herself to the other to recognize the rights of the boys to nurture and the enjoyment of the estate, partitioning the estate as between themselves and the boys, and providing that the surplus income should be accumulated and handed over by each widow to her own son on coming of age. When the adopted son of the elder widow sued the younger widow and her son, it was held that although the boys had no rights under the will, were not validly adopted sons, and were not parties to the *ikrar* as such, the plaintiff was entitled to enforce the terms against the defendants. Lord Hobhouse said, 'The Ranees wished to make the boys the heirs of the Rajah . . . they could, so far as their own interest would go, give them the same benefit out of the property as if they had actually been heirs. Their Lordships hold that the deed expresses this intention, and that by it the Ranees became bound to one another and to the boys to carry it into effect. It is a startling thing to be told that the Ranees could immediately afterwards turn the boys adrift, or that the survivor of them can do so after the arrangement has been in force for five years. . . . It is true they (the boys) are not parties to the *ikrar* . . . but . . . it is one of a series of transactions. . . . Their position in life was substantially altered by taking them away from their families for an indefinite time; it seems to their Lordships im-

[1] *Shivamurteppa Gurappa v. Fakirappa* (1953) 56 Bom. L.R. 354.

possible to maintain that they are strangers in the matter, and that they cannot insist on the performance of the contract. . . .'[1]

Persons about to enter the family by marriage, and their eventual issue, may well take a benefit under the agreement, although strictly as the last illustration shows they were strangers at the time the agreement was entered into. The word 'family' is understood somewhat liberally.

A Hindu father (then a widower) and his son made an arrangement the dominant intention behind which was to provide for succession to the family property otherwise than as the Hindu law allowed, but nevertheless purporting to settle claims against the father by the son. The father contemplated marrying again and the son was (so it seems) claiming an interest in the self-acquired properties of the father (to which he was not entitled). The Bombay High Court held that the second wife of the father and her issue were entitled to possession of the properties allotted to them under the agreement.[2]

What if the 'stranger' does happen to be a blood relation or a relation by marriage, but is not in fact living with the family, whether because he once left it, or because he was too remotely related ever to have been a member? Here the courts have found themselves in a difficulty. At Hindu law the widow of a deceased owner of property took the estate, until 1956, under a limited tenure.[3] On her death the remainder of the estate, indeed normally the corpus of it, passed to that relation of the deceased male owner who would have been his heir if he had died when the widow died. This heir was called the 'reversioner'. Anxious to anticipate, the reversioner often came to terms with the widow. If he had not done so the next reversioner might have survived him and come into the inheritance. Meanwhile the widow often preferred to have half a cake free for her to consume to having

[1] *Surendra Keshav Roy v. Doorgasundari Dassee* (1891) L.R. 19 I.A. 108, 131–2, I.L.R. 19 Cal. 513, 535–6 (P.C.).
[2] *Shriniwas Deorao v. Chandrabhagabai Deorao* (1957) 60 Bom. L.R. 570.
[3] In all text books on Hindu law the topic will be found treated under 'Woman's Limited Estate'. In Derrett, *Introduction to Modern Hindu Law* (O.U.P., Bombay, 1963), it is treated at §§674–99, and family arrangements in this connection are noticed at §687 (where four cases are cited besides those noticed in this paper). A specialist textbook on the woman's limited estate in Bhagwan Das Sirvya, *Hindu Woman's Estate (Non-technical Stridhana)* (Calcutta, 1913). Running into 415 pages, it indicates that even by that date the workings of Equity had produced endless refinements.

the whole cake merely to admire. They seldom found it difficult to come to terms. The Anglo-Hindu law, founded perhaps rather upon notions of equity and of the powers of a life tenant to come to terms with a reversioner or trustee-beneficiary at English law than upon the spirit of the ancient Hindu law, which did not contemplate the enlargement of a female heir's interest, was sensitive to schemes overtly to divide the estate between the presumptive reversioner and the holder for her life, to the defrauding of the remainder of the reversion; but it made no difficulty about an arrangement which was overtly intended to preserve the estate from ruinous litigation! The question would arise whether the reversioner, having entered into such an arrangement, might afterwards repudiate it if, when he actually came into his rights on the widow's death, he repented of any small alienations by the widow that he might have agreed to as a price for his anticipating his accession to the remainder of the estate.[1] The answer was this: the reversioner might be a remote relation, and in general terms a stranger, but the widow was competent to enter into a 'family arrangement' with him, because as between herself and the entire reversion, namely her husband's, say, or her late son's heirs in order of priority, the family relationship did exist, and the avoidance of wasteful litigation which would otherwise ensue upon her improperly alienating parts of the estate could properly be obviated by those two parties coming to an arrangement as to who would be principals in any hypothetical dispute. This must stand solely on the basis of compromise. Naturally it could well be a device to defraud the reversion at large, a division of the estate contrary to the personal law.[2] This did not cause alarm, because of the widow's power to surrender at her option, so that reversioners other than the presumptive reversioner for the time being had no substantial grievance; but then the notion of surrender was also the work of the Anglo-Indian judges. The court will therefore look at an arrangement in the nature of a compromise to see whether the parties entered into it bona fide, to put an end to apprehensions of litigation; and if this is the case the arrangement will bind the parties thereto and the remainder of the potential heirs.[3]

[1] *Sureshwar v. Mst. Mahesh Rani* (1921) L.R. 47 I.A. 233, A.I.R. 1921 P.C. 107 (this was held not a device to divide the estate). *Pandu Pillai v. Lekshmi Lekshmi* (1926) 16 Trav. L.J. 531 (F.B.).

[2] *See Sureshwar* (above).

[3] In *Mansingh v. Nawalakhbali* (1926) L.R. 53 I.A. 11, A.I.R. 1926 P.C. 2, there was no dispute and the transfer was bad. But an honest claim supported a compromise agreement in *Balarama Sastri v. Vasudeva Sastri* A.I.R. 1948 P.C. 7 (1948), 1 Mad. L.J. 47 (P.C.).

When a widow or other limited owner compromises litigation with a presumptive reversioner this is not in any sense an alienation by her. It is not therefore a transfer, and cannot be impeached as such by the eventual reversioner after the limited owner's interest has terminated.[1] It cannot be right that a limited owner must proceed to litigation.[2]

So far we have seen instances where the parties have interests in the property such as a right of maintenance, as in the case of an illegitimate son, or by reason of a reverionary right vested in a total body of relations called the reversion, or a moral right as in the case of the invalidly adopted son. What is the position if the claimants to the property have no interests at law and no moral claim, but only claim by virtue of some act on the part of one or more members of the family? The tendency of the decision is to deny such settlement the status of family arrangement: they are disguised, or professed donations or contracts, to which the ordinary law relating to dispositions of family ought to apply.

R. died in 1859 leaving his mother B., his widow A., and a sister. In 1866 B. gave properties, which she obtained under an arrangement with A., to S., his daughter's son. A. later disputed the title of S. and the dispute was settled in 1867 by an agreement that A. should take one-third and S. two-thirds of them. A. died in 1926 and the reversioner was X. X. sought to recover the property wrongfully alienated by B. and A. respectively. It was urged on behalf of S. that A. was bound by the arrangement of 1867 which was a bona fide settlement of a dispute, and that the reversioner, though not a party to it, was bound by that arrangement. Their Lordships of the Privy Council held that S. had no right to the properties except what he derived by the gift made by B. He had no competing title of his own in respect of the properties in dispute, and there was no family settlement such as would bind the reversion.[3]

A strictly limited exception has been recognized where, along with a valid family arrangement, disputes with strangers are compromised, provided the disputes are *intimately connected with members of the*

---

[1] *Mst. Hiran Bibi v. Mst. Sohan Bibi* A.I.R. 1914 P.C. 44, 27 Mad. L.J. 149, approving *Khunni Lal* (above). Followed in *Ram Charan Das* (below).

[2] *Upendra Nath Bose v. Bindeshri Prosad* (1916) 32 I.C. 468, 482.

[3] *Mathukamalli Ramayya v. Uppalapati Lakshmayya* I.L.R. (1943) Mad. 1, 7–8 (P.C.), (1942) 2 Mad. L.J. 249, 252 (P.C.). *Khunni Lal* (above) was relied upon.

family: in which case the arrangement is not invalid for embracing grants to strangers.[1]

This rule is of great importance, as in India dispositions such as the family law of Hindus would not allow have often acquired an apparent validity because of a bogus claim put up by strangers having no legal interest in the property, and this is purported to be settled by a disposition by some members of the family without the consent of other interested persons, or while others are minors and so inapable of giving their consent.

Yielding up property under the threat of litigation cannot be an act justifiable as a family arrangement, even if scandals are screened thereby. A widower claimed his wife's father's property, though no shadow of title to it could be proved. His wife's female relations, to avoid litigation, relinquished a substantial portion of the estate to him. The reversioner of the wife's father sued to have this set aside. It was held that it was no family arrangement and the reversioner was not bound by it.[2] Further, an invalid gift cannot be supported as a family settlement.[3]

The test must ultimately be whether the arrangement is entered into for the benefit of the family rather than a section of it,[4] and if only the latter is the case the arrangement cannot qualify for the special favours which Equity offers. Fine distinctions may here be made, and in *Ram Charan Das v. Girja Nandini Devi*[5] the Supreme Court of India sailed very close to the wind.

In a series of compromises claims were set at rest which had been raised by (i) a remote collateral of the last male holder of an estate, (ii) the latter's sister's son, and (iii) the last male holder's grandfather's elder brother's grandsons. Claim (i) was that the mother of the last male holder had no right to partition the estate, (ii) that the claimant was the preferential heir by virtue of a statute as to certain items, and (iii) that as to those items the source whence the last male holder obtained them was without title by reason of a defective testamentary capacity in their ancestor. Their Lordships held that

---

[1] *Sultan Ahmad v. Sirajul Haque* I.L.R. (1938) All. 125, A.I.R. 1938 All. 170, 179.

[2] *Himmat Bahadur v. Dhanpat Rai* (1916) I.L.R. 38 All. 335, 338.

[3] *Phaul Bee Bee v. R. M. P. Chettiar Firm* (1935) 13 Rang. 679, referred to in *Syed Sulaiman Sahib* (above).

[4] *Krishnan Velu v. Narayanan Velu* (1935) 25 Trav. L.R. 1,183.

[5] (1966) 1 S.C.J. 61, 66–7, A.I.R. 1966 S.C. 323.

the various withdrawals of claims showed that all the disputes were finally settled, and the several compromises constituted a single family arrangement. In *Ramgouda Annadouda v. Bhausaheb*[1] the Privy Council had held that three alienations by a widow on the same day were a family settlement, so that the descendant of the alienee under one (the reversioner) could not challenge the alienations to others (who included non-family members, e.g. the widow's brother and her son-in-law). Here, the Supreme Court felt the case was stronger. Their Lordships add, 'The word "family" in the context is not to be understood in a narrow sense of being a group of persons who are recognized in law as having a right of succession or having a claim to a share in the property in dispute.'

The second requirement: the arrangement must be intended to settle a bona fide claim

In order to bind minors or other members of the family not capable of giving consent, it is essential that if a claim is urged as the root of the arrangement, the settlement of which is the consideration or part of the consideration supporting the alienation or rearrangement of pre-existing interests, it should be urged bona fide.[2] This, evidently, applies only to compromises. It does not mean that those who urge a claim have adequate legal advice, or that their claim could have been sustained in court.[3] Indeed quite flimsy or even illusory claims can be sufficient for the purpose, provided that those who press them do so under the sincere, but mistaken, impression that if their claim were pursued it would have good chances of success.[4] To hold otherwise would mean to impose upon the family the expense of seeking legal advice and of testing opinions in litigation, which is the thing to be avoided.

In the leading case of *Ram Nirunjan Singh v. Prayag Singh*[5] the Calcutta High Court held that though a dispute between two brothers was founded on a mistake of law the compromise would bind both parties. Pretensions which now seem vain were then thought not unfounded, and independent opinion then thought the

[1] (1927) L.R. 54 I.A. 396, 53 Mad. L.J. 350 (P.C.).

[2] *Authi Lakshmi v. Annasawmy Iyer* (1912) 15 I.C. 723 (Mad.).

[3] *Prakkateri Parkum V. C. K. Kittooli v. Kumathi V. Koram* (1912) 14 I.C. 294 (Mad.).

[4] *Mst. Gangabai v. Punau Rajwa Teli* A.I.R. 1956 Nag. 261. *Sital Singh v. Gajindra Bahadur Singh* (1928) I.L.R. 4 Luck. 57.

[5] (1881) I.L.R. 8 Cal. 138, 142, 143. Referred to in *Gandharp Singh v. Nirmal Singh* (1919) 54 I.C. 325, 329.

terms fair. Caution had been used and the younger party was held bound. So in *Mst. Hassan Bibi v. Faẓal Kadir*[1] the sons who were fully entitled gave a female relative benefits which at law she could not have claimed, but the parties seem to have been in doubt as to their respective rights and the arrangement was held binding. *Perhaps here the court proceeded as it did under the (mistaken) impression that the arrangement would not have been valid if it were not a compromise of a doubtful claim.*

In *Khajeh Solehman Quadir v. Nawab Sir Salimullah Bahadur*[2] deeds executed in 1846 and 1868 purported to make *wakfs* of certain properties in favour of members of a Muslim family. By an agreement in 1881 the members of the family agreed that the *wakfs* were binding (which they were not) and that allowances fixed thereunder should be paid out of the income to named members of the family and on their deaths to their heirs in proportions to be determined. Their Lordships of the Privy Council held that this agreement, being in compromise of litigation in which some members had alleged (correctly) that the deed of 1846 was invalid, was enforceable as constituting a valid charge.

Thus a doubtful claim to some at least of the estate or estates in contemplation is necessary,[3] if we add, to any true compromise, in order that family peace, honour or property may be preserved. For Uttar Pradesh the apparent conflict between *Raghubir Datt Pande's case* (which held that a doubtful claim at least was necessary to a family arrangement) and *Pokhar Singh's case* (which held that not even a doubtful claim need exist) was settled by the exhaustive judgment in *Mst. Dasodia v. Gangaprasad*,[4] which in fact deserves closer attention than it can be given here. In that case there was not even a doubtful claim. The full bench of the Allahabad High Court held that 'a family arrangement at bottom is nothing but an agreement and the essential thing is that it should be for consideration. Where the object of the arrangement was to maintain good relations, to preserve the family property, to convert the expectancy of reversioners into a certainty, it was a sufficient consideration in law to uphold the arrangement.'

[1] (1909) 4 I.C. 954 (Punjab Chief Court).
[2] (1922) L.R. 49 I.A. 153, I.L.R. 49 Cal. 820 (P.C.).
[3] *Helan Dasi v. Durga Das Mundal* (1906) 4 Cal. L.J. 323, following *Williams v. Williams* (above). *Raghubir Datt Pande v. Narain Datt Pande* A.I.R. 1930 All. 498(2), (1930) All. L.J. 1,541 (see below).
[4] I.L.R. (1943) All. 411, A.I.R. 1943 All. 101 (F.B.), followed in *Laxmi Narain v. Banshi Lal* A.I.R. 1965 All. 522.

Had it been grasped at that time that a compromise could be only a category of family arrangement, the resolution of the apparent conflict would have been even simpler. Their Lordships in fact added that no antecedent title was necessary (which seems true) but the remark was *obiter* as the parties had either present or contingent titles. The decision in favour of the approach in *Pokhar Singh*, relying heavily on *Williams v. Williams*,[1] a case which has obtained great vogue in South Asia in this connection, may obtain approval in other jurisdictions. But the opening for fraudulent conveyances cloaked as family arrangements might seem somewhat widened thereby. Thus it is not surprising that it has subsequently been held in Orissa[2] that a shockingly inadequate consideration is not to be treated as consideration binding upon the party who received it, but, on the contrary, evidence of an imposition which Equity would not countenance. Imposition apart, it is probably safer to adhere, whenever reliance is placed upon an alleged compromise, to another formula, namely that a 'situation of genuine contest' existed.[3] The Privy Council have actually said that provided the parties are related to one another *in some way* and have even *a semblance of a claim*, even on the ground of, say, affection, the arrangement may be effective.[4] This approach may be taken as a hint at the true scope of the institution; or we may regret that their Lordships did not appreciate that in order to validate a family arrangement no question of compromise need arise, unless the parties rely upon it: and in South Asia the choice of allegation and the framing of the pleadings should never shut the court's hand, if the true position between the parties has not failed to emerge.

The test eventually developed in India was that, though the claims might be ill-founded, a conflict must be present which the parties intended to fight out,[5] and this unquestionably neglected the much wider

[1] (1867) 2 Ch. App. 294.
[2] *Sunder Sahu v. Chamra* A.I.R. 1954 Or. 80, 83.
[3] *Mst. Gangabai* (above). *Rai Kumar Singh v. Abhai Kumar Singh* A.I.R. 1948 Pat. 362; *Mt. Kauleshwari Kuer v. Surajnath Rai* A.I.R. 1957 Pat. 456; *Tarkeshwar Prasad v. Nankhu Prasad Singh* A.I.R. 1959 Pat. 523, 526; *Phul v. Sambhu* A.I.R. 1965 Pat. 87, following *Williams v. Williams* (above). See also *Tek Bahadur* (above).
[4] *Rangasami Gounden v. Nachiappa Gounden* (1918) L.R. 46 I.A. 72, I.L.R. 42 Mad. 523, 36 Mad. L.J. 493 (P.C.), followed in *Ram Charan Das* (above), at p. 67.
[5] *Pokhar Singh v. Dulari Kunwar* (1930) I.L.R. 52 All. 716, A.I.R. 1930 All. 687; *Sidh Gopal v. Bihari Lal* (1927) I.L.R. 50 All. 284; *Jang Bahadur v. Rana Uma Nath* (1937) I.L.R. 12 Luck. 639; *Buchibai v. Nagpur University* I.L.R. (1946) Nag. 433.

scope of the family arrangement. It is, therefore, a cause for satisfaction that the Supreme Court has recently held that a conflict is not essential.

There were two brothers in a joint family, B1., who was not very intelligent but managed the farm, and B2. who was very able and made huge gains for the family by money-lending, etc. Both had sons. On behalf of their branches these two agreed that B1. should ultimately take two-fifths and B2. three-fifths of the assets. In a suit for partition brought by the son of B1. against B2. and his sons it was held that the agreement, as a family arrangement, was binding upon B1.'s branch because, though there was no dispute between B1. and B2., B2. would have separated (and so deprived B1.'s branch of his earning capacity) unless this inducement to stay had been offered to him.

The arrangement in that case[1] had not been entered into in order to settle a claim to property, but to prevent losses to the family as a whole which might have accrued had the younger brother exercised his undoubted right to a separation.

The claim, to settle which property was sacrificed, need not be justified in law, but it must have been entertained bona fide. This may turn out to be a subtle distinction if the one who urges the unfounded claim had access to legal advice. If the court finds that the claimant had notice that his claim was not good in law it may well hold that it was bona fide. Similarly the arrangement may well be sustained if the mistake is one of fact and not of law.[2] If ultimately it becomes clear that the concessions made by one side need not have been made if the true state of facts had been known the arrangement is not vitiated provided no party was aware of the true state of the acts.[3] These Indian decisions bear out our submission (above) that where there is no false premise the arrangement will not be upset for mistake.

But a purported family arrangement which is really a cloak for a transfer of property to strangers will be struck down.[4]

[1] *Maturi Pullaiah v. M. Narasimham* A.I.R. 1966 S.C. 1836.

[2] See *Ram Nirunjun Singh v. Prayag Singh* (1881) I.L.R. 8 Cal. 138, 142, where *Kerr on Fraud* is cited. See also *Ram Charan Das* (above).

[3] *David v. David* A.I.R. 1957 T.C. 160.

[4] *Mst. Gangabai* (above) following *Miles v. N. Z. Alford Estate Co.* (1886) 32 Ch. D. 266, 291. See also *Basantakumar Basu v. Ramshankar Ray* (1931) I.L.R. 59 Cal. 859, A.I.R. 1932 Cal. 600, followed in *Chunnilal v. Rukhmabai* A.I.R. 1943 Nag. 92, I.L.R. (1944) Nag. 335.

The third requirement: The arrangement must finally settle the differences between the parties, and must be acted upon by them

In family disputes in South Asia, and perhaps elsewhere, litigation drags on interminably. A compromise may well be intended only to give the parties a breathing space, in which other tactics can be tried. The family arrangement, however, must, in order to qualify for its privileges, be intended to put an end to differences,[1] and any indication that the arrangement was only temporary may be fatal to it. The frequency with which parties seek to resile from genuine arrangements shows that this requirement may often fail. Naturally a fair test whether the parties intended the agreement to put an end to their disputes is whether they acted upon it. An arrangement which is not acted upon cannot be enforced after an interval within which it would, if genuine, have been put into effect.[2]

The fourth requirement: The interests of non-consenting members must be properly consulted

In developing countries, where it is usual for males, and often only senior males, to manage the concerns of the family without more than token assistance or consent from the other members, the senior may be tempted to ride rough-shod over the others.[3] Especially where one branch of the family is represented only by an adolescent lad and his widowed mother (the father having, perhaps, worn himself out with quarrels with his brother) the surviving seniors may well give the weaker branch less than its equitable share. Bullying may often be employed where bargaining precedes, as it often must, a contract. Again, a grandparent may disapprove of his widowed daughter-in-law's method of bringing up her son, and so arrange matters between his collaterals and himself that his own share is incapable of descending unimpaired to his grandson, who may in fact have a birthright in it under the personal law.

Those who rely upon a family arrangement bear the burden of showing that the parties sought to be bound by it, whose consent was not actually taken, benefited, and that the consideration passing to

[1] See *Ram Charan Das* (above).

[2] *Potti Lakshmi Perumallu v. P. Krishnavenamma* A.I.R. 1965 S.C. 825, 828 col. 2.

[3] The point is made by Mr S. K. B. Asante in 'Fiduciary principles in Anglo-American Law and the customary law of Ghana—a comparative study', 14 *International and Comparative Law Quarterly*, pt. 4 (1965), pp. 144ff.

them was not nominal or illusory. It is sometimes said that a fair disclosure of the true state of the family property and the incumbrances or claims pressing upon it must be made to all parties.[1] But this could hardly be a clear responsibility where parties would not fully understand what is disclosed to them. Yet we need not imagine nephews and grandsons making independent enquiries. It is not sufficient to allege that they had the opportunity to make enquiries and to satisfy themselves that the settlement was fair.[2] Therefore the rule is that those who propound an arrangement should be able to satisfy the conscience of the court that the non-participating members' interests were fully and fairly consulted, that advantage was not taken of their ignorance,[3] and that the share or value which they took under the arrangement was equitable in the then circumstances. The further requirement at English law that interested parties must be fully informed of doubtful rights sought to be compromised can hardly be insisted upon in Asia or Africa generally.

In a Punjab case a son entered into an agreement with his father in circumstances suggesting not fraud but at least inadequate consultation of his own sons' interests. G. had two sons, H. and K., and H. had two sons, S. and M. H. released his interest in the joint family property to G. and K. in return for being freed from his share in family debts. This was a bogus consideration, as these debts would be binding on the property in any event and not on him personally. There was no real dispute over the property. The gifts of property by G. to S. and M. taking place on the same date were independent and unconnected. And the release by H. could not operate to disturb his own son's birthright in the family properties.[4]

It is not necessary that all parties should be gainers in any obvious fashion—some may be generous[5] and others may have restrictions fastened upon their previously unencumbered rights.[6] Some may agree to take as gifts what they otherwise might have claimed by right, or

---

[1] *Mariam Bibee v. Shaikh Muhammad Ibrahim* (1916) 48 I.C. 561, 605; *Shyam Lal Ghosh v. Rameswari Basu* (1916) 33 I.C. 273, 282.

[2] *Tate v. Williamson* (1866) L.R. 2 Ch. App. 55, 65.

[3] *Billage v. Southee* (1852) 9 Hare 534, 540; for an instance where advantage was taken see *Shyam Lal* (above).

[4] *Karam Singh v. Surendar Singh* (1932) 135 I.C. 180 (Lahore).

[5] *Cashin v. Cashin* (1938) 1 All E.R. 536 (P.C.), A.I.R. 1938 P.C. 103.

[6] *Ramaswami Chettiar v. Venkatammal* A.I.R. 1965 Mad. 193.

accept as an exchange what they could have claimed out-and-out.[1]
None of these conditions will of itself vitiate a family arrangement.
But where the evidence suggests blackmail, the oppressors sacri-
ficing nothing, the agreement cannot be upheld as a family arrangement,[2] and whether or not it masquerades as a compromise is immaterial.

UPSETTING AN ARRANGEMENT

It is of the utmost importance that the good done by a family arrangement should not be jeopardized by further recourse to litigation. The
court favours family arrangements and will not lightly reopen matters
which the settlement has purported to close. But where the arrangement was procured through fraud, or undue influence,[3] or minors'
interests were unfairly disregarded, the arrangements may be upset.[4]

It is indeed possible to contend that an arrangement cannot be
questioned except in a suit properly instituted for that purpose within
the time allowed by law, otherwise there would be no end to disputes.[5]
This is true enough, assuming that one whom others seek to bind by
an arrangement is adopting as his defence an evident flaw of which he
could easily have taken advantage long previously in a separate suit.
The question of laches will arise. But it is doubtful whether it will apply
when the defendants who seek to escape the conditions or effects of such
an arrangement would not in the ordinary course of events have been
aggrieved until that time by the conditions, or could not practicably
have known of the factor which vitiates the arrangement. Another
question remaining for further consideration is whether a minor is
bound by an otherwise unobjectionable arrangement if he is represented by a *de facto* guardian. An expression of opinion in the Privy
Council strongly suggests that he is not.[6] But a case in Andhra Pradesh
(India) proceeds on the footing that he may be. The main question, it

---

[1] *Sahu Madho Das* (above).

[2] *Sunder Sahu v. Chamra* A.I.R. 1954 Or. 80: the eight principles of family
arrangements are stated at p. 84.

[3] *T. Narayana Bhatta v. Narasimha Batta* A.I.R. 1965 Ker. 189 (1964),
K.L.T. 497; *Gopal Das v. Dhanraj Mal* A.I.R. 1945 Sind 11 (1944), Kar. 325.

[4] *Bishambhar Nath Kapoor v. Amar Nath* A.I.R. 1937 P.C. 105, 167 I.C. 561
(no evidence of unfairness).

[5] *Rukn-ul-Mulk v. R. Vishwanathan* A.I.R. 1950 Mys. 33 (F.B.). See *Jan
Mahomed v. Datu Jaffer* (1913) I.L.R. 38 Bom. 449.

[6] *Partap Singh v. Sant Kaur* (1938) 65 I.A. 213, I.L.R. (1938) Lah. 313.
Compare *Kapila Annapurnamma v. P. Venkata Satya* A.I.R. 1959 Andhra P. 40.

is submitted, should be whether the gain to the family as a whole from the arrangement is commensurate with any apparent losses individuals have borne, taking as the standard for judgment what a member of that family might reasonably believe at the time of the agreement. If that requirement is met we may suspect that the identity of the person representing the minors is not of much consequence. It is very doubtful whether at this juncture the personal laws, with their peculiar rules on guardianship of minors, should for the first time obtrude themselves and introduce distinctions for which we are otherwise unprepared.

CONCLUSION

It is too late in the day to contend, as some practitioners are apparently still contending, that an agreement is not a family arrangement because beneficiaries are not all members of the family in a strict sense, or that not every beneficiary had an antecedent title to a part of the estate or the whole of it. But how far is it necessary to pursue the point that there must have been a 'situation of contest', or a situation in which a doubtful claim may, or must, arise unless action is taken?

The assertion that a doubtful claim, and indeed an antecedent interest, must be present is a reflection of the court's anxiety lest family arrangements be utilized principally for fraudulent purposes, whether to defraud participants or to defraud strangers or remoter relatives having a contingent interest in the estate. The court is only too well aware that the head of a family in collusion with a stranger may enter into compromises which purport to be in the family's interest but actually subserve personal schemes of his own.

But let us revert to English law, and see whether the situation is not as contended for at the commencement of this paper. A family arrangement 'is an agreement between members intended to be generally and reasonably for the benefit of the family either by compromising doubtful or disputed rights or by preserving the family property. . . .' In *Wycherley v. Wycherley*[1] there seems not to have been even the last intention. Provision was made for sisters of the tenant-in-tail, who had no antecedent title, but certainly had a moral right to be provided for. The consideration passing from them was that the parties to the arrangement were relieved of anxiety as to the security of their female relatives: whereas had they remained content with the legal position the entire estate would have gone to the male heir. This

[1] (1763) 1 Cox Eq. Cas. 288.

sort of situation was extremely common until English law was reformed. Instances where the entire property was passed by will to one or more members, whereas the family at large believed that others were entitled to concurrent or other rights in the estate, are numerous: and the rearrangements have always been treated as good family arrangements.[1] It has been suggested that there must be some other consideration besides love and affection, and reliance is placed upon *Williams v. Williams* (above). That was a case in which some other consideration was indeed present; but we are not to suppose from it that without valuable consideration of some size passing from each party or beneficiary a family arrangement cannot be arrived at. On the contrary *Wakefield v. Gibbon*[2] is an instance where the property rights were rearranged in order to make provision for the father, the mother, the brothers and sisters, and in this way the characteristic scheme of primogeniture was modified to everyone's advantage. It cannot be pretended that valuable consideration passed from each of these beneficiaries, but good consideration may well have done. Nor is it necessary to assume, or impute, that there must have been family friction, or incipient family friction, or the makings of family friction—though it might be easy to do this in view of the uncertainties of the law, the lack of knowledge of the parties, and the threats to their comfort constituted by vague, but statutory, maintenance claims. Thus neither some disputed right, nor family friction, is a condition precedent to the formation of a family arrangement. We have seen how a family arrangement may be imputed, though no actual agreement can be proved, and that it may be imputed on the basis of a course of conduct. If the submissions of this paper are correct, developing countries are well placed to take full advantage of the family arrangement.

Thus there is no need to do what is constantly done in India, namely to pretend that a dispute exists where none ever did, the members living in perfect amity. English law is satisfied that moral obligations binding on a family are a sufficient consideration to found a family arrangement: *Hartopp v. Hartopp*.[3] It should therefore be sufficient to show that the members decided that the properties in question should be enjoyed in the manner specified, in order to discharge their obligations to each other, to preserve the family's assets and the family's comfort, and to avoid the jealousies and disputes which might otherwise ensue if such action were not taken. And this

[1] *Cashin v. Cashin* (above).
[2] (1857) 1. Giff. 401.
[3] (1856) 21 Beav. 259. *Halsbury*, where cited, §371.

is a very different matter from a pretence that the action taken was a compromise of doubtful claims. On this footing we can entertain the institution of the family arrangement as readily in less developed as amongst highly developed peoples, the well-to-do and the relatively poor alike.

9

THE MUSLIMS IN MALAYSIA AND SINGAPORE: THE LAW OF MATRIMONIAL PROPERTY

INCHE AHMAD IBRAHIM

Singapore Ambassador to the United Arab Republic

Under Islamic law marriage does not affect the power or status of a woman to own and dispose of her own property and the English common law rule that on marriage the property of the wife vested in her husband has not been applied in the case of a Muslim married woman in Malaysia and Singapore. The position under the Muslim law as applied in Singapore may be summarized by saying that all property belonging to a woman on her marriage, whether movable or immovable and however acquired, continues after marriage to a Muslim husband, in the absence of any special contract to the contrary, to be her own property; and that she may dispose of such property without the concurrence of her husband. The law applicable to the property of a Muslim married woman is the Muslims Ordinance, 1957,[1] which in this respect re-enacts in the main the provisions of the Mohamedan Marriage Act of 1880.[2] This Ordinance provides that the following shall be deemed to be the property of a Muslim married woman:

(a) wages and earnings acquired or gained by her during marriage in any employment, occupation or trade carried on by her;

(b) any money or other property acquired by her during marriage through the exercise of any skill or by way of inheritance, legacy, gift, purchase or otherwise; and

(c) all savings from and investments of such wages, earnings and property.[3]

---

[1] No. 25 of 1957.

[2] No. V. of 1880.

[3] Muslims Ordinance, 1957, S. 50. It has been held that a Muslim woman can be convicted of criminal breach of trust in respect of property belonging to her husband (*Re Ketuna Bibi* [1956] M.L.J. 166); and that a Muslim husband can be convicted of attempting to cheat his wife (*Nuruddin v. Siti Aminah* [1929] S.S.L.R. 146).

Singapore is largely an urban area and besides the Malays there is a large and influential group of Muslims, who are mainly engaged in trade and commerce and in salaried service either in the Government, the professions or in business. There has, therefore, been no real difficulty in the application of the Islamic law. By and large it is the men who are the wage-earners and the women are economically dependent on them. The majority of the women are not gainfully employed but are engaged in looking after the house. The position in the States of Malaya and in the Borneo States is, however, very different. In these places the bulk of the Malays (who in the States of Malaya form the majority of Muslims) are engaged on the land and both men and women work together. The Islamic law as applied by the Prophet and his immediate successors was specially suited to the sociological condition of the Arabs—a nomadic group of people where the most important kinds of property were camels and other flocks and herds, jewellery and money. In the States of Malaya and the Borneo States, however, land is the most valuable property and the influence of the tribal organization and the customary practices relating to the tenure of land led to the adoption of a customary law, which modified and was in some respects incompatible with the Muslim law.

In the States of Malaya and in the Borneo States the law applicable is not the pure Islamic law but this law as varied by Malay custom, or rather the Malay custom as varied by Islamic law. This Malay custom was brought over by the Malays when they migrated from Sumatra, where the prevailing form of tribal organization was matriarchal and exogamous. In the Menangkabau region of Sumatra, matriarchy was developed into an elaborate system of customary law called the *adat perpateh*. The Malays of Negri Sembilan and of the Naning district in Malacca came from this region; they brought their tribal organization with them and in some districts they have preserved it till today. In Palembang, however, during the centuries of Hindu and monarchical influence the tribal organization broke down and the *adat perpateh* ceased to be applicable in its pure form. The other States in Malaya followed the Palembang tradition, called the *adat temenggong*.[1]

The main object of the *adat perpateh* is to provide for the continuance of the tribe through its female members and to prevent alienation of the landed property, so that there will always be sufficient to provide maintenance for the women through whom alone the tribe can con-

[1] R. J. Wilkinson, *Malay Law*, Papers on Malay Subjects, Singapore, 1908, p. 2.

tinue. From the principle that the matriarchal tribe is the social unit, four cardinal principles emerge:

(a) all property vests in the tribe, not in the individual;
(b) acquired property once inherited becomes ancestral;
(c) all ancestral property vests in the female members of the tribe; and
(d) all ancestral property is strictly entailed in the female.[1]

Property is either ancestral or acquired. All ancestral property belongs to the tribe; it vests in the female members but they hold it as trustees for their tribe, rather than as owners. A person may acquire property and such property is not entailed in the first instance, unless of his own volition he expressly entails it, and he is at liberty to dispose of it during his life; but, the moment he dies, it becomes entailed and he therefore cannot dispose of it by will[2] and an agreement made during life to vary the succession is void.[3] From the basic principle that property is tribal rather than personal and that the man passes into his wife's tribe on marriage, it follows that all property owned by a married couple is joint property and that it belongs to the tribe of the wife so long as the marriage subsists. Even if the jointly acquired property is land in another State, the rules of the *adat* (custom) apply to it.[4]

Acquired property is divided into two classes according to its origin —*charian bujang*, or property acquired by a man or woman which belongs to his or her tribe, and that acquired by the joint efforts of a married pair, *charian laki bini*, in which both the tribes are interested. *Harta pembawa* means the personal property of a married man, the property brought by him to the tribe of his wife into which he passes on marriage; it may include property of three kinds, that is, his own earnings as a bachelor (*charian bujang*), his share of the earnings of any former marriage and any ancestral property of his own family in which he has an interest. *Harta dapatan* means the separate property of a married woman and also includes three kinds of property, that is, her own acquisitions as a spinster, divorcee or widow (*charian bujang* or *janda*), her share of the earnings of a former marriage and her ancestral

[1] E. N. Taylor, *Customary Law of Rembau* (1929), Journal of the Malayan Branch of the Royal Asiatic Society, p. 39f.
[2] *Re Kulop Kidal decd.* reported in E. N. Taylor, *Customary Law of Rembau*, op. cit., p. 92.
[3] *Romit v. Hassan*, in E. N. Taylor, *Customary Law of Rembau*, op. cit., p. 63.
[4] *Sadiah v. Siakim*, ibid., p. 65.

property. *Charian bujang* thus becomes *harta pembawa* or *dapatan* on marriage.[1]

The fundamental principles of division of property among the members of the tribes are:

Pembawa, kembali;
Dapatan, tinggal;
Charian, bagi;
Mati laki, tinggal ka-bini;
Mati bini, tinggal ka-laki,[2]

that is to say, what is brought by the man to the woman's house at the time of marriage goes back with him on divorce, or to his heirs (*warith*) on his death; that which is in the possession of the wife at the time of the marriage remains with her on divorce or it goes to her customary heirs on her death; that which is acquired during the period of wedlock is to be equally divided between them on divorce, and on the death of the husband it goes to the wife and vice versa, provided there is no issue from the marriage. The debts of a married couple and the burial expenses of both are charges on the *charian laki bini. Maskahwin* (*mahr*), however, is the property of the wife, payable to her separately and does not constitute a joint debt.[3]

Harta charian bujang, or property acquired by a man while he is still single, devolves on the nearest female relatives of the deceased. Property given to a son by his parents ranks as *charian bujang,* and becomes *harta pembawa* on his marriage and this reverts to his heirs (*warith*) on his death. Similarly a gift to a married man by his family also ranks as *harta pembawa* and not as *charian laki bini* of the marriage. Both *harta pembawa* and *harta dapatan* must be declared before the elders at the time of the marriage and, in the event of death, claims for the return of *harta pembawa* must normally be made on the hundredth day funeral feast. On marriage, the man moves from his tribe and goes to live with the tribe of his wife.[4] It has been held that a wife can refuse

[1] ibid., p. 14f.
[2] Husband's property returned
Wife's property remains;
Joint earnings are shared;
On the death of the husband, they go to the wife;
On the death of the wife, they go to the husband.
[3] Ahmad Ibrahim—Islam and Customary Law in Malaysia, *Intisari*, Singapore, Vol. 2, No. 2 (1965), p. 66. See as regards debts the cases of *Re Dahil decd.* and *Mahawa v. Manan* in E. N. Taylor, *Customary Law of Rembau,* op. cit. pp. 113 and 111 respectively. [4] ibid.

to leave the ancestral land if the land to which she is asked to remove has not been registered in her name.[1]

Under the *adat* or custom it is not possible for a married woman to take up new land as her separate estate, even with her husband's consent.[2] There can be no gifts between husband and wife.[3] Ancestral property is at all times strictly entailed but for certain limited purposes the holder may charge or sell it; if she does so, her immediate heirs have a customary option to buy it or to hold the charge in priority to all others and her tribe has such an option in priority to strangers. It is now provided by statute that such entailed land cannot be disposed of except to a member of the same tribe.[4] There is provision for the registration of ancestral land and land acquired by females (at their option) as 'customary land' but it has been held that, if the deceased was a member of a tribe, his property would devolve according to the *adat*, even though the titles are not marked 'customary land'.[5]

The customary law as to matrimonial property in the other Malay States was originally very similar to the law in Negri Sembilan and Naning, but owing to the breakdown of the tribal organization and the increasing influence of Muslim teaching, the law applicable has been gradually modified. In the State of Perak, for example, it was the custom for the lands and homes of the deceased to descend to his daughters equally, while the sons divided the personal property, as the sons were supposed to be able to create landed estates for themselves by clearing and planting land which they may select or at all events to obtain the use of land by marrying women who may have inherited it. It was customary too, among Malays of rank or position, for a husband to appropriate a particular home to the use of his wife at the time of the marriage. She was entitled to live there during coverture and, if she was divorced by the husband, the home was regarded as hers and was assigned to her for her use during her life.[6] The mukim registers in the Malay districts also show that a very large number of holdings were

---

[1] *Hasmah binte Omar v. Abdul Jalil* (1958) M.L.J. 10.

[2] *Hassan v. Romit* in E. N. Taylor, *Customary Law of Rembau*, op. cit., p. 63.

[3] *Nyai Ampar v. Impam*, ibid., p. 67.

[4] Customary Tenure Enactment (Cap. 215 Laws of Federated Malay States) and Negri Sembilan Customary Tenure (Lengkongan Lands) Enactment, 1960.

[5] See Ahmad Ibrahim, Islam and Customary Law in Malaysia, op. cit., and the cases of *Re Haji Mansor bin Duseh* [1940] M.L.J. 110, *Sali v. Achik* (1941) M.L.J. 14, *Haji Hussin v. Maheran* [1946] M.L.J. 116 and *Maani v. Mohamed* [1961] M.L.J. 88.

[6] R. J. Wilkinson, *Malay Law*, op. cit., p. 36f.

from the first in the names of women, and that the widow frequently inherited the whole of her husband's estate. About 1886, the Perak State Council ordered the land of a major chief, Tungku Lang Jaafar, to be transmitted in the female line.[1] Since then, however, the Islamic law has been extensively adopted and the customary laws in the States of Malaya (other than Negri Sembilan and Malacca) have only survived in relation to the rights of divorcees and widows.

In the States of Malaya, the Married Women Ordinance, 1957, applies to Muslim married women subject to the provisions of the Islamic law and the custom of the Malays governing the relations between husband and wife. The Ordinance provides that a married woman shall be capable of rendering herself, and being rendered, liable in respect of any contract, debt or obligation, or of suing and being sued in respect of any such contract, as if she were a *femme sole*. The Ordinance also provides that a married woman shall be capable of acquiring, holding and disposing of any property in all respects as if she were a *femme sole*. The property of a married woman is liable for all her debts and obligations, and she is subject to the law relating to bankruptcy and to enforcement of judgments and orders. Moreover, a married woman has in her own name, against her husband, the same remedies and redress for the protection of her property as if she were a *femme sole*. But criminal proceedings concerning property cannot be taken by a wife against her husband while they are living together, nor while they are living apart concerning any act done while living together, unless such property was taken by the husband when leaving or deserting or about to leave or desert his wife.[2]

There are no statutory provisions relating to the property rights of married women in the Borneo States but it would appear that the position is similar to that in the *adat temenggong* areas of Malaya. In Sarawak it is enacted that if the husband, contrary to the usual custom, asks the wife to leave her family and stay with his family, she will not be required to do so unless the husband can provide a separate house for her in her *kampong* or village or in some other suitable place. If, however, the husband has to stay at a particular place because

---

[1] R. J. Wilkinson, *Malay Law*, op. cit., p. 36f.

[2] Married Women Ordinance, 1957 (No. 36 of 1957), Ss. 4–9. As regards criminal proceedings see the cases of *Re Ketuna Bibi* [1955] M.L.J. 166, where it was held that a Muslim woman can be convicted of criminal breach of trust of property belonging to her husband; and *Public Prosecutor v. Tahir* in E. N. Taylor's *Customary Law of Rembau*, op. cit., p. 102, where it was held that a husband may commit criminal breach of trust in respect of his wife's *harta dapatan*.

of his work, then the wife must accompany him to that place.[1]

In the parts of Negri Sembilan and of Malacca where the matriarchal *adat perpateh* is followed, the distribution of property on divorce follows the *adat* or customary law. Briefly, in all cases of dissolution of the marriage, not only the *charian laki-bini*, but the whole of the property of both parties, movable and immovable, must be brought into account irrespective of its origin and of the name in which the land is registered. Marriage property falls into three classes. That which is acquired during wedlock is called *harta charian*. That which the husband brought at the time of the marriage is called *harta pembawa*. That which belonged to the wife at the time of the marriage is called *harta dapatan*. The property with which the marriage commenced must be restored or made good to the respective parties; *dapatan tinggal*, the wife's separate estate, remains with her or her tribe; and *pembawa kembalek*, the personal estate brought by the man, returns to him. The *charian laki-bini* is divided equally on divorce between husband and wife, irrespective of who is to blame for the divorce, and irrespective even of the wife's adultery or of the number of children. There is, however, one exception to the rule of equal division on divorce; in the case of *cherai ta'alik* (divorce on breach of some condition), the wife retains the whole of the property.[2]

As under the customary law the children remain with the mother on divorce, it is usual for the father to agree to give part of his share to his children. The husband has power to grant as much as he pleases of his own share to the issue, or to the wife as their trustee if they are still children; this is called *tentukan* and is optional. The wife cannot claim more than half as of right; any excess is for the children only and should be protected by a caveat. Where the marriage has subsisted for a long time and the issue are adult, they can claim *tentukan* of a reasonable proportion of the property and the balance only is divided equally between the husband and the wife.[3]

In Rembau, by a rule of practice the Kathi's certificate of divorce cannot be issued until all questions of property are settled. Claims to partition of *charian laki-bini* must be made at the time of the divorce. The division in respect of divorce can be enforced afterwards provided

---

[1] Sarawak *Undang-Undang Mahkamah Melayu*, Sarawak (Laws of Sarawak, 1958, Vol. VII, p. 673) Ss. 43 and 44.

[2] Taylor, op. cit., pp. 20 and 111, citing *Mahawa v. Manan*.

[3] Ibid., op. cit., p. 26, citing *Pesah v. Dollah* at p. 119 and *Ujang v. Bujok* at p. 116; G. A. de Moubray, *Matriarchy in the Malaya Peninsula*, London, 1931, p. 155f.

it was claimed at the time of the divorce.[1] The Kathi is precluded from issuing the certificate of divorce until he is satisfied that all questions of property have been adjusted and, if any such question has been taken to the Court or the Collector of Land Revenue, the Kathi must obtain the leave of the Court or Collector before issuing his certificate. In *Hasmah binte Omar v. Abdul Jalil*[2] it was held that the custom in Kuala Pilah is different from that in Rembau, and that according to the custom in Kuala Pilah proceedings to recover land can be commened after divorce.

There is an important exception to the ordinary rules for distribution of *charian laki-bini*. *Charian laki-bini* land which is *kampong*, *sawah* or *dusun* is regarded as peculiarly the property of women; on divorce the wife is entitled to retain the whole of such property, instead of dividing it, at any rate if she has children.[3]

In the other parts of the States of Malaya and in the Borneo States, the distribution of property on divorce is also based on the Malay custom. As Snouck Hurgronge said, 'In districts where it is the custom for the wife to assist the husband in his employment, the property accumulated during the marriage by their respective toils is in the event of a divorce divided in equal shares between the man and the woman or their respective heirs. Where one of the two dies, the survivor obtains, in addition to this half-share, his lawful portion of the heritable property to which the other half of their common earnings is regarded as belonging. Thus we find in Acheh the same peculiarity that exists in Java and Madura and most Malayan countries, viz. that is where the woman is the fellow-worker of her husband there gradually grows up a kind of partnership between the two.'[4] This Malay custom was accepted and absorbed as part of the law when the Malays became Muslims and at first the property was described as *harta sharikat* or partnership property. Subsequently, however, the Muslim jurists in Malaya held that *harta sapencharian* is not the same as *harta sharikat* and therefore property acquired during marriage cannot be called *sharikat* unless there is either a written or verbal agreement to that

[1] *Saudah v. Siman* and *Rahim v. Sintah* in E. N. Taylor, *Customary Law of Rembau*, op. cit., pp. 104 and 114, and *Jasin v. Tiawan* (1941), M.L.J. 247.
[2] (1958) M.L.J. 10.
[3] Taylor, op. cit., p. 24; G. A. de Moubray, *Matriarchy in the Malay Peninsula*, op. cit., p. 165f; *Kampong* is high land planted with coconut and fruit trees and therefore an actual or potential homestead site, *sawah* is irrigated rice fields and *dusun* is holdings of jungle containing durian and other fruit trees.
[4] Snouck Hurgronge, *The Achenese* (Leyden, 1906), Vol. I, p. 365.

effect. The basis of the doctrine was then found by the Muslim jurists in the principle that a wife is entitled to claim for labour undertaken by her during marriage, not only in assisting in outdoor and household work, but also in looking after the children of the marriage, if any. Subsequently in Perak, for example, it was held that as the Ruler has a discretionary power in applying certain laws, the custom of *sapencharian* is allowable by Islamic law when given effect by the Ruler of the State.[1] Until recently claims to such jointly acquired property, or *harta sapencharian*, were brought either before the Collectors of Land Revenue or the High Court, but recent legislation in the States of Malaya has given the Court of the Chief Kathi or the Court of the Kathi jurisdiction to hear claims for *harta sapencharian*. According to the Malay custom the guardians at a lawful marriage should enquire as to the separate property of the man and the woman so that on divorce it may be returned to the owner, while property acquired during marriage is divided equally. If the separate property has diminished during the marriage, and the joint property acquired during the marriage is large, then the separate property is made good and the residue is the joint property; losses, too, are divided. If the husband wants to divorce his wife for no fault, then the joint property is divided into three, the man taking one share and the woman two.[2]

The Malay custom of the division of the *harta sapencharian* on divorce applied throughout Malaya but, in the former Straits Settlements (that is, Singapore, Penang and the non-customary part of Malacca), it has been held that this custom has been abolished by Statute. The Muhammadan Marriage Ordinance, 1880, provided that Islamic law shall be recognized by the courts of the Straits Settlements only so far as it was expressly enacted in the Ordinance; and as there was no express provision for the application of custom in the division of property on divorce, it has been held that the English law and not the Islamic law applied, so that the wife had no claim to joint earnings during coverture, which were under the English law the property of the husband.[3] In Malacca and Penang, the Kathis' Courts are now given power to deal with claims for *harta sapencharian* on divorce, but the law has not been altered in Singapore.

The position, therefore, is that throughout Malaya except in Singa-

[1] See *Laton v. Ramah* in E. N. Taylor, *Malay Family Law* (1937), Journal of the Malayan Branch of the Royal Asiatic Society, p. 35f and p. 41f.
[2] J. E. Kempe and R. O. Windstedt, *A Malay Legal Miscellany*, 1952 Journal of the Malayan Branch of the Royal Asiatic Society, Part I, p. 6.
[3] *Tijah v. Mat Alli* 4 Kyshe 124.

pore a divorced wife is entitled to a share of all property acquired during marriage. Where she has in fact assisted in cultivating the land she is entitled to one-half of the property, and in other cases to one-third of the jointly acquired property (*harta sapencharian*) of the marriage.[1]

In Perak the matter was settled by a Perak State Council minute dated January 18, 1907. In that minute the Council declared and ordered to be recorded:

'That the custom of the Malays in Perak in the matter of dividing up property after divorce, when such property has been acquired by the parties or one of them during marriage, is to adopt the proportion of two shares to the man and one share to the woman, and the gifts between married persons are irrevocable either during marriage or after divorce.'[2]

Claims to such property were dealt with by the Court or Collectors of Land Revenue (in the case of land registered in the Mukim Registers), but Kathis were called in as advisers on questions of principle. The claim of the divorced wife to one-third of the value of the lands acquired during the marriage is not defeated even if it is proved that she was divorced for adultery,[3] nor would she lose her right on *tebus talak* (*khula*) unless the consideration for the *tebus talak* was the waiver of her claim to the *harta sapencharian*.[4] The divorced wife's share may be increased to one-half depending upon the nature of the work actually done by her on the jointly acquired property. In *Re Elang, Re Kulop Degor* and *Lebar v. Niat*,[5] Mr E. N. Taylor, Collector, said:

'The evidence of the six witnesses who were examined before me establishes that in the Perak River kampongs there is a custom almost invariably followed by which on divorce the property acquired during the marriage is divided between the parties—the division depending on the circumstances—and is arranged by the two families and the *ketua kampong*; if the woman assisted in the actual cultivation she can claim half; if she did not work on the land she received a smaller share—perhaps one-third. If a man of

[1] *Rasinah v. Said* in E. N. Taylor, *Malay Family Law*, op. cit., p. 29.
[2] E. N. Taylor, *Malay Family Law*, op. cit., p. 70.
[3] *Teh Rasim v. Neman*, ibid., op. cit., p. 18.
[4] *Wan Mahatan v. Haji Abdul Samat*, ibid., op. cit., p. 25.
[5] E. N. Taylor, *Malay Family Law*, op. cit., p. 48.

this class earns a salary (e.g. as a Government servant) and property is bought out of his earnings the wife's share is one-third.'

There is some doubt as to the position where the man earns a salary (e.g. as a Government servant) and property is bought out of his earnings. In *Re Elang*, deceased (*supra*), it was stated that in such a case the wife's share is one-third but in the case of *Wan Mahattan v. Haji Abdul Samat* (*supra*) evidence was given that where a woman married a person who earned wages and the wife merely looked after the household, the property obtained by the husband during the marriage is not held in partnership with the woman but is appropriated to the husband alone.

In Pahang the Chiefs and Kathis gave their opinion in 1930 that a woman can claim *harta sapencharian*, according to Pahang custom, on divorce or on the death of her husband. The claim can be made in respect of land and movable property. There is no fixed rule as to the share of the divorced wife, but either equal or unequal shares may be awarded pursuant to an agreement between the parties or confirming a gift or by judgment of the Kathi.[1]

In Kedah it has been stated that on the dissolution of a Malay marriage the property acquired by the husband and wife is divided between them, but there is no established rule or principle to guide the Court in deciding the respective shares.[2] However, in *Habsah v. Abdullah*[3] it was held that on divorce a woman in Kedah is entitled by customary law to half of any property acquired during the marriage by the joint effort of the spouses and such a claim is not barred or extinguished by her remarriage.

In nearly all the States of Malaya there is now legislative provision which gives the Courts of the Chief Kathi and of the Kathis jurisdiction to hear and determine all actions and proceedings relating to the division *inter vivos* of *sapencharian* property. The earliest provision to this effect was made in Selangor in 1952, and since then this legislation has been followed in Kelantan in 1953, Trengganu in 1955, Pahang in 1956, Malacca and Penang in 1959, Negri Sembilan in 1960 and Perlis in 1964.[4]

[1] E. N. Taylor, *Malay Family Law*, op. cit., p. 72f.
[2] *Wan Nab v. Jasin*, ibid., op. cit., p. 20.
[3] (1950) M.L.J. 60.
[4] Selangor Administration of Muslim Law Enactment, 1952, S. 45(3); Kelantan, Council of Religion and Malay Custom and Kathis Courts Enactment, 1953, S. 48(1); Trengganu Administration of Islamic Law Enactment, 1955, S. 25(1); Pahang Administration of the Law of the Religion of Islam Enactment, 1956,

In Kedah, while the Court of the Chief Kathi and the Court of the Kathi are given jurisdiction to deal with any disputes as to the disposition of or claim to property arising out of marriage or divorce, there is no express reference to *jarta sapencharian*.[1]

The only States where the Kathis have not expressly been given such jurisdiction are Perak and Johore. Perlis is the only State where it is expressly provided that a woman who has been divorced may apply to a Kathi for her share of the common property called *harta sapencharian*.[2]

In Sarawak it is provided in the *Undang-Undang Mahkamah Melayu*, Sarawak, that if both parties join in acquiring the matrimonial property, for example a farm or rice field, then on divorce the wife is entitled to one-half of the matrimonial property. If, on the other hand, the husband is the only earner, then on divorce the wife is entitled to one-third of the matrimonial property.[3]

In the States of Malaya, before the British period, the law of the Malays relating to the inheritance of property was, in Negri Sembilan, *adat perpateh*, and, in the other States, *adat perpateh* in decay or the *adat temenggong*. The Malay Rulers were Muslims but it is doubtful whether they introduced any more Islamic law into the other Malay States than was introduced in Negri Sembilan. About 1886 the Perak State Council ordered the land of a major Chief, Tengku Long Jaffar, to be transmitted in the female line, but since then Islamic law has been more extensively adopted. It is probable that among country people many estates are still divided according to *adat kampong*, but that can only take place by consent. The Islamic law has been applied so frequently by the Collectors of Land Revenue and the courts that the law of inheritance is now, except as to the special rights of spouses, the Islamic law. Questions of property and inheritance are seldom litigated between a woman and her own children or between the kindred of an intestate. Such matters are usually settled by agreement, and the tendency has been that in such agreements the widow usually receives more than her share under Islamic law. In the vast majority of Malay

S. 37(3); Malacca Administration of Muslim Law Enactment, 1959, S. 40(3); Penang Administration of Muslim Law Enactment, 1959, S. 40(3); Negri Sembilan Administration of Muslim Law Enactment, 1960, S. 41(3); Perlis Administration of Muslim Law Enactment, 1963, S. 11.

[1] Kedah Administration of Muslim Law Enactment, 1962, S. 41(3).
[2] Perlis Administration of Muslim Law Enactment, 1963, S. 94.
[3] Sarawak *Undang-Undang Mahkamah Melayu*, Sarawak, S. 41.

families, one-eighth of the estate does not provide the widow with subsistence. The matter was, therefore, regulated by Malay custom rather than by Islamic law. The fact that the Islamic law allows distribution of the estate of a deceased person to be settled by consent of the heirs has enabled many arrangements which are in reality applications of the *adat kampong* to pass as distributions according to Islamic law.[1]

In all the States of Malaya (with the exception of those parts of Negri Sembilan and Malacca where the *adat perpateh* is followed to the exclusion of Islamic law) the Islamic rules of inheritance or intestacy are followed. These rules are, however, subject to the following modifications in the Malay States:

(a) on the death of a person his widow is entitled to a special share in his estate, as her share in *harta sapencharian*, unless provision has been made for her *inter vivos*, as for example by registering land in her name. If the deceased had no children and the estate is small she may take the whole estate; in other cases she takes a half or less according to circumstances;

(b) the residue of the estate is distributed according to Islamic law but, in as much as the widow's special share is discretionary, her one-eighth or one-quarter share can and should be taken into consideration in assessing the special share.[2]

In Selangor, Kelantan, Trengganu and Pahang the Court of a Chief Kathi and Courts of Kathis, and in Perlis the Courts of the Kathi and Assistant Kathi, are given power to hear and determine actions and proceedings relating to (a) the division of and claims to *sapencharian* property; and (b) the determination of the persons entitled to share in the estate of a Muslim deceased person and of the shares to which such persons are respectively entitled; but such actions and proceedings can also be brought in the ordinary courts.[3] In the other States of Malaya actions relating to the distribution of the estate of a deceased are heard and determined in the ordinary civil courts.

The rule as to *harta sapencharian* originated as a rule of Malay

[1] E. N. Taylor, *Inheritance in Negri Sembilan* (1948), Journal of the Malayan Branch of the Royal Asiatic Society, Part II, p. 47f.

[2] Ibid., p. 50.

[3] Selangor Administration of Muslim Law Enactment, 1952, S. 45(3); Kelantan Council of Religion and Malay Custom and Kathis Courts Enactment, 1953, S. 48; Trengganu Administration of the Law of the Religion of Islam Enactment, 1956, S. 37(3); Perlis Administration of Muslim Law Enactment, 1963, S. 11(4).

custom. In the early days when ownership of land rested in bare occupation without any registration of title neither the executive nor the courts were often concerned with disputed succession to small holdings. When land was registered, matters of succession to such land came to be dealt with by Collectors of Land Revenue, who in general accepted the division agreed on by the next of kin. Where there were disputes the matter was dealt with according to the Islamic law as varied by local custom. The local Kathi who was called to give expert evidence usually declared the *adat*, that is '*harta sapencharian*', to be a rule of Islamic law and in some such cases this property was described as *harta sharikat* or partnership property. It is clear from the resolutions of the Perak State Council in 1907, and the Pahang Committee of Chiefs and Kathis in 1930, however, that this rule is a rule of Malay custom. It is in fact the rule '*chari bahagi*' (earnings are divided) of the *adat perpateh*.[1]

In Selangor there is no reported case which gives a share in the *harta sapencharian* to the widow. In *Laton v. Ramah*[2] the trial Judge held on the evidence of Kathis that a widow is entitled to one-half of the value of the immovable property of the deceased husband at the time of his death, but on appeal the Court of Appeal held that the evidence of the Kathis was not admissible and they ordered a retrial. In *Haji Ramah v. Alpha*[3] it was merely held that a widow is entitled to claim *upah* or compensation for her share in the work of cultivation of land.

In Pahang it was held in *Haji Saemah v. Haji Sulaiman*[4] that the evidence called in that case did not prove the existence of any custom that the widow is entitled to more than her Quranic share in her

---

[1] E. N. Taylor, *Inheritance in Negri Sembilan*, op. cit., p. 49.

[2] (1926) 4 F.M.S. L.R. 16. It was there held by a majority that the Islamic law was the law of the Federated Malay States; it was not 'foreign law' within the meaning of the Evidence Ordinance and evidence as to *harta sharikat* was therefore improperly admitted. This led to the passing of the Muslim law and Malay Custom Determination Ordinance, 1930, which enabled any Judge or Collector before whom a question of Muslim law or Malay custom arose to draw up a statement of facts and submit the question to the Ruler in Council for decision.

[3] (1924) 4 F.M.S.L.R. 179. In that case the Kathi gave evidence that if a wife helped her husband to clear or plant or even cultivate his land she is entitled to compensation (*upah*). This was what the widow claimed and there was no mention of *harta sapencharian* in the case.

[4] [1942] M.L.J. 17; (1948) M.L.J. 108. In that case only the *Penghulu* gave evidence of the custom but the Kathis who were called said that the widow was not entitled to more than her Quranic share, except by agreement of the other heirs. The Kathis appear to have given evidence contrary to the views expressed by the Chiefs and Kathis of the State in 1930.

deceased husband's estate and the widow's claim to a half-share of the
lands of her deceased husband's as *harta sapencharian* was dismissed.
But in *Teh binte Chik v. Kalsom binte Haji Abbas*[1] it was assumed that
claims for *harta sapencharian* can be validly and successfully made in
Pahang. It was held in that case, however, that *harta sapencharian* is
only applicable to property acquired during marriage and not to
property acquired before marriage. Where property has been acquired
before marriage and either spouse has contributed money or labour to
that property, *harta sapencharian* does not apply, but either spouse is
entitled to claim what is known as *upah* or remuneration for work done.
In 1930 the Chiefs and Kathis of Pahang gave their opinion that a
woman can claim *harta sapencharian* according to Pahang custom on
divorce or on the death of her husband. The claim can be made in
respect of land and movable property. There is no fixed rule as to the
share of the widow but either equal or unequal shares may be awarded
either by gift or by judgment of the Kathi.[2]

In *Hujah Lijah v. Fatimah*[3] it was held in Kelantan that a suit for
harta sapencharian can be brought as an ordinary suit in the High
Court. J. Briggs in that case said:

> The claim by a widow for *harta sapencharian* is not a claim for a
> share of the deceased's estate, but a claim adverse to the estate for
> property of claimant held in the name of the deceased; this branch of
> the Malay *adat* is recognized throughout Kelantan among peasant
> landowners and the share usually considered to belong to the widow
> is one-half, apart from any question of her claim to a distributive
> share in the deceased's estate.

The claim to *harta sapencharian* arises most frequently in practice in
applications for summary distribution of small estates, and the practice
is to regard such a claim as one of the factors to be considered in
attempting to formulate an agreed scheme of distribution. Such agreed
schemes very often give full effect to the claim.

The Perak State Council Minute of 1907 referred to claims to *harta
sapencharian* by a divorced wife and Raja Sir Chulan expressed the view
that the widow would only get what she is entitled to under the law of
inheritance in case of her husband's death and would lose her claim to
what she had earned during marriage.[4] In *Re Elang* (deceased),[5] how-

[1] [1939] M.L.J. 289.
[2] E. N. Taylor, *Malay Family Law*, op. cit., p. 72f.
[3] [1950] M.L.J. 63.
[4] E. N. Taylor, *Malay Family Law*, op. cit., pp. 41–2.
[5] ibid., p. 48.

ever, it was held that in the Perak River kampongs the property acquired during a marriage is divided between the parties on the death of either spouse. If the wife had assisted in the actual cultivation she could claim half the property; otherwise her share was smaller—perhaps one-third. It has been questioned whether the rule applies where the man earns a salary (e.g. as a Government servant) and property is bought out of his earnings. In *Re Elang* (deceased), *supra*, it was said that in such a case the wife's share is one-third, but in the case of *Wan Mahatan v. Haji Abdul Samat*[1] it was stated by the Kathi of Larut that, where a woman married a person who earned wages and the wife merely looked after the household, the property obtained by the husband during the marriage was not held in partnership with the woman but belonged to her husband alone. In *Re Noorijah*[2] the facts were that the deceased was the wife of a public servant and left land registered in her name. The land was bought by the husband but registered in the name of the wife. There was no evidence of any gift to the deceased by her husband. It was held that the husband was solely entitled to the property and that it should not be regarded as the estate of the deceased.

In Penang and Malacca it is provided that the estate and effects of a Muslim dying intestate after January 1, 1924, shall be administered according to the Islamic law, except in so far as such law is opposed to any local custom which prior to January 1, 1924, had the force of law; but any next of kin who is not a Muslim shall be entitled to share in the distribution as though he were a Muslim. In an application for probate or letters of administration in the case of a deceased Muslim, the petitioner is required to state the school of law to which the deceased belonged. Questions of succession and inheritance according to the Islamic law are dealt with by the ordinary courts, and it is provided that in deciding such questions the court shall be at liberty to accept as proof of this law any definite statements in all or any of certain specified books, among which is the translation of Nawawi's *Minhaj-at-Talibin*.[3]

While the position in the States of Malaya can be defended in accordance with the Islamic law by the argument that the distribution of the estate (including the giving of more than her Quranic share to the widow) is agreed to by all the heirs and that the custom of the distribu-

[1] E. N. Taylor, *Malay Family Law*, op. cit., p. 25.

[2] ibid., p. 59.

[3] Straits Settlements Muslims Ordinance (Cap. 57 of 1936 Editions), Ss. 27–9. Prior to 1924 the Statute of Distributions applied to the estates of Muslims. There has been no reported case where the custom of *harta sapencharian* has been recognized in Malacca and Penang.

tion of *harta sapencharian* is sanctioned by the Ruler, no such arguments can, it is submitted, be used to justify the application of the *adat perpateh* in tribal areas of Negri Sembilan and Malacca.

There is clearly a conflict between the Islamic law and the Malay custom in this matter and it is accepted that in this respect it is the custom and not the Islamic law which is followed. It is significant that in Negri Sembilan the Council of Muslim Religion is only given power to aid and advise the Ruler in matters relating to the Muslim religion and that the Courts of the Chief Kathi and Kathis in Negri Sembilan have no power to deal with the distribution of property on a person's death. While the Courts of the Chief Kathi and Kathis are given power to issue inheritance certificates to certify how an estate should be distributed on death, this only applies where the estate is to be distributed according to Islamic law. There is in fact a Council of the Yang di-Pertuan Besar and the Ruling Chiefs constituted under the State Constitution to advise the Ruler on questions relating to Malay custom.[1]

The rules as to distribution of ancestral property under the *adat perpateh* are simple in theory although they may be sometimes difficult to apply in practice. The basic principle is that all the ancestral property of the family is to be divided equally *per stirpes* among the direct female descendants—but due regard must be had to any partial distribution which may already have been made. The rule applies only to the proper share of the proprietor, so that if the deceased was registered as the holder of all land derived from her mother and left one sister, the sister would be entitled to half, and the daughters of the deceased to the other half in equal shares.[2]

The rules for the distribution on death of acquired property under the Malay custom are as follows:

(1) The *harta dapatan* or *pembawa* reverts on death to the *warith* of the deceased, that is the nearest female relative in the tribe of the deceased (in the case of a man his sister, in the case of a woman her daughter).

(2) The *charian laki-bini* is apportioned—

(a) on the death of either spouse without issue of the marriage, the whole remains to the survivor;

(b) on the death of the husband leaving issue, the whole remains to the widow and issue;

[1] Negri Sembilan Administration of Muslim Law Enactment, 1960, Ss. 4, 41 and 44; Laws of the Constitution of Negri Sembilan, First Part, Chapter 6.
[2] E. N. Taylor, *Customary Law of Rembau*, op. cit., p. 14f.

(c) on the death of the wife leaving issue, it is divided between the widower and the issue, but not necessarily equally; the principle of the division, by agreement or otherwise, is to make sufficient provision for the issue. If the wife dies leaving issue of the marriage and there is little *charian laki-bini* property the widower may not be entitled to any share.[1]

If the *harta pembawa* has been increased in value by the joint efforts of husband and wife the increase, which is called *untong*, ranks as *charian laki-bini* and must be apportioned accordingly. The principle of *untong* does not apply to the wife's ancestral property, but appears to apply to *harta dapatan*.[2]

There are two classes of property which are excluded from the ordinary rules for distribution of *charian laki-bini*. *Charian laki-bini* land which is *kampong*, *sawah* or *dusun* are regarded as peculiarly the property of women; on the death of the husband such property devolves on the widow and the female issue to the exclusion of sons, and on the death of the wife it devolves on the female issue to the exclusion of the widower. The other type of excluded property is *tanah tebus*, ancestral land which has been purchased in the exercise of the customary option by the immediate heiress; such land will devolve not as *charian* but as ancestral land on the immediate heiress of the transferee, but the widower of the purchaser may be entitled to reimbursement by the heiress-in-tail of the exact amount of *wang charian* (money jointly acquired) expended, but without any allowance for improvements.[3]

The Small Estates (Distribution) Ordinance, 1955, provides that in making any distribution order in respect of land where the deceased is a member of a tribe in the Districts of Jelebu, Kuala Pilah, Rembau and Tampin in Negri Sembilan, the Collector shall apply the following principles:

---

[1] Taylor, op. cit., pp. 29–30. Sons and daughters are equally entitled to inherit rubber land and movable property (*Re Puan*, p. 164, 167) but daughters have an exclusive right to *kampong*, *sawah* and *dusun*, *Temah v. Haji Zakaria*, p. 125, *Re Rahmat Pakeh*, p. 126, *Re Hahi Munap*, p. 127. See also *Taib v. Uchang*, p. 135, where it was held that on the death of a wife if there is little *charian laki-bini* property the whole is inherited by the female issue; and *Re Kering*, p. 136, where it was held that if a wife dies leaving issue of the marriage and there is little *charian laki-bini* property the widower may not be entitled to any share.

[2] ibid., p. 22f, citing the case of *Napsiah v. Samat* at p. 83.

[3] ibid., p. 24, citing the cases of *Re Rahmat Pakeh*, p. 126, *Re Haji Munap*, p. 127, and *Temah v. Haji Zakaria*, p. 125.

(a) if any land appears to be ancestral customary land, though not registered as such, it shall be transmitted to the customary heiress, subject if necessary to life occupancy;

(b) if any property is found as a fact to be *harta pembawa* or *harta dapatan* it may be transmitted to the customary heirs of the deceased, subject to the right of any other person to a share or charge over that property according to the principle of *untong* (or increase), where applicable, and on registration of the order the Collector may, if necessary, add the words 'customary land' to any title affected, but he shall not be bound to do so;

(c) if any property is found to be as a fact *harta charian bujang* or *harta charian laki-bini* it may be transmitted according to the custom of the *luak* (tribe), and on registration of the order the Collector may, if necessary, add the words 'customary land' to any title affected, but he shall not be bound to do so;

(d) the Collector shall give effect to customary adoptions where they are satisfactorily proved;

(e) in all cases regard shall be had to any partial distribution of property made or agreed upon in the lifetime of the deceased and to the existence of any property which is affected by distribution or agreement though not part of the estate;

(f) wherever practicable the Collector shall avoid transmitting undivided shares in any one lot to members of different tribes;

(g) where funeral expenses are by the custom chargeable on specific property and the party on whom the property ought to devolve has not paid them, the Collector may require such party to pay the funeral expenses as a condition of inheriting that property or may by order charge that property with the amount of the funeral expenses.[1]

In the non-tribal parts of Negri Sembilan (Seremban and Port Dickson) the tribal organization had ceased to be effective by 1874, and it would appear that the practice adopted was the *adat temenggong*. In general the distribution follows a family settlement of *pakat*; but where there is dispute the distribution tends to follow the rules laid down by the *adat temenggong* (which is not as definite as, but tends to follow, the

[1] Small Estates (Distribution) Ordinance, 1955, Ss. 20–5. Funeral expenses are a matter of great importance in Malay Custom. They include not only the actual burial expenses but also the expenses of the last illness and the cost of the customary feasts which are held on the third, seventh, fourteenth, fortieth and hundredth days—see Ahmad Ibrahim, Islam and Customary Law in Malaysia, Intisari, op. cit., p. 71f.

adat perpateh), although in some cases the rules of Islamic law were followed.[1]

An illustration of the application of the *adat kampong* or *adat temengong* is given in the Seremban case of *Shafi v. Lijah*.[2] In that case the question was whether the inheritance of certain real property should be in accordance with the *adat* (custom) or the Islamic law. The land was acquired during wedlock (*charian laki-bini*) but the title of the land was not endorsed 'customary land'. It was held that the lack of endorsement on the titles of customary land precluded, in the absence of strong evidence to the contrary, the *adat perpateh*. It was held further on the evidence that it was clear that the deceased intended some form of local customary law to apply and that therefore the *adat temenggong* should be applied and the estate distributed equitably between the claimants.

J. Callow in this case said:

'I am satisfied that in the absence of strong evidence to the contrary, which was not forthcoming, the lack of endorsement on the titles of customary land precludes the *adat perpateh*. It is always open to a landowner to request the endorsement of title as customary, and it could be inferred from the omission in this case that the late Abdul Majid did not desire the land to be subject to the *adat perpateh* although I do not believe inheritance or succession in accordance with the law of the *Shafi* sect of the *Sunni* school of Islam was ever contemplated. But although the more defined tenets of the *adat perpateh* may not in this case be adhered to, there remains the still older and perhaps more fundamental *adat temenggong*, which one might perhaps almost term the common law behind the more statutorized *adat perpateh*, though whereas in England statutory law evolved from the common law, in this country one might almost conclude the reverse—that the *temenggong* is from the law or codes of bygone generations. I suggest this notwithstanding Wilkinson's observations at page 40 of his work, "The true *adat temenggong* of Malaya was an unwritten law"; it was and is unwritten, deriving its origin from the lawgivers of ancient times. Another simile is that the *adat temenggong* was as the royal prerogative, and exercised in suitable cases where strict adherence to the *adat perpateh* would cause hardship. The holder of the Ministerial Office of *temenggong* exercised on behalf of the ruler the prerogative which could not be

---

[1] E. N. Taylor, *Inheritance in Negri Sembilan*, op. cit., p. 80.
[2] [1948–9] M.L.J. Supp. 49.

challenged. It was an autocratic decree and should in proper circumstances the *adat perpateh* conflict or differ from the code of conscience the *adat temenggong* could be invoked and so overrule the former. It seems to be clear, and I accept the evidence of Lijah accordingly, that the deceased Abdul Majid acquired this property for the benefit of his widow and adopted daughters. He did not contemplate the administration of his estate in accordance with the inheritance law. He intended some form of local customary law to apply, although he was probably quite vague as to detail or principle. Therefore, although the *adat temenggong* is deprecated by Wilkinson (page 45), and although Taylor regards it as essentially the same as the *adat perpateh* (Royal Asiatic Society Journal, May 1937, page 3), I distinguish the two *adats* and rule that the *adat temenggong* should apply. This means that the estate should be distributed equitably between the claimants, such division being decided by the circumstances of the particular case before the court. It is not a division necessarily to be followed in every such case.'

In Singapore it is provided that the estate and effects of a Muslim dying intestate shall be administered according to Islamic law, except in so far as it is opposed to local custom. There has been no reported case in Singapore where local custom has been relied on to vary the Muslim law. Questions of succession and inheritance according to the Islamic law are dealt with by the ordinary courts and it is provided that in deciding such questions the court shall be at liberty to accept as proof of the Islamic law any definite statement on that law in all or any of certain specified books, among which is the translation of Nawawi's *Minhaj-at-Talibin*.[1] It has been held in Singapore, in the case of *Re Mutchilim*,[2] that where a deceased Muslim belonging to the Shāfi'ī school of law dies intestate leaving a widow but no next of kin, the widow is entitled to only a one-quarter share of the estate and the doctrine of *radd* or return does not apply to make her entitled to the balance of the estate; in such a case the remaining three-quarter share escheats to the State.

In Sabah it is provided that nothing in the Probate and Administra-

[1] Singapore Muslims Ordinance, 1957, S. 44.
[2] [1960] M.L.J. 25. According to the doctrine of *radd*, or return, if there is a residue left after the claims of the sharers and the residuaries have been satisfied, the residue reverts to the sharers in proportion to their shares. In the early history of doctrine neither the husband nor the wife was entitled to take by return but a later development in the Ḥanafī School in India has given a right also to the husband and the wife.

tion Ordinance shall affect any rules of Islamic law as varied by local custom in respect of the distribution of the balance of the estate of a deceased person after debts have been satisfied. Special provision is made in the Administration of Native and Small Estates Ordinance for the administration and distribution of small estates, that is estates not exceeding 5,000 dollars in total value at the date of the death. Application for administration may be made to the Collector of Land Revenue who, after hearing the application, shall make an order for distribution and in making such order shall give effect to any division of the estate agreed upon by any surviving spouse, issue and parents, and shall, where no such agreement exists, in the case of a Muslim distribute the estate according to the Islamic law or custom having the force of law applicable to the deceased.[1]

In Sarawak the Administration of Estates Ordinance provides that on obtaining probate or letters of administration the executor or administrator, as the case may be, shall after payment of all debts distribute the residue of the estate among the beneficiaries or heirs of the deceased according to the will of the deceased or, as the case may be, in the shares to which they are entitled by recognized law or custom. Islamic law is therefore applicable in the distribution of the estate of a deceased Muslim dying intestate.[2] It is provided in the *Undang-Undang Mahkamah Melayu*, Sarawak, that if both the husband and wife have joined in working on or acquiring the matrimonial property the widow will be entitled to a half-share, while if it is the husband who is the earning partner then the wife is entitled to one-third share and in addition will be entitled to her share under Islamic law on the death of the husband.[3] The effect of this is shown in the case of *Haji Mohidi v. Spiah*[4] where it was held that on the death of the deceased leaving no issue his widow was entitled to one-third of the deceased's estate plus one-quarter of the remainder. The custom of *pencharian* under which half of the property goes to the widow has been recognized and applied in a number of cases in Sarawak—*Men v. Dan*[5] and *Serujie v. Sahah*.[6]

---

[1] This would appear to be the effect of S. 10 of the North Borneo Administration of Native and Small Estates Ordinance (Cap. 1) as amended by the Intestate Succession Ordinance, 1960 (No. 1 of 1960), and the Administration of Native and Small Estates (Amendment) Ordinance, 1961 (No. 8 of 1961), and S. 2 of the Intestate Succession Ordinance, 1960.

[2] Sarawak Administration of Estates Ordinance (Cap. 80 of the 1947 Edition of the Laws of Sarawak), S. 17.

[3] *Undang-Undang Mahkamah Melayu*, Sarawak, S. 41.

[4] (1951) S.C.R. 22.

[5] (1952) S.C.R. 13.

[6] ibid., 40.

Custom has played an important part in the development of Islamic law. The Muslim legal system recognizes the force of custom in establishing rules of law. The validity of such law rests on principles somewhat similar to those of *ijmā'* or consensus which is one of the accepted sources of Islamic law. The customs and precedents which prevailed in Arabia in the time of the Prophet are accepted where they have not been abrogated by the holy Qur'ān or the practice of the Prophet. As to customs which have sprung up or which are found since that time, their validity can be justified on the authority of the tradition which lays down that whatever the people generally consider to be good for themselves is good in the eyes of God. In the Shāfi'ī school, too, it is accepted that where the Ruler orders his court to follow some accepted opinion or doctrine, this is obligatory and should be applied. Custom has come to be an important source of law in some Muslim countries, especially in Morocco, where the principle of *'amal* or judicial practice has been developed by the jurists. In Malaysia too the *adat* has played an important part in the development of the Islamic law and there would appear to be no reason why it should not continue to do so, especially in those spheres where it helps to maintain the status and position of women in society. A synthesis between the *adat* and Islamic law is possible if, on the one hand, the principles of the Muslim law as contained in the Qur'ān and the *Sunnah* are subjected, as they were in the early days of Islam, to the free activity of interpretation through *ijtihād* and *ijmā'* to meet ever-changing social and economic conditions, and if, on the other hand, the *adat* itself is modified to meet the needs of such social and economic conditions. The custom of the division of *harta sapencharian* appears to be generally accepted throughout Malaysia, though it has not yet been applied in Singapore. It is significant that at the Regional Conference of the World Muslim Congress held at Kuala Lumpur in January to July 1964, a resolution was adopted to the effect that in order to build up a stable and happy family system in accordance with the teachings of Islam, it was necessary to ensure that the Islamic law is so administered as to protect and maintain the strength and happiness of the family and in particular (*inter alia*) to ensure that the wife has an adequate share of jointly acquired property on divorce or on the death of her husband.[1]

[1] Report of the Regional Conference for South-East Asia and the Far East in *World Muslim League Magazine*, Singapore, Vol. 1, No. 5 (March–April 1965), p. 53f. The resolution was moved by the only lady delegate present, Mrs M. Siraj, of Singapore.

IO

COMMUNITY OF PROPERTY IN THE MARRIAGE LAW OF BURMA

ALAN GLEDHILL

Professor Emeritus of Oriental Laws in the University of London

Macaulay might have said that every schoolboy knows that, on assuming political power in India, the East India Company set up courts which gave Hindus and Muslims the benefit of their personal laws in family and religious matters. Many books of today and tomorrow represent or will represent the absorption of Burma in the Indian Empire as naked imperialism, notwithstanding that the Burmese Wars were provoked, that there were three bites to the cherry and that it was after considerable hesitation that the Indian Government ultimately decided to put an end to the Burmese kingdom. In the years immediately following the first Burmese War, local administrators were allowed considerable latitude in the selection of their machinery of government but, once it had been decided to bring Burma within the Indian orbit, then just as Hindus and Muslims had been given the benefit of their personal law, Burmese Buddhists were given the benefit of what was described as Burmese Buddhist law.

But, whereas the Hindu law and the Islamic law are primarily applicable to the followers of the Hindu religion and of Islam, as such, the same is not true of the Burmese Buddhist law. Gautama was extremely careful not to encroach on the field of the secular power; he advocated indifference to worldly affairs; and he never attempted to lay down laws governing those who did not assume the yellow robe. The Buddhists of India have never been governed by the rules applicable to Burmans. The rules applied in the courts of the Kingdom of Burma to disputes affecting the clergy and to religious matters were not those laid down in the Vinaya.

In the early days of British rule in Burma a myth was created that the Burmese Buddhist law was of Hindu origin. In the Burmese Dhammathats the juristic oracle is called Manu and some texts in the Dhammathats reproduce word for word texts found in the Hindu Manu. For example, the text which requires the dhobi to use soft wood instead of rocks to beat the dirt out of linen mentions the same wood in both versions. Jardine and Forchhammer are mainly responsible for the perpetuation of this myth. The former was known to believe it; he offered a prize for an essay on the origins of Burmese Buddhist law, which was won by Forchhammer's essay, strongly supporting the myth. It is difficult to understand how Jardine, after his Indian experience, failed, as Judicial Commissioner in Burma, to recognize the fundamental differences between Hindu law and Burmese law.

Hindu law has a religious basis which persisted after the jurists had recognized the distinction between the moral law and positive law, as is evidenced by the son's pious obligation to pay his father's untainted debts, the law of adoption and the sacramental nature of marriage. Burmese law is essentially secular; the spouse relict, not the son, is the preferential heir; there is no religious purpose in adoption; marriage is contractual, and so is divorce. Hindu law is patriarchal and long denied women property rights. In Burmese law agnates have no rights as such; and equality between the sexes was recognized far beyond what was allowed in England before the Married Women's Property Act was passed in 1882. The Hindu law assumes the social unit to be the large joint family, consisting of all descendants of a male; in Burmese law the social unit is a man, his wife and their unmarried children.

In 1952 Professor R. Lingat published the first volume of *Les Régimes Matrimoniaux*, showing that the basic principles of the law of marriage are identical in Burma, Siam, Cambodia, Laos and Vietnam. His weightiest piece of evidence relates to the written code found by the French, when they first seized the sceptre in Northern Vietnam. This code, which embodies the patriarchal principles of Chinese law, was based on the Chinese dynastic codes (Vietnam having been subject to Chinese cultural influence), but the French administrators were puzzled by the discrepancies between the code and the practices of the people—until they discovered an earlier code, embodying the traditional system in South-East Asia. The obvious conclusion is that the writers of the earlier Dhammathats had access to the Hindu Dharmaśāstras, from which they borrowed the eighteen titles, some terms of art and some texts, more for the felicity of their language than their substantial importance, for the substance of the Dhammathat law is the common law of South-East Asia, with inevitable local variations.

The Anglo-Burmese courts used the Dhammathats in the same way as the Anglo-Indian courts had used the Hindu law books; but there are no schools of law, and the Dhammathats do not display the evolution and development to meet social and economic changes, which we find in the Hindu law books. If the Sastric law was an ideal law, not intended to be as rigidly applied as a statutory code of rules, that is even more true of the Dhammathat law. The judges of the Kingdom of Burma were not always learned in the Dhammathat law, and those who were did not always attempt to apply it. No development of the law by creating a body of precedents was contemplated.

As has already been said, the Buddhist religion had nothing to do with marriage, which was essentially secular and pragmatic. No ceremony was necessary; Burmans distinguish between a married couple and a couple who are cohabiting, though it is difficult to lay down the criteria on which the distinction is drawn. In 1930 Sir John Baguley, then a judge of the Rangoon High Court, defined Burmese marriage as cohabitation with a present common intention to create a valid marriage.[1] The definition is circular but I cannot find anything better.

As there are no formalities to marriage, so any marriage may be dissolved without formalities or the intervention of a court; the agreement of the parties is sufficient. But the decree of a court may be necessary for the partition of the property of the marriage, if not effected by agreement or unofficial arbitration. If the husband deserts the wife and does not maintain her for three years, or if the wife deserts the husband for a year and is not maintained, the deserted spouse acquires the right to put an end to the marriage; an approach to the court is not essential, but the deserted spouse must in some way manifest his or her decision,[2] and it may be necessary to invoke the jurisdiction of the court to partition the property of the marriage. Decisions of the courts are few and not uniform, but it would probably be correct to say that, if the desertion was without cause or combined with another matrimonial fault, the deserting spouse might be deprived of his or her interest in the property of the marriage; but, if there was some excuse for the desertion, the partition might be on the same basis as in a divorce by mutual consent. The intervention of the court is essential when a spouse claims a divorce for a matrimonial fault other than desertion and a claim for partition of the property of the marriage is usually joined. Adultery by the husband, even in the matrimonial home, is not a matrimonial fault.[3] Cruelty by the husband does constitute such a fault, although the Dhammathats give the husband the right to beat the wife; but it is the Anglo-Burmese courts could not recognize, as it is an offence under the

[1] *Ma Hla Ma v. Mg. Hla Baw* (1930), I.L.R. 8 Ran. 425.
[2] *Dr Tha Mya v. Daw Khin Pu* (1951), B.L.R. 108.
[3] *Ma Thein Nyun v. Maung Kha* (1929), I.L.R. 7 Ran. 451.

Penal Code. The Dhammathats also seem to regard only physical cruelty as actionable; but some Dhammathats provide that a husband who is guilty of ill-treatment may be required to enter into a bond not to repeat it and, if he declines to comply, the marriage will be dissolved on the basis that the husband is guilty of a matrimonial fault. If, on the other hand, he enters into the bond and then breaks it, the wife will be granted a divorce on the same basis as if it were a divorce by mutual consent. A rescript of King Bodawpaya in 1784 forbade any divorce to be granted on the first complaint of any matrimonial fault.

But the concept of cruelty in the Anglo-Burmese courts is not identical with that at present held in England. Sir John Baguley held that *mens rea* in the form of indifference to or delight in the other's pain was necessary,[1] a view subsequently accepted by Sir Mya Bu[2]—who also thought that what was sauce for the goose was sauce for the gander, though there is no case of a husband claiming a divorce on the grounds of cruelty on the part of the wife. The courts do not seem to restrict actionable cruelty to causing physical pain, for there is at least one case of a wife securing a decree against a husband who persistently made false accusations of adultery against her.[3] The courts have always shown reluctance to divest a guilty spouse of his property and, on a divorce for cruelty, the property will be divided as on a divorce by mutual consent, unless the husband has rejected the *locus poenitentiae* offered by the wife.

Most Dhammathats give the wife a right of divorce if the husband takes a second wife without her consent, but the Anglo-Burmese courts have been unwilling to enforce this rule on the ground that polygamy is recognized by law and practice. The judges, however, never felt very happy about their attitude and in 1918 a full bench of the Chief Court held that a husband could take a second wife without the consent of his first wife only in certain circumstances, set out in the Dhammathats in a different context,[4] such as when the first wife is barren, or bears daughters only, or does not conduct herself according to the rules of her class, or does not love her husband, or is leprous or insane. The practice of taking a second wife without any such excuse is not uncommon but the first wife usually accepts this as an occupational risk, so that there is very little case law on the subject. Though the Dhammathats provide that a husband who breaks this rule should forfeit his in-

---

[1] *Mg Kywe v. Ma Thein* (1929), I.L.R. 7 Ran. 790.

[2] *Daw Pu v. Mg Tun Kha* (1946), R.L.R. 125.

[3] *Mg Po Aung v. Ma Nyun* (1904), 10 L.B.R. 132.

[4] *Mg Hme v. Ma Sein* (1918), 9 L.B.R. 191.

terest in the property of the marriage, the courts order division of the
property as on a divorce by mutual consent.

The Dhammathats recognize the right of a wife, whose husband
dons the yellow robe without her consent, to remarry. Though some
say that the husband can revert to secular life seven times and reclaim
the wife, Manugye, recognized as the principal authority on the British
period, says she can remarry seven days after he enters the order. But
Buddhist males habitually make short retreats to the monasteries, so
that the courts have refused to recognize ordination as a ground for
divorce, unless undergone with intent permanently to renounce the
world.[1] Such ordination divests him of his property.[2]

I have now indicated that the method of distribution of the property
of the marriage on divorce may differ in the case of a divorce by
mutual consent, or deemed to be by mutual consent, from the method
used when the divorce is for a matrimonial fault. It also depends on
whether the spouses are in the *nissaya-nissita* relationship, i.e. one is
the supporter and the other the dependant; there is one law for the rich
and another for the poor spouse. It also depends on whether the
spouses have been previously married, in which case each may take
back the property brought to the marriage. But the courts have always
leaned, as I have indicated, in favour of a distribution as on a divorce by
mutual consent and have been reluctant to make a penal division.

My subject is the property of marriage, for which there is no Pali,
Sanskrit, or Burmese term of art; but there are terms of art to describe
the different categories of property comprising the property of the
marriage, the criteria of which are the source from, and method by,
which it was acquired. *Payin* or *atetpa* is what was brought to the
marriage by a spouse. If the spouses were not previously married, on a
divorce by mutual consent each takes one-third of the other's *payin*.

There are three kinds of *lettetpwa*, which is property acquired during
coverture. Inherited *lettetpwa* is what is inherited by a spouse during
marriage; on divorce by mutual consent each spouse takes one-third of
the *lettetpwa* inherited by the other.[3] Ordinary *lettetpwa* is acquired
during marriage by the individual exertions of one spouse; the other
spouse again gets one-third on a divorce by mutual consent. *Hnapazon*
is property acquired during marriage by the joint exertions of the
spouses; and on a divorce by mutual consent, this is equally divided.
Payin retains its character so long as it is identifiable; but it may be-

[1] *U Ohn Kin v. Daw Ohn Bwin* (1936), Civil 1st Appeal 156 of 1935.
[2] *Ma Pwe v. Mg Myat Tha*, 2 U.B.R. (1897–1901) 54.
[3] *U Pe v. U Maung Maung Kha* (1932), I.L.R. 10 Ran. 261.

come *lettetpwa* when dealt with by the spouses, as when husband and wife buy a house with their *payin*.

From these rules, derived from the Dhammathats, the Anglo-Burmese courts evolved the notion that each spouse had, during coverture, an interest in the property of the marriage equal to that he or she would have on partition on divorce by mutual consent—an interest which, to some extent, resembles the interest of a Hindu coparcener in the joint family property. This immediately raises the questions who is the manager, what are his powers of alienation and what powers of alienation the spouse who is not the manager may have. Most Dhammathats assert that the husband is the manager; but anyone with even a brief experience of Burma knows that the old grey mare is often the better horse, and that the supremely confident wife, conducting the family business in penny-wise fashion (while the husband does nothing in particular except enjoy an ill-founded local reputation as a philosopher, poet or alchemist), is a well-known figure in Burmese society. Were the courts to enforce a rule more honoured in the breach than in the observance? Though they are not too clear on the point, the Dhammathats seem to forbid either spouse to alienate *lettetpwa* without the consent of the other; similarly, a spouse may not alienate the *payin* of the other, but a previously married spouse may alienate his or her own *payin*, except to a concubine or paramour. There is an obvious inconsistency between these Dhammathat rules and the notion developed in the courts that each spouse has an interest in the *payin* of the other.

In 1874 the Special Court, consisting of the Recorder of Rangoon and the Judicial Commissioner, decided that neither spouse could alienate *hnapazon* without the consent of the other, that neither spouse could oust the other from possession, but that the husband held it in trust for both.[1] In a case decided in 1891 after prolonged enquiry into the custom followed, it was held that, when both spouses had mortgaged their joint property but the husband had subsequently given the mortgagee a bill of sale, this did not affect the wife's right of redemption; the husband had no power of alienation, unless he was acting as the wife's agent, which might be implied if he conducted the wife's business with the wife's consent.[2] Two years later it was held that only the husband's interest in the property of the marriage was liable to be taken to satisfy a decree against him alone.[3] In 1892 it was

[1] *Mg Ko v. Ma Me* (1874), S.J.L.B. 19.
[2] *Mg Thu v. Ma Bu* (1891), S.J.L.B. 578.
[3] *Ma Me v. Mg Gyi* (1893), 2 U.B.R. (1892–6) 45.

held that the spouses were tenants-in-common;[1] and in 1899 that the spouses were partners, and that an act of either, in pursuit of the family business, bound the other, except when immovables were alienated.[2] Though this exception may seem surprising at first sight, it is to be remembered that alienations of land to satisfy a debt were not generally permitted in the time of the Burmese kings and a debtor might be compelled to work off a debt by becoming his creditor's slave. Up to the end of the British period, judgment-debtors, whose land had been sold in execution of decrees against them, usually regarded themselves as still the owners of the land.

In 1905 the Chief Court, which had displaced the Judicial Commissioner in 1902, held that a sale by the husband of *hnapazon*, without the wife's consent, effectively transferred the husband's interest in the property;[3] but in 1927 the Judicial Committee approved the view that the spouses were partners.[4] In the same year *Ma Paing*'s case came before the High Court, which had supplanted the Chief Court in 1922. A Burmese husband and wife carried on a business, in the course of which they incurred heavy debts. The creditors sued the husband, got a decree and attached property of the marriage; but the wife got the attachment removed from her interest in the attached property. This property, less the wife's interest, was sold by court auction and the auction purchaser was put in possession. The wife then sued for a declaration that she had a half interest in the attached property and for possession, but the trial court dismissed the suit. She then appealed to the High Court and the question whether the property was partible was referred to a full bench, which held:

(1) Husband and wife are partners in respect of all kinds of property of the marriage.
(2) The partnership can only be dissolved by death or divorce.
(3) Until such dissolution, neither spouse is entitled to separate possession of any share of the property or profits of the partnership.
(4) If the husband's interest is sold in execution of a decree for a debt incurred during coverture in a business carried on while living with his wife, the buyer does not acquire the right to partition, he cannot obtain possession of that part of the property which represents his interest.

[1] *U Guna v. U Kyaw Gaung* (1892), 2 U.B.R. (1892–6) 204.
[2] *Mg Twe v. Raman Chetty* (1901), 1 L.B.R. 11.
[3] *Ma Shwe U v. Ma Kyu* (1905), 3 L.B.R. 66.
[4] *Ma Thaung v. Ma Than* (1927), 3 B.L.J. 333.

(5) Either spouse may represent the partnership when dealing with a third person and the presumption will ordinarily be that debts contracted by either bind the partnership and are recoverable out of the partnership property.

(6) A suit brought against a spouse is presumed to be a suit against the partnership; the spouse not joined is presumed to be represented by the other, so that a decree against either can be executed against the partnership property, provided that the decree was against the judgment-debtor as representing the partnership.[1]

The bench before which the appeal had first been opened, which included Sir Benjamin Heald, a strong partisan of the partnership doctrine, then held that Ma Paing's claim was not sustainable; the husband's share was impartible and his interest indeterminate, so that it was not such an asset as was liable to attachment and sale under the Code of Civil Procedure, 1908.[2] Though the auction had to be set aside, the decree holder was entitled to attach the whole property of the marriage and bring it to sale in execution of his decree.

But in 1931 a case came before the High Court in which the husband and wife had both been previously married; and the wife had incurred a debt before the subsisting marriage had been solemnized. She was sued after her second marriage by the creditor, who got a decree and in execution attached a house built during this marriage with funds brought to the marriage by the husband. After his objection to the attachment had been rejected, he sued for a declaration that the house, being joint property of the marriage, could not be taken to purge a pre-nuptial debt of the wife. This was successful. The creditor then appealed, and the bench hearing the appeal (which included the Chief Justice, Sir Arthur Page, to whom the partnership doctrine was anathema) referred to a special bench not only the question whether such an attachment was legal but also the question whether *Ma Paing*'s case was correctly decided. This was a noteworthy event. *Ma Paing*'s case, having been determined by a full bench, was a judgment of the court, not liable to be reversed except by the Judicial Committee; but when, as happened in this case, a special bench disapproved of a full bench decision, the latter was subsequently disregarded.

Obviously the particular attachment involved was unjust by any equitable standard, and one judge cited texts from Manugye to the

[1] *Ma Paing v. Mg Shew Hpaw* (1927), I.L.R. 5 Ran. 478.

[2] Under S. 60 of the Code of Civil Procedure, 1908, all property over which a judgment debtor has a disposing power which he can exercise for his own benefit is attachable.

effect that neither spouse could alienate the *payin* of the other and that the *payin* of each was liable to purge only that spouse's antenuptial debts. But the court agreed that *Ma Paing*'s case had been wrongly decided. Only the interest of a spouse in the joint property of the marriage could be attached and sold in execution of that spouse's antenuptial debt. It is not possible to execute a decree by attachment and sale of a spouse's interest in joint property, unless that spouse has been impleaded and is bound by the decree. The spouses hold as tenants in common, each having a vested interest liable to attachment and sale in execution of a decree against the spouse holding that interest. There is no analogy between a Burmese marriage and a business partnership; and there is no presumption that a Burmese spouse is the agent of the other spouse or that the wife consented to the acts of the husband.[1]

Sir Arthur Eggar, as he later became, was at this time Government Advocate. Though he did not appear in the case last cited, he was a member of the special committee to report on the Bill which became the Indian Partnership Act, 1932, and it was presumably his influence which caused the statute to state categorically that Burmese spouses were not partners. In the year 1932 the Judicial Committee held that, when a deserted wife made a gift of the property she had inherited from her father, it was good to the extent of her two-thirds interest and that the spouses were tenants in common.[2] There seems to have been no advance from this position since independence. In 1935 the High Court held that the spouses were tenants in common, that neither spouse could partition, that either spouse could dispose of his or her interest and that the interest of either party could be attached in execution of his or her judgment debt.[3] In another case in the same year it was held that the husband could not alienate property of the marriage, whether *payin* or *lettetpwa*, except with the wife's consent or when acting as her agent.[4] In a case decided in 1955, where the marriage had been solemnized in 1944, the husband bought a house in 1947 from the appellant; in 1949 he was captured by rebels and vanished; and in 1951 the wife sued for possession of the house, of which the appellant claimed to be in possession under a covenant for resale. It was held that she could not proceed without joining her husband, and that the trial court was wrong in awarding her a half.[5] In 1958 in a case in which the wife sold a house

[1] *N. A. V. R. Chettyar Firm v. Maung Than Daing* (1931), I.L.R. 9 Ran. 524.
[2] *U Pe v. U Maung Maung Kha* (1932), I.L.R. 10 Ran. 261.
[3] *Ma Ohn Kyi v. Daw Hnin Nwe*, B.L.R. 1953 H.C. 322.
[4] *Ma Htwe v. Ma Tun U*, B.L.R. 1953 H.C. 29.
[5] *Daw Sar Yi v. Ma Than Yi*, B.L.R. 1955 H.C. 44.

which was property of the marriage, with the knowledge and consent of the husband, it was held that the sale was binding on him.[1]

I have no information about the activities of the courts established by the present military régime but presumably a time will come when decisions are again reported and will form precedents for subsequent decisions. But it is not likely that the courts now operating will completely ignore the decisions I have mentioned.

I think it fairly obvious that, from the development of the law which I have outlined, satisfactory solutions of the problems raised have not yet emerged.

In the days of the Burmese kings no difficulty arose, for the Dhammathat law was an ideal law and there was no doctrine of precedent; an upright judge could make such order as he thought would do justice to the facts of each case. But the Anglo-Burmese courts had no such liberty. A text of a Dhammathat could be rejected as contrary to the custom or practice of the Burmese, or because it was opposed to public policy or conflicted with a statute; otherwise it had to be followed. It could be glossed, but the object was to establish by successive precedents rules from which a legal practitioner could predict with reasonable certainty what the judgment would be on a given set of facts. This perhaps was not the judicial system the Burmese wanted, for the young advocate's first step on the road to brieflessness was to advise a client that he had no case to put before a court. The Anglo-Burmese courts followed the practice of the Anglo-Indian courts, of which it used to be said that they had made the law rigid without removing its uncertainty; and the Anglo-Burmese courts had less time than the Anglo-Indian courts in which to create a coherent system. The Burmese law, applicable only to family and religious matters, was only a part of the law administered by the courts, most of which was statutory; and, in case of conflict, the Burmese law had to yield. This was especially true of the Code of Civil Procedure, which made liable to attachment anything over which the judgment-debtor had a power of disposal for his own benefit.

When the special bench rejected the doctrine of partnership between Burmese spouses, they said that the doctrine would preclude any business relations with a married Burman. If this is true, has there been any improvement in his position? A Burmese husband and wife commonly carry on business together. Now, if an outsider contracts with one spouse and subsequently seeks damages for breach, he can only proceed against the *interest* of that spouse in the property of the mar-

[1] *Daw Nyein Mya v. U Ba Ohn*, B.L.R. 1958 H.C. 248.

riage, unless he can establish agency; and the interest of the spouse with whom the contract was made may be negligible; it may have been already alienated. The person contracting with a Burmese spouse is, therefore, put on his enquiry about that spouse's interest in the property of the marriage. Today commerce cannot proceed unless A, dealing with B, can assume from B's position in life that B is likely to be able to pay such debts as he may incur to A without the danger of C claiming an overriding interest in the property against which A had a prima facie right of resort.

But I am not going to suggest that a reversion to the doctrine of partnership is desirable. The history of the property of the marriage in the Anglo-Burmese courts exhibits the danger of the practice of applying terms of art used in the common law to indigenous institutions having some resemblance to them. This was probably inevitable, since community of property is unknown to the common law and an English lawyer in Burma might doubt the wisdom of attempting the reconciliation of two different systems by borrowing notions from a third. But when Professor Lingat, who had been a judge of the capitulary court in Saigon, started collecting material for his *Régimes Matrimoniaux*, the essential similarity between the property of the Burmese marriage and the *communauté des biens* of France and other northern European countries struck him at once. Where this institution prevails, it is not sufficient that there should be unity of bodies or even of souls; no marriage is complete unless it results in community of gains accruing during coverture. Of course, marriage settlements are possible, and tycoons and intellectuals may prefer to have separate estates; but the average marriage contract modifies rather than extinguishes the ordinary rules governing the community. The Code Napoléon excluded immovables from the community, but at that time immovables were the most important form of wealth. Most settlements today exclude from the community all assets which each spouse acquired before marriage.

Under the Code the husband manages the wife's separate estate, which she can neither alienate nor charge. But an amendment of the law in 1907 placed the acquisitions of the wife, otherwise than in the household or in the course of the husband's business, in a reserved fund, over which she exercises powers of enjoyment and alienation for so long as the community continues. On its determination, the reserved fund is distributed with the community. A wife who enters into a contract binds herself, her husband and the community, unless the debt resulting was not contracted in the interest of the household or in the course of following her profession. The husband is liable for all debts incurred by the wife as his agent, and agency is presumed in transactions relating to the household. Since 1942 it has been possible for the husband to deprive the wife of her right to make him liable for debts incurred by her only where he has sufficient cause. Thus the husband and the community are not liable for debts incurred by the wife in pursuing a business or profession, if the husband has declared his opposition to her indulging in such activities; but since 1938 the wife may move the court to nullify the husband's objections, if they are not justified in the interests of the family. Amendments have also enabled the wife to dispose of her own assets, her husband's and the community, when this is necessary and the husband either cannot or will not do so. Nevertheless, banks are very cautious when dealing with a married woman's alienations, usually requiring strict proof that the asset involved is part of the wife's reserved fund or insisting on the husband's countersignature to the transaction.[1]

Now I do not think that, despite the comparative fragility of the Burmese marriage bond, the Burmese are less prone than the French to regard marriage as a union of property; but I think that the Dhamma-thats did not contemplate a social development resulting in an important minority of Burmans of both sexes following professional careers, for which community of property is not ideal. I also think that the power of the courts to develop the law governing the property of the marriage is exhausted and that it is time for the legislature to intervene. If I am told that now is hardly the time to amend the Burmese law of marriage, I would reply that in Pakistan considerable amendments have been made in the personal law of Muslims during the martial law period, and these are now, it seems, generally accepted. Obviously it is not for me to say what the law of Burma ought to be, and I only offer some suggestions as a basis for discussion. I think the right of the spouses to contract out of or modify the incidents of community might be recognized. I see no reason why the existing fractional interests of the spouses in the different kinds of property should not be retained; in particular, the rule that a previously married spouse should retain his or her *payin* intact is a good rule, for it protects the interests of the children of the previous marriage. I would vest management in the husband, who is, after all, always liable to maintain the wife; but I would make it possible for this power to be transferred to the wife by registered deed, and enable the wife to sue for the transfer of the right to her if the husband was incapable of management. I do not think it is necessary

[1] D. M. Aird, *Civil Laws of France*, pp. 151 seq.

to declare that, in particular transactions, the wife will be presumed to be agent of the husband as manager. I would vest in the husband a power of alienation of the property, other than the *payin* of a previously married spouse, to meet community debts or debts of either spouse; and I would allow a judgment-creditor to attach the undivided interest of a spouse in the property of the marriage. Generally I would retain the rules for distribution of the community on divorce by consent and either abolish the rules for a punitive division or restrict them to a few specified extreme cases. I would also abolish the *nissaya-nissita* rule, for which modern courts have shown little respect.

PART THREE

GENERAL

II

THE ECLIPSE OF THE PATRIARCHAL FAMILY
IN CONTEMPORARY ISLAMIC LAW

J. N. D. ANDERSON

*Professor of Oriental Laws, Director of the Institute of Advanced Legal Studies and
Dean of the Faculty of Laws in the University of London*

First, a word or two about the title of this chapter. I am painfully
aware that I have used the word 'patriarchal' in a vague and general,
rather than an exact and technical, sense—if, indeed, the term really
has any precise meaning. Sociologists speak, much more exactly, of a
system of inheritance which is 'patrilineal' or a system of marriage
which is 'patrilocal'. But in choosing the term 'patriarchal' I shall, like
Humpty Dumpty, make it mean precisely what I intend it to mean: in
other words, the type of family set-up which has been typical of Islamic
law throughout almost all the centuries of its development. And here I
refer not so much to the tribal system of the Arabs as to the characteristic family of Islamic history.

This family may, I think, be said to have the following features.
First, it was polygamous—at least potentially, and often actually—
with the Sunnīs, or orthodox Muslims, allowed to have up to four
legal wives at a time; with the Shī'īs allowed to have *mut'a*, or temporary, wives as well; and, in the past, with a considerable number of
families also including slave concubines. Secondly, these wives were
always threatened by the possibility of repudiation or divorce at the
unilateral discretion of their husbands, for any reason or for no
reason. It is true that Muslims agreed that to divorce a wife for an inadequate reason was sinful; but the divorce, if pronounced, was none
the less regarded as legally valid and binding. Thirdly, no similar
latitude was accorded to the wife, whether in the indulgence of poly-
andry or in any right to repudiate her husband. Add to this that a
duty of obedience in certain specified matters was owed by a wife to
her husband; that in case of disobedience the husband had the right, in
the last resort, to submit his wife to personal chastisement; and that if
the wife ran away he could bring an action for what we should call
restitution of conjugal rights—and, in a number of Muslim countries

at least, this would be executed by the police, who would march the wife back to the matrimonial home.

Then again, the guardianship of children always vested in the father. It is true that the mother, if divorced, normally had a right to the custody of very young children while they were dependent on a woman's care; but, even so, the actual right of guardianship vested in the father. When, therefore, the age of custody came to an end, he was entitled to demand that the mother should hand the child over to him, however fond she had become of him during the intervening years. Similarly, the father—or, if he were dead, the father's father (in most of the schools of law)—had the right of guardianship in marriage, by which he (and other guardians in the Ḥanafī system) had the right to contract their minor wards, whether male or female, in compulsory marriage—and this was extended, in some of the schools, to the giving of female wards in compulsory marriage up to almost any age, provided only that they had not been married previously. Even where there was no right of compulsion, moreover, a woman could, in most schools, contract a marriage only through the intervention of her marriage guardian; and even in the Ḥanafī system, which allowed an adult woman to give herself in marriage, the agnatic guardian had the right to object if she contracted a marriage with a man who was not her social equal, or for less than her customary dower.

Finally, in this same context, there was the special position in the law of inheritance of the agnates, or male relatives whose relationship to the deceased could be traced through males. This was the universal and sole system of inheritance, so far as we know, in pre-Islamic Arabia. It was radically modified by the Sunnīs as a result of the revelations of early Islam, but in their systems it still obtains. Thus, should a man be survived, say, by one daughter and a number of distant agnatic cousins, the daughter would take half his estate according to the text of the Qur'ān, but the remainder would go according to the pre-Islamic system to the nearest agnate, or tribal relative, however distant he might be.

Such, in broad outline, was the typical family structure and family law of the past. But much has changed in the last few decades, in almost all Muslim countries. And it is the purpose of this paper to give a panoramic view of the changes which have taken place.

First, let me deal with the marginally relevant subject of concubinage —for slave concubines were a fairly common component of the medieval ḥarīm. The law on this subject was that sex relations in Islam are lawful only between husband and wife and between master and his own female slave. Indeed, at the time of the enormous expansion of early Islam, a woman of any community which fought against the Muslims, whether she was married or not, might be taken by the victors as a slave concubine. This was one of the worst features of the Islamic conquests. Something rather similar has, moreover, occurred from time to time in those parts of Africa in which Muslims have indulged in slave raiding expeditions. But, for the most part, the slaves were either bought or born to that status.

Now today, self-evidently, all this is largely a thing of the past, for slavery has been abolished almost everywhere. All the same, relics of concubinage remain. To begin with, slavery was only very recently abolished in Saudi Arabia, although the slave trade was prohibited at a slightly earlier date. If, moreover, one goes to a country such as Northern Nigeria, where slavery was abolished years ago, one still in fact finds women who occupy the legal position of slave concubines. It is true that they are not slaves by civil status, for they could walk out, free, at any moment. But, because they are women who would have been the slaves of the man with whom they live, had slavery not been abolished, they are regarded by the religious courts as having the legal position of his slave concubines. Similarly, of course, if a man who would have been the owner of such a woman, had slavery not been abolished, were to 'give' such a woman to one of his friends, she would be regarded as his lawful slave concubine, however free she might be in the eyes of the civil law. And if one goes further afield—to the Gambia, for instance, where I have done some field work, and other parts of West Africa—one finds Muslim families where the husband may have many more than four wives, but would say, if questioned on the subject, that he had only three or four free wives, while the others were slave wives. In reality, of course, there is no provision in Islamic law for slave wives allowable to a man in addition to his maximum quota of legal wives; the only concession concerns slave concubines. What such a man means is that he has married one or more women of a rather lower social status, and that, in order to keep himself within the broad limits of what he imagines to be Islamic law, he regards them as having a different legal status, too. But here, in fact, Islamic law fades into customary law, and in other parts of the Gambia you will find quite pious Muslims, according to local reputation, openly keeping more than four wives without any distinction of status whatever.

So this question of concubinage is largely, though not entirely, today a thing of the past. But here I want to emphasize a very important phenomenon: that the virtual extinction of concubinage did not come about through any change in the essentially Islamic family law, but rather through the statutory abolition of slavery by the civil and criminal law. And this principle has been typical of many other reforms also. One could say, in fact, that law reform in the Muslim world in the last century or so has had three main phases. First, radical reforms were introduced in such subjects as commercial law, criminal law, and to some extent the law of obligations, by a series of legislative enactments; for in these matters Muslim Governments were prepared largely to abandon the Islamic law—as happened in the Ottoman Empire, in Egypt, and in a number of other countries—and substitute in its place a codified law of mainly Western inspiration. In the middle of the last century, indeed, this procedure, which might seem to many of us the most radical possible action for a Muslim Government to take, was not regarded at all in this light by many thoughtful Muslims. On the contrary, they preferred to retain the sacred law, intact and inviolate, as the law which they believed had once been fully applied, and would no doubt be applied again in the golden age to come, even if this meant putting it quietly on one side, in this workaday world, in favour of a different sort of law forced upon them by the exigencies of modern life. Such action was no doubt regrettable, but much better in their eyes than to allow any profane meddling with its immutable provisions. As a consequence, one finds a clear-cut dichotomy in the law of most Muslim countries from the middle of the last century; part was secular and codified, and part—the family law, broadly speaking—was still Islamic and uncodified.

The second of these three phases began in 1915, when the Ottoman Government felt itself compelled to introduce changes even within the sacred sphere of the Islamic family law. It was the miserable position of Ḥanafī wives which forced the first action in this context, but numerous reforms in family law have been promulgated in most Muslim countries in the last few years. Within this sphere of family relations, however, Muslims felt that there could be no wholesale substitution of some system of an alien inspiration in place of their own religious law. Instead, they insisted that the family law must remain distinctively Islamic—except, of course, in Turkey and among the Muslims of Cyprus. So they were faced with the major problem of how to change and reform a law which was regarded as divine and in some sense immutable.

This was in fact done, if I may outline it in the broadest terms, by one or more of four ingenious expedients. Sometimes it was effected by a procedural device, by which no pretensions whatever were made of changing the substantive law. Instead, orders were given to the courts that they were not to apply this law in specified circumstances. In other words, the law in its substance remained unaltered, but it would no longer be enforced by the national courts. The second device— and this was by far the most widely used expedient of reform—was an eclectic choice of suitable provisions, by which Muslim Governments refused any longer to be bound by the dominant view of any one school of law. Instead of being Ḥanafīs, Mālikīs, Shāfiʿīs or whatever it might be, they claimed to be merely Muslims; so they felt at liberty to pick and choose between all the *dicta* of the recognized jurists of the past, and to select those principles which seemed most in keeping with the needs of modern life. They even went to such lengths that they sometimes chose part of one opinion and part of another and put them together in a provision which was really new, although each component part could claim the most respectable ancestry.

The third expedient was the reinterpretation of the ancient texts. Where no recourse to traditional authority would avail them, then the reformers felt at liberty to go back to the ancient texts and to reinterpret them in a fashion more in accordance with what they believed to be the needs of contemporary life. And the fourth expedient was to introduce administrative regulations imposing the results reached by one or more of the other three devices. These regulations could, moreover, be given at least a semblance of Islamic authority by calling in aid the injunctions in the Qurʾān and the traditions which make it a duty for Muslims to obey their rulers. Such was the second phase in law reform.

The third phase, which is very much to the fore today, is for Muslims to say: 'Well, if we can go back to the original sources of our law and reinterpret them in the sphere of family law, why not in other spheres too? Why have a commercial law, or a criminal law, which is almost entirely of foreign inspiration? Why should we not, instead, reinterpret our own law, or apply it in a new way?' So codes are being brought into operation today which are partly of Western and partly of Islamic inspiration, and the sharp dichotomy between different parts of the law which came into being in the first phase of law reform is now tending to become much less clear-cut.

To return to my main subject. We have dealt with the question of slave concubines; but what about the relationship of husband and wife? As I have observed in passing, the first reform in the family law of Islam—and it took place in the Ottoman Empire—was to provide relief for two classes of unhappy wives. It was quite common at that time for Muslims to visit Istanbul from other parts of the world, to marry local women, and then at the end of their stay to sail away home sometimes without even bothering to divorce their wives; and these unfortunate women were left, for the rest of their lives, bound in marriage to a husband from whom they could get no maintenance or companionship or anything else, but from whom they could never get a judicial divorce. Similarly, women sometimes found themselves married, without their knowledge or consent, to men who were lepers or imbeciles.

It was comparatively easy to provide relief in such cases, for this was readily available in the Mālikī and the Ḥanbalī, and to some extent in the Shāfi'ī, schools. And today major reforms have been introduced in this matter almost all over the Muslim world, as a result of which a wife can nearly everywhere now get a judicial divorce if her husband fails to support her, if he treats her with cruelty, if he is afflicted with some disease which makes married life dangerous, or if he deserts her physically for more than a specified period. In Tunisia the reformers have gone a good deal further than this, and a wife can always insist on a divorce today if she is determined to do so, provided that she is prepared to pay her husband such financial compensation as the court may decree. And in Pakistan recently, the courts have followed an alleged tradition from the Prophet in granting a wife a divorce in return for financial consideration in circumstances of what might be termed temperamental incompatibility, where the wife insists on this sufficiently strongly. All this may appear to undermine the stability of marriage—and no doubt it does, from one point of view. But one needs to remember that what is sauce for the goose is sauce for the gander; and if the husband can repudiate his wife at any moment, for any reason or no reason, it may well be the first step in reform to make divorce equally easy for the wife.

It proved much harder, in one Muslim country after another, to restrict the ridiculously wide scope of validity previously given to formulae of repudiation pronounced by Muslim husbands, which formerly brought the marriage relationship to an abrupt end even where this was not really desired by either party. It was comparatively easy to deal with divorces pronounced under compulsion, intoxication, or such anger as to make the husband temporarily almost insane—although even these formulae of repudiation, strange to say, were valid and binding in the classical Ḥanafī law. It was considerably more difficult to invalidate divorces pronounced as an oath, a threat or an inducement. I have lived in the Arab world for a good many years, and it used to be very common, when buying a carpet, for the merchant to swear an oath of triple divorce that he himself bought it for twice its apparent value. In such cases he would usually be telling a lie; so his wretched wife—according to the law—would *ipso facto* become unlawful to him. Almost certainly the couple would in fact continue married life as before, since no one would take the matter to court; but the '*ulamā*', if consulted, would have decreed that they were living in adultery.

It was far from uncommon in most of these countries, moreover, for a husband who wished to discourage his wife, let us say, from buying any more jewellery, to pronounce a suspended divorce should she do so; and the divorce would at once become valid and binding as soon as the condition was fulfilled. But such a divorce is no longer effective, in Egypt, unless the husband really intended the marriage relationship to be ended in such circumstances. And suspended or conditional divorces have recently been declared to be invalid in Morocco and Iraq regardless of the husband's intentions. It was equally difficult to reduce the triple formulae ('I divorce you, I divorce you, I divorce you', or some such phrase), itself an innovation not dreamed of by the founder of Islam, to a single, and therefore revocable, divorce— but that, too, has been done in Egypt and nearly all the Arab countries.

It was even more difficult, of course, to go further than this; yet some attempts have been made. It was provided in Syria in 1953, for instance, that a man who divorces his wife without adequate reason, and in such circumstances as to cause her financial injury, should be forced by the court to pay her a sum of money by way of compensation; and similar provisions, but without reference to any specific financial detriment suffered by the wife, were included in the Tunisian law of 1957 and the Moroccan Code of 1958. This might, indeed, have proved a considerable safeguard were it not that, up to date, the amounts decreed have been miserably inadequate.

In Tunisia, in 1957, the daring step was taken of declaring that no divorce pronounced outside a court of law would have any legal validity whatever; instead, every divorce must be judicially decreed whether on the basis of mutual consent, on one of the grounds specified in the law, or on the insistence of either of the parties—in which case the court would decree that the party so insisting must make some financial compensation to the other. Similarly, in Pakistan, the Muslim Family Laws Ordinance, 1961, provided that no divorce, whatever formula had been pronounced—and this is a drastic departure from the classical law—would have any effect until ninety days after being reported to the President of the relevant Union Council. This interval—which was chosen, I suppose, because of its similarity to the 'idda period—was to provide an opportunity for an arbitration committee to attempt conciliation; and if this succeeded, then the divorce, whatever formula had been used, would fall to the ground. From the point of view of Muslim orthodoxy, this is a drastic expedient, but it still allows the husband to insist on divorce whenever he really wants to do so; and it would certainly have been possible to have provided a more effective safeguard for wives with less scandal to Muslim sentiments. In Singapore, under the Muslims Ordinance of 1957 (as amended in 1960), it is decreed that in default of mutual consent between the parties a divorce may be registered only by the Sharī'a Court itself; and here, too, conciliation will be attempted, regardless of the formula which was used. I have myself on several occasions met and conversed with the Muslim lady responsible for attempting conciliation in such circumstances, and there is no doubt that she has had a most astonishing measure of success.

We turn, next, to the problem of polygamy—the practice of which is still very common in some Muslim countries, including parts of Africa, although it is extremely rare in others, such as India, Pakistan, Tunisia and Egypt. The first attempt to tackle this problem was in the Ottoman Law of Family Rights, 1917, the introduction to which includes a most moving passage about the evils to which polygamy gives rise. But the reformers finally contented themselves in that law with providing that, if a wife stipulated in her marriage contract that she should be the only wife, this stipulation would be valid and binding—at least to the extent that should her husband, after accepting the stipulation, subsequently marry a second wife, the first wife would have the right to a judicial divorce. Previously, according to the Ḥanafī, the Mālikī, and the Shāfi'ī law, this was not the case; for all these schools take the view that the implications of marriage have been laid down by the divine Lawgiver, and cannot be varied by the unilateral decisions of the parties. If, therefore, a wife accepted a proposal of marriage only on the basis of a stipulation that she should never have a co-wife, or should be allowed to continue her practice as a doctor, or should never be submitted to personal chastisement, and if her husband married her on this condition, the law decreed that the marriage was valid and the stipulation void—so the husband could marry other wives, prevent his wife from continuing her career, or submit her to suitable chastisement, as he saw fit. But the Ḥanbalī jurists never took this view. They pointed out, very sensibly I think, that while Islam allowed polygamy, it had never made it incumbent on a Muslim to marry more than one wife; that while it allowed a husband to prevent his wife from going out to practise a profession, it did not make it incumbent upon him to do so; and that the same applied to corporal punishment. So there was nothing contrary to the essential nature of the marriage relationship in a stipulation of this sort; and if a husband voluntarily accepted such a stipulation, he should be bound thereby.

The second attempt to tackle polygamy was made in Egypt, in 1927, when the Egyptian Cabinet, following the suggestions of the great reformer Muhammad 'Abduh, accepted a draft law providing that a man who already had one wife should now be allowed to marry another woman without consent of court. The court, moreover, might refuse such permission if it was not satisfied that this particular husband was capable of treating two or more wives with equal justice, as provided in the verse of polygamy in the Qur'ān. This was certainly a step in the right direction, but seems to presuppose that judges have the gift of prophecy! The court might also refuse permission—and this was much more feasible—where it considered that this particular husband was not in a financial position to support his existing dependants and also assume further obligations. But this draft law was never promulgated in Egypt, owing to the opposition of King Fu'ād. It was not until 1953, and in the Syrian Law of Personal Status, that a provision was introduced making judicial permission for polygamy obligatory, and laying it down that such permission should be withheld in the absence of financial competence. Then, in 1957, President Bourguiba in Tunisia characteristically went the whole way, and completely prohibited polygamy. He justified this, moreover, on two quite different grounds. The first, which I suspect was his real reason, was that there were certain institutions, such as slavery and polygamy, which made sense at an earlier stage in human development, but which were offensive to most peoples' consciences today. But he also gave a second reason, which was much more acceptable to orthodox opinion, when he quoted the verse of polygamy in the Qur'ān as teaching that a man should not marry more than one wife if there was any fear that he would not treat them with equal justice, and when he observed that history had proved that no man other than a prophet was capable of such a feat!

The next development was in Morocco in 1958, where the reformers were considerably more cautious. First, they decreed that, if a wife stipulated in her first marriage that she should be the only wife, this would give her a right to divorce if her husband were to indulge in a polygamous marriage. Next, they included a general statement that, where any injustice was to be feared between co-wives, polygamy was not permitted; and they also provided that, where the first wife had not included any such stipulation in her marriage contract, she could still request a divorce if she was injured by her husband's second marriage—and that the contract with the second wife would not be valid at all unless she had been duly informed about the existence of the first marriage. In Iraq in 1959 the reformers went a little further still, but not so far as in Tunisia. They decreed that judicial permission must be obtained before a second wife was married, and that the court might refuse such permission where the husband lacked financial competence, where there was no lawful benefit in the second marriage (which I suppose was intended to cover such cases as the sterility or sickness of the first wife) and where there was any fear of injustice. Originally too, in Iraq, a polygamous marriage contracted in defiance of this rule was itself invalid. But since the new régime of 1963 came to power this last point has been changed—and it certainly represents a hotly debated problem among Muslims. There are, indeed, still penalties in Iraq for anyone who contracts a polygamous marriage in defiance of the regulations, but the marriage itself is now regarded as valid. Even in Tunisia this was a vexed point at the time of my last visit to that country, for there is no provision in the Code of Personal Status which specifies that such a marriage, though forbidden, is itself invalid. But President Bourguiba, when I discussed the matter with him, assured me that it would in fact be so regarded; and he pointed to the Civil Code, which says that any contract which is contrary to public policy is void, and argued that, since polygamy is expressly forbidden in the Code of Personal Status, any such contract must be considered contrary to public policy and therefore without effect.

In Pakistan, under the Muslim Family Laws Ordinance, 1961, a man who has one wife and wants to marry another must seek the consent of the Chairman of the local Union Council, who will set up an arbitration committee composed of himself, a representative of the husband, and a representative of the existing wife or wives, to consider the question. The decision will depend largely on whether the existing wife gives her consent; but not exclusively so, since it is provided that permission will be given where this is 'necessary and just'. A second marriage contracted without such permission is regarded as valid, but the full dower owed to the first wife is payable at once, a penalty will be imposed in the form of fine or imprisonment (or both), and the first wife has the right to a judicial divorce. In Singapore, again, the consent of the Chief Qāḍī has to be obtained before a polygamous marriage is contracted, and he has to assure himself that there is 'no lawful obstacle'. The law does not specify what these obstacles are, but I understand that permission is in fact seldom given—which is an outstanding example of law reform not by legislation, but by administrative action.

At this point I want to make a few more general observations. First, I think it would be true to say that the degradation of womanhood which Muslims themselves acknowledge to have taken place in a number of Muslim countries, and the acute suffering of many Muslim wives, has been due much more to the ease and frequency of divorce than to polygamy. In many Muslim countries today polygamy is not a major problem—partly for economic reasons, and partly because men have come to realize that a polygamous household is seldom happy. Divorce, on the other hand, is still appallingly common in some Muslim countries, though comparatively rare in countries like India and Pakistan. So the contemporary picture is not of a man indulging in simultaneous polygamy, but rather, in many countries, what may perhaps be termed 'successive polygamy'.

Secondly, it is obvious that to prohibit, or even severely restrict, polygamy, but without tackling divorce in an equally radical way, may do more harm than good from the point of view of Muslim wives. This happened, I believe, in Pakistan, where the regulations about polygamy were at one time so stiff that a middle-aged husband who was determined to marry a younger woman, but who would previously have kept his middle-aged wife as well, felt himself compelled, if he were to follow his inclinations, to divorce his first wife before marrying the second—which certainly did not help the older woman.

I must deal with the remaining points as briefly as I can. The duty of a wife to obey her husband in a number of specified respects remains wherever Islamic law is applied, so far as I know; but what about the right of personal chastisement? I have already stated that a wife may claim a judicial divorce in many Muslim countries today for cruelty; but the problem is where to draw the line between personal chastisement and cruelty. The formula used in Egypt, and I think elsewhere, is that a wife may claim a divorce for cruelty where she is subjected to such treatment as is intolerable to persons of her social status—which, significantly enough, represents a variable standard. As for the restitution of conjugal rights, this is very seldom today executed by force. A court decree will be given; then, if she refuses to go back to her husband, she will lose her right to maintenance, but no further action will be taken.

When we turn to the guardianship of children, there has, again, been little change—except in regard to guardianship in marriage. It is true that in Egypt, and one or two other places, the age up to which a mother is entitled to the custody of her child has been somewhat extended—from seven to nine in the case of a boy, and from nine to eleven in the case of a girl—where the court feels that this is advisable in terms of the welfare of the child. This is a very minor reform, particularly since the Mālikīs give the mother the right of custody for considerably longer, and the Shāfi'īs give the child the right to choose, after the age of seven, whether he or she will live with mother or father. The Shī'īs, on the other hand, grant a mother the right to the custody of a male baby only up to the time of weaning.

It is noteworthy in this context, perhaps, that in many parts of the world, and particularly where there has been any British legal tradition, a tendency is manifest today for the courts to take the welfare of the particular child into account in such cases, rather than follow rigid rules; and in some countries specific provision has been made by statute law on this subject, regardless of the religion of the parties concerned.

In regard to guardianship in marriage, on the other hand, much progress has been made. Very severe restrictions have been placed on child marriage, in one country after another. In Egypt this was done by a procedural device, which provided that, if a father gave his infant ward in marriage, that marriage could not be registered; and if the marriage was subsequenly disputed, the courts would be precluded from entertaining any matrimonial cause arising therefrom. This meant that the wife, for example, could enforce none of her rights, so fathers tended to abandon the practice of giving their infant daughters in marriage. In most countries, moreover, minimum ages for marriage have been laid down, to which only very limited exceptions are allowed. But not only has child marriage been virtually abandoned in most (though not yet all) Muslim countries, but the compulsory marriage of an adult, but previously unmarried, daughter has now been virtually forbidden in Morocco and the Sudan, where the Mālikī law previously allowed it, although it is still allowed in Singapore, where the Shāfi'ī law prevails.

Similarly, the guardian's right to intervene, even in the Ḥanafī law, if an adult woman contracts herself in marriage to a man who is not her 'equal', or for less than her 'proper' dower, has been considerably curtailed. Where she marries herself for an inadequate dower, the right to intervene is today almost dead; and where she marries herself to someone who is not her social equal, in most Arab countries the guardian's intervention, to be effective, must now be made before pregnancy is apparent—and in many countries, such as India, I believe the right of intervention on these grounds is virtually extinct.

A further development of deep significance concerns the special position of agnates in the Sunnī law of intestate succession. In this context a number of reforms have been effected during the last few years. In Tunisia, in 1959, the law was so changed that not only will a son or son's son—as before—exclude all brothers, sisters and more remote cognates from inheritance, but the same is also true of a daughter or a son's daughter—by a new and unorthodox extension of the doctrine of the 'return'. In Iraq, in the same year, the Islamic law of inheritance was completely abandoned, and the law previously applicable only to succession to government land (*arāḍī amīriyya*), which was based on German law, was extended to cover property of all descriptions. But after the *coup d'état* in 1963 this provision was repealed, and the basic essentials of the Shī'ī system were adopted, and made incumbent upon all Iraqis, whether Sunnīs or Shī'īs. This means that any child or grandchild, male or female, will exclude all cognates. In Pakistan, a revolutionary provision was included in the Muslim Family Laws Ordinance—designed, primarily, for quite a different purpose—that grandchildren by a predeceased son or daughter will have the right to 'represent' their dead parent; and this, too, sometimes has the effect of excluding cognates in favour of grandchildren. This problem of the disinherited grandchild has been dealt with rather more intelligently, perhaps, though much less drastically, in several of the Arab countries by a quite different device which is known as the doctrine of 'obligatory bequests'; but, however that may be, the tendency today is clearly to favour the basic family unit at the expense of tribal heirs.

I will conclude with a few final observations. First, I suppose, one inevitably asks oneself whence the impetus and the inspiration for these reforms originally came. Was it from within Islam, or from outside it? Initially, as it seems to me, the impetus and the inspiration came from outside—from Christian missions, and from the general impact of Western life and standards. But certainly this impulse from outside soon met a ready response from a number of Muslim reformers. Qāsim Amīn in Egypt, about the turn of the century, wrote a book in Arabic entitled *The Liberation of Women*; the great Egyptian reformer, Muḥammad 'Abduh, did much to help; and so did men like Ameer Ali in India. The arguments of these reformers were, of course, based on

Islamic sources, whether their original inspiration came from there or elsewhere. Sometimes they relied on an eclectic choice of opinions from among the doctrines of the past, as we have seen; sometimes on a reinterpretation, which might be more or less convincing, of the ancient texts; and sometimes they put their primary emphasis on the needs of contemporary life.

But the question remains: how far can such reforms go? They are appearing all round the Muslim world; and details could be quoted from one country after another. But can they go far enough? To this, I think, there is no ready answer. It depends, obviously, on how radical the reformers are prepared to be. With regard to polygamy, we have seen that the restrictions which have been imposed in several countries, and even its prohibition in Tunisia, have aroused comparatively little opposition. What is a much more vexed question is whether a polygamous marriage in defiance of these rules is itself valid or invalid. Public opinion seems to be generally prepared to accept the imposition of a penalty on one who transgresses government regulations in this matter; but many feel it to be contrary to their religion that such a marriage should itself be held null and void.

What, then, of divorce? There is a verse in the Qur'ān which says that, where discord is feared between spouses, the court should appoint arbitrators, one from the family of each, to try to reconcile their differences. So it has been suggested in some Muslim countries that legislation should be introduced penalizing a husband who divorces his wife without such recourse to a court as would enable it to bring this procedure into effect. Another suggestion which has been made— and, indeed, imposed in Tunisia—is that any repudiation outside a court of law should be refused all judicial recognition. Where, moreover, one party insists on divorce without just cause, then financial compensation, at a much more adequate rate than that accorded at present, might well be decreed. But the question remains whether the reformers are prepared to go so far as to refuse any right of divorce whatever except in specified circumstances.

The only other possibility, and with this I close, is that in some of these countries, with the unification of the courts and the increasing power of the bureaucracy, a civil law of marriage, divorce and inheritance will be promulgated, applicable to all citizens without distinction of religion. Obviously, there are many arguments in favour of such a development. But it seems to me most unlikely that this action will in fact be taken in the foreseeable future in most of the countries of which we have been thinking.

12

RELIGIOUS LAW AND THE MODERN
FAMILY IN ISRAEL

Z. W. FALK

Senior Lecturer in Jewish Law, Tel-Aviv University; Legal Adviser, Ministry of Interior; Fellow of the Hebrew University of Jerusalem

The object of this paper is to say something about the development of law in Israel, both in respect of religion and the modern family. However, my readers must not expect the description of a model system. We are as yet far from the ideal of Isaiah that 'out of Zion shall go forth the law'. On the contrary, I shall try to illustrate some of the confusion which is the inevitable result of the ingathering of the exiles and of the clash of their respective cultures. The difficulties seem to be insurmountable, yet they may in the end bring about a better understanding of the dynamics of the family and the machinery of the law. Thus the experience of a new State confronted by an old tradition is perhaps typical of the intellectual revolution taking place in all parts of the world.

Most of the difficulties which I am going to mention could be overcome by certain reforms in religious law and technique. Indeed, until quite recently many of my friends, and I myself, have been of the opinion that sooner or later this would be the solution. However, to this day any proposal of reform has been rejected by the rabbinical establishment while, on the other hand, anti-religious feeling is getting more and more militant.

Eventually, there will be no other way out than to introduce civil marriage and divorce, at least as an optional form in cases where the religious ceremony is not possible. This will go together with the abolition of the exclusive jurisdiction of religious courts in family matters and the adjudication of such cases by the civil courts. But while this solution may be satisfactory from the legal point of view, it will not take care of the uniqueness of Jewish tradition and the repercussions of a secularist Jewish state on the future of the Jewish people both in the diaspora and in Israel.

Let us first look at the legislative background of the present situation. Under the Ottoman rule of Palestine, jurisdiction in all matters was vested in the Muslim State Courts. However, according to the so-called 'Millet System', the various religious communities not professing Islam were granted autonomy in the administration of their institutions and in the adjudication of conflicts arising therefrom. The family, being guided by custom and religion, was included in the sphere of exclusive communal jurisdiction. Another limitation put upon the ordinary jurisdiction was the result of the so-called 'Capitulations', which provided for the special status of foreigners in matters of marriage and divorce.

The British Mandatory Government adopted the same policy. The privileges of the Jewish and Christian communities were confirmed, as was also the more favourable status of the muslim courts. But there were two conditions: each community was to create a court of appeal, to which lay a right of appeal from those of first instance. Matters of intestate succession, moreover, were exempted from the exclusive jurisdiction of the non-Muslim communities. Thus any heir disqualified under religious law, such as a woman under Jewish custom, was entitled to apply to the civil court for a succession order according to Ottoman law. This law was based on the German code and did not disqualify anybody on the ground of sex. The courts of the religious communities also started giving orders according to the civil law, so as to be able to compete with the civil courts. Thus, except for the extraordinary cases of common consent, the religious law here became practically defunct.

Jewish and Christian religious courts kept exclusive jurisdiction in matters of marriage and divorce, alimony, confirmation of wills and the administration of charities. Besides, these courts were entitled to deal with other questions where all parties concerned had agreed to their jurisdiction. While the activity of the religious courts was, thus, somewhat limited, the application of religious law was extended. Even the civil courts were to use the personal religious law of a party in all matters of his or her personal status, subject, of course, to any statute promulgated by the State.

The State of Israel, ruled for most of the time by a coalition government including the orthodox parties, followed this *modus*. Meanwhile, however, the legislator has sometimes overridden the religious law or restated it. Let us mention here the most important of these statutes.

Any disqualifications still existing on the basis of sex and any limitations attached to married women's property were abolished by the Women's Rights' Equalization Law, 1951. But this law did not purport to affect the rules of marriage and divorce. Thus, under the procedure of the rabbinical courts, a woman is still not considered competent to act as a witness at the marriage ceremony.

The death of absentees and victims of World War II may be declared by the civil court under the Death Declaration Law, 1952. Again, such a declaration is limited to matters of succession and is of no effect for the purpose of remarriage. Rabbinical courts, on the other hand, will not dissolve a marriage in absentia and will not give licence to remarry to a woman whose husband may be presumed to be dead.

Personal status is also affected by the Names' Law, 1956. This statute provides, *inter alia*, for the need of the father's consent where an unmarried mother wants to give the father's family name to the child. However, there is no such need where the mother is the father's 'reputed wife'.

The status of *de facto* marriages has been dealt with by Israeli legislation on various occasions. Since 1949 nine laws on pension rights have provided for equal rights of the reputed and the lawful wife. The same idea appears in the Estate Duty Laws, 1949 and 1964, the Tenants' Protection Law, 1955, and the Succession Law, 1965.

The fierce opposition of the orthodox parties in Parliament has left significant imprints on some of these laws. Twice the legislator gave rights to the surviving reputed wife, while the rest of the laws provided also for the surviving reputed husband. Once it was said that the reputed wife was entitled to a pension only if the deceased man had not been otherwise married at the time of his death. According to the other versions, the married wife has no priority. In three cases, including the recent Succession Law, 1965, the reputed wife is accorded rights only if she is not legally married to another person. The other laws do not make this a condition.

Most of the laws deal with pension rights and the question always arises what is the position of the lawful wife, if there is one? Is the State to pay twice or is the amount to be divided between both women? The recognition accorded to the reputed wife, obviously, affects the rights of the legal wife. Some of the statutes provide that the legal wife who has lived apart from her husband for a certain period should be considered as having been divorced. In other laws she loses her right only if she has wilfully deserted her husband or where she has lost the right of alimony.

The instability of legal policy in such a basic question is somewhat unsatisfactory. It reflects the polarity of opinion among the various political groups.

The Legal Capacity and Guardianship Law, 1962, defines the status of minors and insane persons, and the rights and duties of parents and guardians. One section is included on the equality of father and mother and the overriding 'benefit of the child'. Another section provides that the rules of marriage and divorce shall be unaffected.

According to both Jewish and Muslim tradition the age of marriage was rather low. This was a result of the patriarchal structure of society and served as a means to prevent pre-marital relations between the sexes. Nowadays, early marriage has been found convenient even among non-traditionalists to save a girl from army service or from undesirable influences.

In 1963, 12.5 per cent of Jewish brides and 24.1 per cent of non-Jewish brides in Israel were less than 17 years old. The average age of a Jewish bride in 1953 was 22.8, and in 1963, 21.9, and the average age of a non-Jewish bride only 20.6.

Against this tendency the Marriage Age Law, 1950, was enacted, raising the minimum age for women to 17. Marriage under age can be contracted only by special licence of the civil court. However, the law did not declare marriages contracted in contravention of its provisions to be void. It only imposed a penalty on the parties celebrating the marriage and it made the illegality a ground for divorce. A petition to this effect could be made by a social worker as well as by either of the spouses. But this provision remains a dead letter, for a rabbinical court, for instance, will not grant a divorce on this ground only.

The most important statute regarding the Jewish family is the Rabbinical Courts Jurisdiction (Marriage and Divorce) Law, 1953. It provides for the exclusive jurisdiction of Jewish religious courts in the matters mentioned, while actions for maintenance can be filed by the wife, according to her option, in the rabbinical or the civil court. Marriages between Israeli Jews must be celebrated in Israel according to talmudic law. Rabbinic judgments of divorce or release by the dead husband's brother can be enforced by imprisonment by way of contempt of court proceedings. But an order can be made only by the civil court on the application of the Attorney-General, not by the Rabbinical court itself.

The duty of relatives and in-laws to support a needy person is regulated by the Family Law Reform (Maintenance) Law, 1959. This is mainly to relieve the National Assistance authorities but not to define the obligations of the spouses towards each other. These obligations are still governed by religious law, as is the duty of support of one's minor children.

The prohibition of bigamy and the administration of rabbinical licences for remarriage of a husband were the object of the Criminal Law Reform (Polygamy) Law, 1959. Cases of real bigamy happen mainly among the Muslim population, while licences are given by rabbinical courts to husbands of insane or absent women where an ordinary divorce is not feasible. The same law also imposes a punishment upon anybody celebrating a marriage knowing that it was illegal or anybody effecting a divorce without prior court decision.

Adoption of minors was given legal status by the Children's Adoption Law, 1960. It is possible only where parents and child are of the same religion, it does not affect any impediment of marriage existing before the date of adoption and the court may limit the effect of the adoption order in other respects.

In the recent Succession Law, 1965, the rules of intestate and testate succession are codified. The traditional disqualification of Jewish women, who are merely supported from the estate, and the right of primogeniture, i.e. the double share of the firstborn, are applied only by mutual consent of all parties concerned. Otherwise the civil code is binding on religious as well as civil courts.

Finally, the Population Register Law, 1965, provides for the registration of personal data, including those governed by family law. But no formula for this function could be found in Parliament. The only guidance for the Registrar as to whether a person should be registered as married or not, or as to his religion, are administrative circulars issued by the Minister. We will mention a leading decision criticizing this state of affairs, but the position has not yet been changed.

Quite a considerable part of family law has, therefore, been codified by Parliament and the various statutes will eventually form a complete code. Meanwhile, however, the customary religious law is applied in the following matters: form and capacity of marriage (except for monogamy and minimum age), validity and annulment of marriage, rights and duties of spouses and parents, affiliation, and the causes, form and results of divorce.

Let us now make some remarks on the social background of marriage and of the discussion going on about the family law of Israel.

While the marriage rate of Israel is decreasing, it is still quite high. In 1951, there were about 114 marriages per 10,000 people and, in 1964, 77 marriages. The number of unmarried persons of marriageable age is therefore low. Out of 100 Jewish marriages contracted in 1963, in 82.5 both the bridegroom and the bride married for the first time, while in 17.5 per cent one or both spouses had already been divorced or widowed.

This is not only the result of the youthfulness of the immigrant population but also of Jewish tradition. Judaism is positive towards life and favours marriage and remarriage. Moreover, the incidence of marriage can be explained by the difficulty of living conditions and the loneliness of immigrants in a new country. People long for a home of their own, to be a castle against the adversities of life and to compensate them for the loss of other values.

An interesting process in favour of marriage may be recognized among those sections of society living in the collective settlements and generally among the immigrants of two generations ago. Until World War II, the average couple in left-wing circles would not bother to marry. Instead, they used to apply to the committee of the settlement for a room of their own and the allocation of such a room practically amounted to the status of marriage. This practice was an expression of the idea of 'free love' with emphasis on content rather than on form. This attitude was also favoured by collectivist ideology. Communal life was considered all-embracing and society was ill-disposed towards any particularist loyalty.

Nowadays, this practice and ideology are almost extinct. Members of collective settlements, as well as urban society, insist on the proper celebration of marriage. The choice of one's companion is becoming more and more an intellectual decision and everything is done to protect one's interest in the future. Nevertheless, beside the ordinary couple married according to law and tradition, there still exist a certain number of families, both in urban and rural districts, which do not have a marriage ceremony as a basis. These so-called 'de facto' marriages depend only on the criterion whether the couple are reputed husband and wife. Naturally, there are no statistical data available, but from a sample chosen these cases seem to be about 1 per cent of the population. The same sample shows that the phenomenon is more current among well-to-do people born in the country or who immigrated long ago than among the poor and newcomers. This furnishes an explanation why this status was recognized by Parliament. Many such cases were known personally to members and met with the latter's sympathy.

These then are the same circles who considered all marriage 'old fashioned'. They did not believe in the renunciation of love and happiness in favour of law, form and convention. Moreover, the law of compulsory religious marriage is not favoured by the secularist majority in Parliament. It is a burden to be borne in the interest of the coalition Government and out of piety towards the past. Wherever this law causes hardships, the majority of members, while not wishing to abolish it, at least show understanding for borderline cases. Finally, the question comes up mainly after the death of one of the spouses. At this stage the feeling of piety towards the deceased person's wish is an important factor. By treating the woman who had been living with the man as his widow, honour is given to his memory.

What are the reasons for an individual couple preferring this quasi-marriage to an ordinary one, though the former is not favoured even in modern society? The answer is that in almost all these cases an ordinary marriage under Jewish law could not be obtained. The woman may have been divorced on an adultery charge in which her present companion was co-respondent. One of the two may still be legally married to somebody else without being able to obtain a divorce. The man may be from a priestly family, while the reputed wife is divorced; or there may be other impediments making the desired union illegal.

Where the man and the woman do not wish to abide by the rabbinical decision, they can either celebrate the marriage outside Israel or put up with the status of *de facto* marriage. As long as they do not need an official document there will be little difficulty. But the right of support and other matrimonial rights will not arise from such a union. Rabbinical courts will dismiss any action, except for nullity proceedings, and so perhaps will the civil courts. On the other hand, the position of the children is not affected by the lawfulness of their parents' marriage. The Population Register does not recognize *de facto* marriages and no consequences arise from unions beside those expressly provided for in the above-mentioned laws.

The main opponents to the recognition by the law of this state of affairs are the orthodox parties. The question has become part of the 'kulturkampf' between religion and state. The rabbinical courts, while generally showing much understanding for cases of individual hardship, do not agree to legislative action. They consider these cases as mere contraventions against the law and do not see the necessity to give them any status at all. The secularists, on the other hand, have made these cases part of their argument for the separation of religion and state. They do not realize that legislation of this type is inconsistent with legal logic and public order. The recognition accorded to *de facto* marriages, in their view, will be a step towards the introduction of civil marriage. Meanwhile, it has rather become an expression of legal anarchy, which will not be cured by civil marriage.

There is a certain irony in the fact that talmudic law itself recognizes *de facto* marriages. According to the early sources, there was no need for the participation of a rabbi at the marriage ceremony. If the marriage formula was recited and the consideration given in the presence of witnesses, the vinculum was complete. Even if no ceremony had taken place, a reputed husband and wife were presumed to have undergone the ceremony at some date. This presumption existed only where there was no impediment preventing a legal marriage, because nobody was presumed to have broken the law. Meanwhile Jewish law has insisted on the participation of a rabbi to solemnize marriage, at least for guidance in the particulars of the ceremony. A person choosing *de facto* instead of religious marriage may nowadays be presumed to have done so on purpose. The lack of form could thus be construed as an indication of the intention of the parties not to create a legal marriage. Nevertheless, no rabbinical court would grant a decree of nullity on the ground that the ceremony had not taken place. Except for the case where marriage between the parties was impossible, as for instance if the woman is married to somebody else or if she is within the prohibited degrees, the court will not declare a *de facto* marriage void but will demand a divorce for the dissolution of the bond.

The secular faction, recognizing *de facto* marriage, therefore follow to a certain extent the ancient Jewish law. The orthodox, on the other hand, rely on the modern concept of 'public order' to justify their opposition to this recognition.

This brings us to the problem of the marriage ceremony, especially to the conflict between religious and civil marriage in Israel. In the Talmud, marriage is regarded as a civil contract creating, incidentally, a covenant relationship between the spouses and thus coming under the supervision of God. In post-exilic times the contract was introduced by a series of benedictions invoking the divine presence, describing the creation of mankind, referring to the idea of holiness and praying for the joy and success of the newly wed. There was no need for the presence of a competent person but only of two witnesses, and no licence was required.

In my study on 'Jewish Matrimonial Law in the Middle Ages' (Oxford, 1966) I have tried to show how Jewish marriage became more formal. Nowadays in Israel the ceremony must take place before a rabbi and, according to a recent regulation issued by the Chief Rabbinate, the rabbi must have been authorized by the Chief Rabbinate. All the same, a marriage solemnized by an unauthorized person in the presence of two witnesses would not be considered void or even voidable. A rabbinical court dealing with the validity of such a marriage would examine the religious reliability of the witnesses and the elements of the ceremony. Under no circumstances would the *clandestinum matrimonium* by itself be ground for annulment.

However, the Marriage and Divorce (Registration) Ordinance, 1919, one of the first enactments of the British Mandatory Government, brought a change in this field. All marriages and divorces performed by clergymen of the various denominations were to be registered with the District Commissioner. The Commissioner, on his part, did not supply the necessary forms for notification to all clergymen applying, but only to those who were authorized by their communities to perform marriages and divorces. Thus the ordinance indirectly came to regulate not only the procedural aspect of registration but also the material rules of the ceremonies. The powers of the person performing marriage and divorce were derived from his title as registrar, since little practical value attached to an unregistered marriage or divorce.

The power of the District Commissioner in this respect is now vested in the Minister of Religion, who has most of the time been a member of the orthodox party. Accordingly, the authority to perform marriages is reserved to those rabbis who are recognized by the Chief Rabbinate and to clergymen recognized by the heads of their communities. The forms of marriage certificates issued by the respective Registrars are printed and distributed by the Minister. Thus a couple married in private or before an unauthorized person will not get a certificate and the marriage will not be included in the Population Register until they can furnish a declaratory judgment to this effect.

Now in 1949 a man significantly named Aaron Cohen (Aaron, the Priest) wanted to marry a divorced woman and applied to the local Rabbinate. Since this was not allowed under biblical law and since his name was considered an indication of his priestly ancestry, his application was refused.

After two years' waiting the couple were married according to talmudic rite before their lawyer. Having advertised his intention in two newspapers, the lawyer on the fixed date performed the ceremony in the presence of witnesses and of a police officer who was going to charge him. He drew up a private 'certificate of marriage' and notified the Population Register of the change of status. The Registrar refused to register the marriage and the couple's petition for a declaratory judgment was dismissed. Thereupon the lawyer appealed to the Supreme Court and the appeal was allowed by a majority. These judges relied on the original character of Jewish marriage, while the minority took into account also the latest development of Jewish law, i.e. the regulation of the Chief Rabbinate. In their view, the appellants had violated these regulations and caused a public mischief, so that they should not be granted the equitable relief of a declaratory judgment.[1] The lawyer

---

[1] *Cohen v. Buslik*, C.A. 238/53, Pisqe Din Israeliim (Israel Law Reports, hereinafter abbreviated: PDI) viii (1954), 8–57.

was prosecuted and found guilty of causing public mischief and his appeal was set aside by the majority decision of the Supreme Court.[1]

The Rabbinical Courts Jurisdiction (Marriage and Divorce) Law, 1953, though expressly providing that Jewish marriages in Israel were to be celebrated according to rabbinic law, did not change the legal position. Though private marriages are against recent regulations, they are not void. Such a decision would certainly have been a novelty with regard to the traditional attitude but would have helped to enforce the recent regulations. The abuse of any such action on the part of the Rabbinate made further attempts to undermine the law possible and opened the door to continuous trouble.

Meanwhile, a group of intellectuals, left-wingers and extreme secularists had constituted themselves into a 'League against Religious Coercion'. Their object is the separation of religion and state and the introduction of civil marriage. Though having a small membership, the League made itself heard in public by means of a number of demonstrations and legal proceedings. The following cases were tested through the initiative and with the financial support of the League.

During the last few years various couples who were unable to marry under rabbinic law had gone for a visit to nearby Cyprus, had married before a civil authority and come back to Israel with a foreign marriage certificate. One of them was a Jewish Israeli man and a Christian woman of Belgian nationality. Having obtained the Cyprian certificate, the woman had her marriage entered into her Belgian passport. The couple then notified the Population Register and upon its refusal applied to the Supreme Court for an order of mandamus. A majority of the judges, making the order absolute, held that the Registrar of Population had no discretion in the discharge of his duty. Once an official document had been filed, he was not entitled to question its validity but was to register its contents.[2]

A year later a further attempt was made to introduce private marriage into Israeli law. A man had applied to the local Rabbinate for marriage with a divorced woman. He was asked to furnish proof that he was not of priestly parentage, but was found to be so. Upon the refusal of the Rabbinate, the marriage was celebrated by a lawyer and a private certificate of marriage was drawn up by him. The Registrar refused to register the marriage and the parties applied for an order of mandamus. The majority judgment of the Supreme Court revoked the order-

[1] *Ganor v. A.-G.*, Cr. A. 208/53, PDI viii (1954), 833–840.
[2] *Funk-Schlesinger v. Minister of Interior*, H.C. 143/62, PDI xviii (1963), 225–258; cf. Z. W. Falk, in HaPraqlit (Israel Bar Quarterly) xix (1963), 199–205.

nisi and referred the petitioners to the rabbinical court for a declaratory judgment. According to the Rabbinical Courts Jurisdiction (Marriage and Divorce) Law, 1953, this matter referring to Jews was within the exclusive jurisdiction of the rabbinical court. But the Supreme Court even at this stage expressed its sympathy with the petitioners. In an *obiter dictum*, the enforcement of the biblical rules of priesthood was said to be in conflict with liberty of conscience. On the other hand, the court put emphasis on the need for a public marriage ceremony and criticized the fact that the petitioners had taken the law into their own hands. The judgment also justified the refusal of the Population Register to register the marriage without an official document or declaratory judgment. The minority of the judges agreed to give the order forthwith.[1]

Next the couple applied to the rabbinical court for a declaration on the validity of the private marriage. The court refused, so as not to give support to an illegal act. However, the judgment included a clause that the parties were bound to divorce each other and that they could not remarry third persons until they had been divorced.[2] The couple then applied again to the Population Register, and this time the registration was made. This was actually against the intention of the rabbinical court, but the Minister of the Interior felt he could not follow their way of reasoning. If the spouses were asked to divorce each other and if they could not meanwhile marry another person, this was tantamount to a declaration of validity. Though the court had not wanted to deliver a declaratory judgment, it had in fact done so. Had the Minister followed the view of the rabbinical court, the applicants could easily have obtained an order of mandamus against him.

While in the above-mentioned cases the parties had resorted to private marriage after their application to the Rabbinate for a legal marriage had been refused, there followed a purely demonstrative private marriage without any such cause. In November 1964, twenty-five young couples celebrated private marriages in one of the collective settlements. None of them had ever applied to the rabbinical authorities and there did not exist any cause to prohibit these unions. The formula used on this occasion was the traditional one, except for the fact that no mention was made of the 'Law of Moses and Israel'. A petition to a civil court for a declaratory judgment was then filed by

[1] *Gurfinkel-Haqlai v. Minister of Interior*, H.C. 80/63, PDI xviii (1963), 2048–2072.

[2] 465/5724, *Pisqe Din shel Bate haDin HaRabaniim beIsrael* (Rabbinical Courts Law Reports) v (1964), 219–224.

the parties but it was rejected for lack of jurisdiction. During the same week the rabbinical judges of the country convened to decide on the line to be taken if an application should be filed in one of their courts. No such application was made, however, and no statement was made regarding the rabbinical attitude to these marriages.

Another attempt to obtain official recognition of private marriages was made under the provisions of the Names' Law, 1956. Two members of a collective settlement, married in private, gave notice to the Population Register of the woman's change of name. The Registrar asked whether that change was the result of marriage. Upon an affirmative reply, the registration was refused and the woman was required to furnish a declaratory judgment. She applied to the Supreme Court for an order of mandamus but failed to get the order.[1]

A later move was made by way of proxy. According to Jewish law, a betrothal may indeed take place through the act of a proxy representing bride or bridegroom, or even between two representatives only. This is not possible with regard to nuptials. On these grounds a couple filed with the Population Register a document drawn up in Mexico, witnessing a marriage contracted by way of proxy. The act had taken place between the two representatives in Mexico, while bride and bridegroom were both in Israel. The Registrar refused to make the registration and no further steps were taken in the matter.

During the last few weeks news has reached Israel that one of the Supreme Court judges of a priestly family married a divorced woman while on a visit to the United States. Public discussion is now going on as to how far a judge should be allowed to evade the law of the land or whether this is his private affair only. Thus the question of religious or civil marriage has come to a further climax just at this very moment.

The combination of a kind of religious 'common law' with the statutory law of the State sometimes causes difficulties. Talmudic law, like any other law, is based on an equilibrium of the rights and duties of the spouses. The husband is to maintain his wife according to his standard of living or according to the standard of her family, whichever is the higher one. As a consequence the husband is entitled to administer his wife's property and enjoys the usufruct.

When civil legislation intervened, the equilibrium was disturbed. The Woman's Rights Equalization Law, 1951, mentioned above, abolished the husband's right of usufruct. Henceforth a husband is not entitled to the rent or other income from his wife's property. However, even after the coming into effect of this Law, rabbinical courts took the

[1] *Stand v. Minister of Interior*, H.C. 71/65, PDI xix (1965), vol. 1, 501–502.

income into consideration when dealing with an action for maintenance. Such an action, they held, should be adjudicated according to the totality of talmudic law, including the possibility of a counterclaim by the husband. Therefore the husband was allowed to claim a set-off in the amount of the wife's income. The same view was held by a civil court, but on appeal the decision was reversed by a majority of the Supreme Court. It was held that the husband could neither claim the usufruct in a direct action nor bring it up by way of set-off in an action for maintenance. One of the judges upheld the view of the rabbinical courts and the civil court below. In his opinion, the new Law had repealed only the direct rule concerning married women's property, but not its reflection on the right of support. If the legislator disallowed the claim of set-off, he would enlarge thereby the husband's duty of support. In his view, there was no indication of such an intent.[1]

As a result of this decision, the wife has achieved not only equality of rights but is more favoured than the husband. The logical conclusion from this decision would have been the imposition of an obligation of support also on the wife of a needy husband. This could have been included in the Family Law Reform (Maintenance) Law, 1959. But no such step was taken, lest a husband should meet any claim of maintenance by a counterclaim. Thus, in order to prevent the misuse of such a provision, it was not adopted even for cases where it would be justified.

Let me now make some remarks on the law and practice of divorce. While the ideal of Jewish marriage is that of a permanent union, Jewish law does not insist on the maintenance of this union at all costs. A certain percentage of marriages have always come to an end by divorce, but in modern Jewish society the divorce rate is considerable. In 1951 there occurred among Israeli Jews 8.2 divorces against 100 marriages, in 1954 there were already 10.5 and five years later even 14.5 against 100 marriages. About 30 per cent of all married couples undergo a crisis at some stage and apply to the courts; but fortunately most of them do not reach the stage of divorce. The divorce rate of 1964 was again somewhat lower, viz. 12.3.

What are the causes for this increase in the breakdown of marriages? There is first the great change in moral values, the rising standard of living and the shortage of employment. Among the Oriental immigrants there is also the difficult transition from the patriarchal system to the industrialized-urbanized type of family. Poor housing and interference by relatives are further factors undermining marriage. Since

[1] *Balaban v. Balaban*, C.A. 313/59, PDI xiv (1960), 285–292.

people marry quite young, and often without adequate preparation or acquaintance with each other, there often follows a big disappointment leading to divorce. From the beginning, some consider marriage as a mere trial, which can be abandoned in case of failure.

The most common ground in divorce proceedings, in fact the one most favoured by the rabbinical courts, is mutual consent. True, according to talmudic law divorce was a unilateral act of the husband, with no participation by the wife or by a court. But during the Middle Ages the Jewish communities allowed divorce only by consent and sometimes even required a prior judgment or licence. Nowadays, therefore, both spouses must take part in the divorce proceedings and the court will force one or other of them only when there is a clear cause for such action according to talmudic sources. The husband especially cannot be compelled to deliver the writ of divorce, if the duty to do so is not expressly imposed upon him. Thus in cases of cruelty and desertion the wife will get a divorce under the circumstances codified in the sources but not in analogous cases. While sympathizing with the wife, the court will usually advise her to enter into negotiations, so that the ground for the divorce will eventually be consent. Unfortunately, this state of affairs often gives rise to extortion. The husband can withhold his consent until he gets consideration either in cash or by release of any claims which may be made against him.

A frequent cause of divorce is adultery by the wife. Once the court has been satisfied of this fact, or even where the fact can reasonably be inferred from the wife's behaviour, the order of divorce will be made without delay. Condonation is no bar in this case, for the husband is under a religious obligation to part from the unfaithful wife. There is, equally, no need for 'clean hands' on the part of the petitioner.

Impotence, mental defect or serious disease are grounds for divorce, especially if they existed before the marriage and were not disclosed to the petitioner. Where a marriage was contracted in violation of religious law or when after ten years the couple was still without child, each party is entitled to demand a divorce.

On the other hand, refusal of intercourse or of support, cruelty or illegal demands made by the respondent against the petitioner, are only qualified grounds for divorce. The petitioner must come to court with clean hands, he must not have condoned the act and the respondent must have been persistent in his behaviour. In these cases an action is usually brought for the restitution of conjugal rights or for maintenance and the court will grant a divorce only after a long period of litigation.

The main weakness of present-day divorce law in Israel is its enforcement. Marriage cannot be dissolved by a court decision but only by the delivery of a bill of divorce by the husband to the wife. Although the husband can no longer put away his wife at will, action by him is still needed after the court has made its decision. The wife's consent, likewise, is needed for the act, though its absence is not as fatal as that of the husband.

In most cases the court gives an order that the parties should be divorced but no provision is added for enforcement. Where the husband does not pay any attention to this kind of 'advice', he is ordered to pay alimony *in terrorem*. He can free himself from this obligation only by delivering the bill of divorce. According to the rules of execution, the husband can be put in prison for failing to pay maintenance or alimony. Where the wife is the one refusing the divorce in spite of the judgment, another course is taken. The court will give her warning that licence for remarriage will be issued to the husband without divorce, whereas the wife would remain unable to remarry.

However, the Supreme Court has ruled against both these practices. The rabbinical court was held to be unable to enforce its decision by imposing payments which were beyond the amount of alimony proper. Such a decision was declared *ultra vires* and the execution office was not to enforce it.[1] Similarly, it was held that the rabbinical court could use its power of licensing bigamy only in cases where Jewish divorce was technically impossible. Such cases are the wife's insanity or long absence. But no use should be made of this competence to compel a recalcitrant wife to receive a divorce.[2]

Thus there remains only the way of enforcement provided by the Rabbinical Courts (Marriage and Divorce) Law, 1953. According to this law, whenever a rabbinical court has made an order for compulsory divorce, the recalcitrant party may be imprisoned until he or she agrees to take part in the ceremony. But the order of imprisonment cannot be made by the rabbinical court itself. The interested party must apply to the Attorney-General who, if he thinks fit, files a petition in the civil court. Only if the court makes the order will the rabbinical judgment become effective. But even then there have been cases where a husband preferred prison to the delivery of the bill of divorce. The spouse and the court, in such cases, will just wait and see.

Moreover, execution can take place only where the rabbinical court

---

[1] *Rosenzweig v. Chief Execution Officer*, H.C. 54/55, PDI ix (1955), 1542–1560.
[2] *Streit v. Chief Rabbi and others*, H.C. 301/63, PDI xviii (1965), vol. 1, 598 ff; cf. Z. W. Falk, in HaPraqlit xxi (1965), 148.

has not only made an order for divorce, but included also a provision that the parties should be compelled to obey. We have already said that such a provision will be included only in the more serious cases, such as adultery of the wife, impotence or defects existing before the marriage, illegality of the marriage or childlessness. In cases of cruelty or desertion an order of compulsion will not, usually, be made. Therefore, some divorce petitions go on for years without coming to any practical result. The party desiring the divorce is finally compelled to buy his or her right from the respondent and to accede to exorbitant demands.

Sometimes even a clear compulsion order will be of no help to the party in whose favour it was given. In a case where the sole ground for the divorce had been childlessness, the Attorney-General refused to lend a hand in the enforcement. Thus he practically acted as if he was a court of appeal from the rabbinical court.

But the greatest difficulty lies in the Jewish concept of divorce. Since the act is executed by the spouses and not by the court, the rules of legal capacity apply to it. True, the husband of an insane wife can be granted a licence to remarry after having deposited the bill of divorce and the amount due to his wife. But no parallel arrangement is known where the husband is insane. The rabbinical court will look for lucid intervals to effect the divorce. Sometimes the proceedings even take place in an asylum and the court gives these cases its utmost care. But if a man is really insane, there can be no divorce, and his wife remains bound by the vinculum throughout his life. The same rule applies where the husband has deserted his wife or is absent for a long time. Nothing may have been heard of him for years, he may be presumed to have died, but as long as there is no positive evidence to that effect the wife cannot remarry.

Such a woman, as also a childless widow whose brother-in-law refuses to perform the ceremony of unshoeing or is insane or absent, is usually called 'angunah', i.e. a bound, imprisoned woman. The talmudic sources and present-day rabbinical courts show much understanding for her fate, they make efforts to trace the husband or brother-in-law, and they interpret the law rather leniently in favour of the woman. Nevertheless, there remain hard cases with no solution. We have seen that the husband in the opposite case can get a licence for remarriage. This is, of course, a residue of the original polygamous character of Jewish marriage and of its insistence on the faithfulness of the Jewish wife.

Another peculiarity of Jewish law lies in the position of the child. While no difference is made between children born in or out of wedlock, much emphasis is put on legitimacy in another sense. A child born of parents who are within the prohibited degrees, or of a married mother by adultery, is illegitimate. So is a child whose father is unknown. When coming of age these children will have difficulties in marrying into an ordinary Jewish family and there will be no way of legitimization. But these impediments are not as serious as those mentioned before and, once the child has married, the act is valid. Such a person registering his marriage will usually not disclose his blemish to the rabbi and the rabbi will not make particular inquiries about a possible illegitimacy.

There are hard cases where a child was born to a woman who had married his father after a civil divorce only. According to the view of rabbinical courts, no rule of Private International Law can validate a divorce which was not arranged under Jewish law. The woman is still regarded as the first husband's wife and her children are illegitimate. These cases are all the more unsatisfactory in a country of immigration like Israel.

A child born to a Jewish father and a non-Jewish mother is not Jewish while, in the opposite case, he or she is. The reason is the idea that there is no legal marriage between Jew and Gentile, so that the patriarchal system cannot apply. Now, there are in Israel quite a number of such persons feeling themselves to be Jewish although not born of a Jewish mother. The rabbis insist that they undergo the procedure of proselytism, but there is sometimes opposition on the part of the persons concerned. Here again, a conflict arises between religious law and the concept of everyday life of modern society.

Moreover, this system may cause a conflict of laws as to the status of such a person. Take, for instance, a child born in Israel to a Jewish mother and a Muslim father. Jewish religious courts will consider the child Jewish, while in the opinion of the Muslim qāḍī he or she is Muslim. The question is of far-reaching importance for jurisdiction, viz. which court is competent to decide on the status of such a person, and who is to perform his marriage or to decide on his divorce.

The administrative side of the question, i.e. how to register this person in the Population Register, has come up several times. It has caused at least one major Government crisis and is still unsettled by the civil law. While the present Minister of the Interior professes to act according to Jewish religious law, he has lately yielded to secularist demands. In two cases of children born to non-Jewish mothers the Supreme Court had given an order-nisi against the Minister as to why he should not have them registered as Jewish. In both cases the petitioners declared themselves Jewish and were of no other religion. The Minister thereupon agreed to register them according to their wishes, and the question on principle is, therefore, still unsettled.

Formal adoption and the consequential change in the child's status was not known in Jewish law. The Children's Adoption Law, 1960, therefore met with certain criticisms from the orthodox parties. Thus they did not agree to the total severance of links between the child and its natural parents, relying, as they did, on the commandment: 'Honour your father and mother'. As a compromise, a provision was included in the law that an adopted child coming of age was entitled to know the names of his or her natural parents. Moreover, the court making the adoption order is entitled to limit its effect, for instance with regard to name or registration.

According to Jewish law, the rules of consanguinity applying to the child prior to the adoption are not affected by that act. An adopted child is not, for example, allowed to marry his sister or aunt by the natural parents. How, then, was one to preserve the knowledge of the former status to prevent such a marriage? The law, therefore, safeguards the application of the rules of marriage and divorce. Any Registrar of Marriages is entitled to inspect the otherwise secret Adoption Register. Licence will be given to adopted persons only after the verification that the intended marriage is not within the prohibited degrees. In order to draw the attention of Registrars to the fact that an applicant is an adopted child, a hidden sign is included in the birth certificate.

We have spoken of the conflict of laws being the result of religious jurisdiction in family matters. Jewish law is, indeed, the personal law of the Jewish people, wherever they live. Rabbinical courts will decide on the validity of a marriage or divorce according to the Jewish rule only and will completely disregard the *lex loci contractus* or similar principles of Private International Law.

This means, for instance, that where one of the spouses is not Jewish the couple will not be deemed to be married even though their marriage had been contracted under the law of the land. On application the rabbinical court will give a decree of nullity and it will not hear any action of maintenance between the parties. But such an action can also be filed in a civil court and there the rules of Private International Law will be applied. Thus, a conflict of laws arises between the various courts of Israel.

But the situation is worse with regard to foreign divorces, as mentioned above. A satisfactory solution could be found only if the rabbinical court would not apply Jewish law to foreign marriages as well as divorces. If such a marriage could be held of no effect under rabbinical law, recognition could be given to the foreign divorce. As a matter of fact this was the rabbinic attitude when part of the Spanish marranos returned to the faith. Since they had not performed divorces according to Jewish law, there arose the question whether the children of divorced women from a second marriage should not be considered illegitimate. The view was then taken that the marriages were also celebrated according to foreign law and thus the divorce was adequate to the marriage.

But here we come to another peculiarity of rabbinical courts, especially during the last few generations. Whereas in other systems of law the judge is required to decide on questions of law in issue, this is not so in Jewish procedure. The concept of a divine law puts a great responsibility on the judge. Any mistake would be of far-reaching consequence for the judge himself. We have mentioned the tendency not to force a divorce on the husband except in entirely clear cases. This is part of the general tendency to refrain from action and decision in order to avoid mistakes. Therefore, although rabbinical courts do not recognize foreign marriages, they demand a Jewish divorce whenever a Jewish marriage could have been contracted between the parties.

Let me, finally, make some generalizations as to how a more satisfactory situation could be created. Any discussion *de lege ferenda* should start with a sociological study. Too often politicians and lawyers jump to conclusions without paying due attention to the facts. Reasoning should be based on the jurisprudence of interests rather than on dogmatic jurisprudence. Undesirable behaviour in the field of family relations is seldom prevented by legal rules. The legislator should always ask himself whether, by being strict on one point, he will not cause some laxity in another, and more important, direction. A considerable proportion of the community, if it does not agree to a certain rule, can prevent its enforcement. Therefore, education and public relations must precede actual legislation, and positive steps are more effective than prohibitive ones. There should be enough positive incentives to make a person refrain from illegal acts and, in any case, an undesirable act should not only be punishable but void.

I have tried to show some of the difficulties of the unique phenomenon called Israel. Here is a nation, living for three thousand years by virtue of its Law, most of the time under foreign rule. Now, when coming back to build an independent political structure, this same nation refuses to obey the Law. For in the meanwhile the civil emancipation of the Jews and their assimilation to the Western world have weakened their allegiance towards their past and their destiny.

Modern society is also less uniform than that foreseen by religious law. Secular man with his eudemonic attitude to life is not ready to abide by a theo-centric law. How can the Jewish State remain loyal to the past and still provide a common platform for all its citizens?

Let us hope together with Isaiah:

'And I will restore your judges as at first
and your councillors as at the beginning.
Afterwards you shall be called the city of
righteousness, the faithful city.'

13

CUSTOMARY FAMILY LAW IN SOUTHERN AFRICA: ITS PLACE AND SCOPE

NEVILLE RUBIN

Lecturer in African Law, School of Oriental and African Studies

Most of the problems with which this paper is concerned are revealed—albeit without any clear solution being offered—in the following exchange, which took place more than eighty years ago, at the hearings of the Cape Native Laws and Customs Commission, between Mr J. Ayliff and Sir Theophilus Shepstone:

'Private rights, or disputes between man and man, are distinct from their political and tribal relations; do you think we ought to legislate contrary to their customs, or in accordance with them, or why can't disputes between native and native be settled by laws based upon the principles of English or Roman-Dutch Jurisprudence?

'—I don't think there is much difference in the principles of these laws and the native laws under which disputes between natives are settled. The difficulty appears to be not in the principles of the law but in the application of them.'[1]

Few people today would agree with Shepstone's confident statement about the character of customary law, but it is not that which makes the exchange so interesting. Nor is it the fact that Shepstone—the author of the 'Natal system' of administration, and the great proponent of legal and administrative differentiations—chose to beg the question. What makes his reply so fascinating is that, more than forty years after the first attempts had been made to define the relations between customary law and the foreign legal system in Southern Africa, he was unwilling to opt for any of the choices with which he was presented by Commissioner Ayliff.

Yet the fact remains that the three basic approaches which were outlined in the question are still clearly to be seen as those which have dominated the thinking of successive governments in the countries of Southern Africa in their attitudes towards the customary law. Nowhere

[1] Cape of Good Hope, Native Laws and Customs Commission, 1883, p. 22.

has this been more clearly evident than in the ways in which the different aspects of customary family law have been dealt with— whether by legislation or by the courts. For the problem has not just arisen in relation to the degree of recognition which is (or has been) given to customary law as a whole; it has also been one of establishing the ways in which the customary rules of marriage and succession should be made to relate to the prevailing general law of Southern Africa—the Roman-Dutch law—over the years.

It would be much easier to deal with this subject if there had been anything like a uniform development of the laws which apply to both topics. But this has not been the case. Far from it. There has been an enormous amount of variation in the approach of the legislatures to the problems of customary family law. And, while it is still possible to say that the fluctuations in attitude have taken place within the basic frame-work of the three choices mentioned by Mr Ayliff, it would also be true to say that every possible permutation and combination of them has been tried, either within the same country or within the region as a whole. It goes without saying that it is not possible to describe—let alone do justice to—all of them within the compass of a relatively brief paper. All that will be attempted is a reference to the more prominent experiments which have taken place within the field, and to single out one or two of the remaining areas of difficulty or obscurity in present-day systems.

But even before I embark on this limited description, it may be of some use to offer a few general comments on the character of the region as a whole, the way in which I have defined it, and my reasons for doing so. It is not, strictly speaking, a unit, in any sense of the term— politically, legally or even geographically. I have taken it to refer to six countries in the southern part of Africa—Rhodesia, South West Africa, the Republic of South Africa, Basutoland (Lesotho), Swaziland and Bechuanaland (Botswana). The decision to do this was based partly on the ethnic similarity of the various tribes living in the area, and the similarity of the systems of customary law under which they live.[1] It was also guided, in part, by the fact that several of them share a number of tribes among their inhabitants. Thus there are substantial numbers of baTswana, baSotho and Swazi living in the Republic of South Africa, where their law is recognized and applied—though in different ways, subject to different rules, and in different circumstances from the way it is enforced in Lesotho, Botswana or Swaziland. Or, to

[1] e.g. the Zulu of Natal and the Ndebele (Matabele) of Rhodesia share a similar language and are of common ethnic origin.

take another example, both South West Africa and Botswana share Bushman (Khoi-khoin) minorities among their respective populations. But these were not the major considerations which dictated my choice. The decision to deal with these countries as if they were a unit stems basically from the degree to which their general legal systems derive from a common heritage.

In broad terms, this common stock of legal background arises in two ways; in the first place, the general law of each of the six countries is the Roman-Dutch law, as found in the principles enunciated by the writers of the early and later Roman Empires and of the Netherlands and received in the Cape Colony from the date of its colonization by Holland in the seventeenth century. Secondly, and more specifically, all of the other countries—and, indeed, Natal and the pre-Union South African Republics as well—derive their general law from the law which was in force in the Cape Colony at a specified date.[1] It would be out of place here to attempt a description of the subsequent history of the Roman-Dutch law in each of these countries, but it should be noted that the development of the general principles has been substantially similar in each, and has been greatly influenced by the fact that the decisions of the Appellate Division of the Supreme Court of South Africa have been either binding on them or at least of strong persuasive authority. Nevertheless, each country has produced its own system of law,[2] compounded if judicial decisions and exegesis as well as legislation; so that it would be untrue to say that they share the same laws, or even the same legal structure.[3] What they do have in common are certain fundamental legal principles—particularly, but by no means only, in the field of family law—drawn from the Roman-Dutch law.

[1] The relevant dates are:
Basutoland (Lesotho): February 2, 1884;
Bechuanaland (Botswana): June 10, 1891;
Swaziland: October 15, 1904.

[2] With the possible exception of South West Africa, which is much more dependent on South Africa for its legislation. Nevertheless, not all South African law applies in the territory—it has to be applied specifically and does not have automatic effect—and the decisions of the South West Africa Division of the South African Supreme Court, though subject to the overriding authority of the Appellate Division, has on occasion differed substantially in its interpretation of the Roman-Dutch law from that given in the other Divisions.

[3] Botswana, Lesotho and Swaziland have an entirely separate appeal structure from the other countries, culminating in appeals to the Judicial Committee of the Privy Council. See, generally, A. N. Allott (ed.) *Judicial and Legal Systems in Africa*, pp. 179–207. The position as regards Rhodesia is uncertain at the time of writing.

But, although this is the extent of their common legal system, it is not the limit of their common legal experience. And an important aspect of this experience has been the attitudes that have been adopted in dealing with customary law. It is to these which I now turn, with no more than a brief explanation of the fact that so much of the description which follows is concerned with South Africa.

The reason is that which has already been indicated—the extremes of diversity which are to be found in the approach of the various South African régimes to customary law. In relation to marriage these have been described, not without a touch of irony, by one writer in the following terms:

'South African legislatures, considered collectively, cannot be accused of indifference or inflexibility in their approach to African marriage. Almost all possible variations were tried out in different territories before Union; a single marriage system for all inhabitants; a marriage law for Whites alone; one law for Whites and for a selected group of Africans who had passed a test of "civilization"; a modified type of marriage with some of the consequences of customary unions; sequences of marriage; marriages and customary unions; a modified type of customary union with some of the consequences of marriage; marriages and customary unions existing side by side without modification and freely available to all Africans.'[1]

Yet, despite—or perhaps because of—their diversity, these systems of recognition (as well as those which have followed them) deserve attention; for they provide the basis, whether by design or otherwise, for those which function in the other countries. As will appear more fully below, moreover, each of them arose in relation to, or because of, problems in the field of marriage and succession.

The South African Colonies and Republic
It is not necessary to dwell at any length on the first 'system' of recognition which was introduced; for, although they were authorised by legislation in 1847 to recognize existing customary law, nothing was done by the British Colonial authorities at the Cape which took acount of particular problems of conflict between the general law and the customary law until 1864, when the Native Succession Act was introduced in the Colony. Until then, a general practice of giving effect to transactions at customary law was followed so long as there was no con-

[1] H. J. Simons, *Marriage and Succession among Africans*, in *Acta Juridica*, 1960, p. 314.

flict with the law of the Colony, and they were not held to be repugnant to 'morality' or 'public policy'. So far as marriage was concerned, the effect was that customary marriage was tolerated; but in the event of any marriage by an African under the general law, an existing customary marriage was automatically dissolved. The new Act did not alter the situation greatly, though it—and subsequent judicial interpretations of its provisions—raised an issue for the first time that has not yet been satisfactorily resolved. It gave limited recognition to customary marriages, by providing that the customary rules of intestate succession should apply to the estates of all Africans—no matter under which system they were married. In the case of Africans married under the Roman-Dutch law, however, the courts later modified the provision by holding that the general law had not entirely been ousted:[1] instead, it was held that a community of property between the spouses had been created, and that the surviving spouse of such a marriage was entitled to succeed to one-half of the joint estate, the other half only devolving according to customary rules of intestate succession. A slightly different approach was adopted in another area of the Cape Colony in the same year on the question of succession and that of the degree of recognition accorded, in that connection, to customary marriages.[2] The Native Succession Ordinance[3] explicitly recognized customary marriages for the purpose of succession, but provided a special rule in the case of a widow by a previous customary marriage which had been superseded by a Roman-Dutch law marriage: she and her issue were placed in the same position as the widow and issue of the Roman-Dutch law marriage. For the rest, customary law applied.

Thus far what has emerged from a consideration of the earliest Cape legislation is a dim awareness of the problems associated with the existence of a dualistic social and legal structure. But there are two other developments in the period which are also worthy of attention, since both reflect attempts to cope with a further set of related issues— though in very different ways. The first is the brief experiment attempted in 1887[4] to provide for the application of Roman-Dutch rules of succession to the exclusion of customary law, in the case of a limited number of categories of Africans, who may roughly be grouped

[1] H. J. Simons, *Marriage and Succession among Africans* in *Acta Juridica*, 1960, p. 315, for a description of the differing decisions leading up to this decision.
[2] *Xasa v. Xasa*, 7 E.D.C. 201; *Tutu v. Tutu*, 2 N.A.C. (1910) 167.
[3] This applied to British Kaffraria, an area which corresponds approximately to the present Ciskeian District of the Cape Province.
[4] Under the Native Registered Voters Relief Act.

as those who had been given a different status from the mass of the African population by virtue of education or the offices they had attained. This experiment—the extreme example of an assimilation policy in Southern Africa—did not last long. But the other—and opposite—trend was to be of far more lasting effect. It occurred in yet another area of the Cape Colony—the Transkei—and was introduced in a series of proclamations between 1879 and 1885.[1] The main features of this system were the following: it provided for the administration of customary law through a discretionary power given to magistrates to apply it in suits between Africans; it gave explicit recognition to customary marriages; further, it introduced a system of qualified registration of customary marriages by providing for the registration of only one such marriage (the first). The husband of such a marriage was not prohibited from entering into a subsequent marriage by customary law, but all questions of divorce, inheritance and guardianship which arose between the spouses of a registered customary marriage were determined by Roman-Dutch, and not customary, law.[2] Marriages under the Roman-Dutch law were still possible, of course; and they operated to dissolve any existing marriage under customary law, and were attended by the proprietary consequences of that system, i.e. community of property. This rule was later altered, so that community of property only resulted from a Roman-Dutch law marriage where the parties had specifically opted for that system—another rule that was to be followed widely in South Africa and elsewhere[3] in Southern Africa.

This, then, was the law—or the variety of differing legal provisions—which operated in the Cape Colony in relation to customary family law at the date of its reception into other countries of Southern Africa where the general legal system was based on that of the Cape.[4] It does not, however, exhaust the varieties of attitudes that existed, even prior to the establishment of the relevant rules in the Union (now Republic) of South Africa. Indeed, two important systems still need description—and again they represent opposing trends: those of the Colony of Natal

[1] Proclamations 110 of 1879; 112 of 1879; 140 of 1885.

[2] For the subsequent history of these provisions, see Simons, loc. cit., pp. 325–6. It is interesting to note that the proposal concerning the registration of a first marriage was revived in Ghana in the Marriage, Divorce and Succession Bill of 1961; and, more recently, in the Report of the Uganda Commission on Marriage, Divorce and the Status of Women, 1965.

[3] See the Swaziland Marriage Proclamation, 1964, and the Native Administration Act, No. 38 of 1927 (South Africa).

[4] i.e. Botswana, Lesotho, Rhodesia and South West Africa.

and the South African Republic (Zuid-Afrikaansche Republiek), now the South African province of the Transvaal. The more significant of the two—mainly because it still operates today—is that of Natal, whose system of legal and administrative differentiation (or segregation) is far too well known for it to need detailed treatment here.[1] It is, with justice, better known for its introduction of a codified system of law (based to a large extent—but by no means entirely—on the dominant customary law of the Colony, that of the Zulu nation)[2] than for its provisions in relation to those Africans who were permitted to marry under the Roman-Dutch law. The Natal system was the most thoroughgoing in its recognition of customary law. Indeed, it gave precedence, in regard to Africans, to the customary law, and legislation in 1849[3] provided that, subject to a 'repugnancy' clause,[4] custom would not be interfered with or abrogated; and, what is more, that so much of the Roman-Dutch law as was inconsistent with it, was repealed. Having thus established the primacy of customary law, it proceeded to make allowance for exemption from its operation in connection with marriage. In this respect its provisions were based on similar exemptions for what may be called an *assimilado* class as those which existed in the Cape from 1887 onwards: such Africans—and there were very few of them—were permitted to enter into a Christian marriage, solemnized by a minister specially licensed for the purpose, after an administrative officer had explained the implications to them, provided they signed a declaration to the effect that they understood what they were doing. Such Christian marriage did not, however, have the effect of removing the parties from the operation of customary law, which still applied to its proprietary consequences and to matters of succession. In terms of the legislation, neither party to such a marriage might enter into another marriage—customary or otherwise—during its subsistence and any such purported marriage would be both invalid and bigamous.

The Natal Code of Native Law applied, then, to all Africans living in

[1] For further material on this subject see E. H. Brookes, *A history of Native Policy in South Africa*; J. S. Marais, 'The imposition and nature of European control', in I. Schapera (ed.) *The Bantu-Speaking Tribes of South Africa*; W. G. Stafford, *Native Law as Practised in Natal*.

[2] First introduced in 1878 in the Colony, later revised in 1891, and reintroduced in further revised form by Proclamation in 1932 in terms of the Native Administration Act, No. 38 of 1927.

[3] Ordinance 3 of 1849.

[4] The phrase used, 'repugnant to the general principles of humanity recognized throughout the civilized world', was reproduced later in the Zuid-Afrikaansche Republiek.

Natal. Its main family law features were the following: (1) it defined the essentials of a customary marriage (namely, the consent of the father or guardian of the bride and, where necessary, the father or guardian of the husband, and a declaration by the bride in public to an 'official witness' at the marriage ceremony that the marriage was contracted of her free will and with her consent); (2) the marriage would not be valid unless all these essentials were complied with; (3) customary marriages were registrable, though this was permissive and not obligatory;[1] (4) a maximum number of cattle (or their equivalent in money) was fixed for marriage consideration;[2] and (5) a specific procedure was provided and grounds specified for divorce from a customary marriage. In addition, the Code makes detailed provision concerning the personal status of persons subject to it, and on the topic of inheritance.

The record of the Zuid Afrikaansche Republiek in regard to customary law stands in stark contrast to that of Natal. Indeed, it hardly involved recognition at all—either of customary marriages or of marriages by Africans. Its first marriage legislation applied only to white persons.[3] This was followed, five years later, by legislation which specifically outlawed both polygyny and marriage consideration.[4] Although the pre-Code Natal provisions were introduced during a brief British interregnum, they were later abolished; and provision was only made for the marriage of Africans in 1897, by a special procedure, under the Roman-Dutch law. Questions of divorce were to be dealt with by a separate court (staffed by the Superintendent of Natives), and questions of succession to the estates of Africans married in terms of the law were governed by the Roman-Dutch law exclusively. The Zuid-Afrikaansche Republiek system—if indeed so attenuated a set if rules can be so called—has been mentioned for three reasons: first, out of a desire to offer a comprehensive, if brief, survey of the main patterns of attitudes to customary law in pre-independence Southern Africa; secondly (and of rather more practical importance), because this law was that received in Swaziland as the foundation of its general legal system; and, thirdly, because it provides the most complete example of the dismissal of customary law in any legal system in Southern Africa. It has, for this reason, been termed a policy of 'assimilation'.[5] It could be, and is, with equal justice described as a policy of legal intolerance.

---

[1] The duty of recording the details concerning the marriage falls on an 'official witness' (Sec. 65).

[2] Sec. 87.

[3] Law 3 of 1871.

[4] Law 3 of 1876.

[5] Simons, loc. cit., p. 320.

The Contemporary Systems and the Place of Customary Law
None of the systems so far described applies today in full—not even in
South Africa. To complete the picture, it is necessary to look at both
the legislation and decisions of the courts in South Africa and in the
other countries concerned.

The South African legal system today recognizes the primacy of the
Roman-Dutch legal rules. It does, however, also provide for the application of customary law, through the provisions of the Native Administration Act.[1] The Act lays down a number of specific rules concerning
questions of status and succession and it provided the basis for the re-
introduction of the Natal Code by Proclamation in 1932; but, for the
most part, customary law has been introduced by a hierarchy of separp-
ate courts which the Act established, and which are staffed by officers of
the Department of Bantu Administration and Development (formerly
known as the Native Affairs Department).[2] It is these courts—and in
particular the Bantu Commissioners' Courts, whose jurisdiction is confined to civil matters—which are empowered to apply customary law in
terms of the following provision:

> 'Notwithstanding the provisions of any other law, it shall be in the
> discretion of the courts of Bantu Affairs Commissioners in all suits
> or proceedings between natives involving question of customs
> followed by natives, to decide such questions according to the native
> law applying to such customs except in so far as it shall have been
> repealed or modified: Provided that such native law shall not be
> opposed to the principles of public policy or natural justice. . . .'[3]

The application of customary law is thus restricted in a number of ways:
(1) it may be applied only in suits or proceedings between Africans;
(2) it may be applied where such suits involve 'customs followed by
natives' only to the extent that these have not been repealed or modified;
(3) it may be applied only where it is not repugnant to principles of
natural justice or public policy; and (4)—most important of all—the
question as to whether or not it is applied at all is a matter for the discretion of the court. It is the last matter which deserves attention here,
since it is unique in the legal systems of Africa, in that it permits either
the general (Roman-Dutch) law or the customary law to be applied in a
particular matter. Although it is generally true that the discretionary

[1] Act 38 of 1927, as amended.
[2] It also coined the term 'customary union' for a customary marriage, reserving
the term 'marriage' for the Roman-Dutch law institution.
[3] Sec. 11(1), Act 38 of 1927.

power of the court must be exercised in a judicial manner, it has been remarked—by a judge of the South African Appellate Division—that the responsibility involved is 'greater than that generally borne by courts of law'.[1] Nevertheless, it is this provision which has resulted in the development of the greater part of the customary law as enforced by the courts. Thus the courts have established the essentials of a customary marriage—rather differently from those which operate in Natal under the Code, e.g. by making marriage consideration an essential element—and the procedure for dissolution of customary marriages, as well as those concerning guardianship and the duties of a family head.[2] It should be noted that, when applying customary law, the Bantu Affairs Commissioners' courts do not require this law to be proved, though they may call for evidence as to the existence of a particular rule if they wish to do so. In the Supreme Court—which does not have original jurisdiction in respect of customary law, but may hear appeals by special leave of the Bantu Appeal Courts, or grant such leave itself—customary law, on the other hand, must be proved. The system described above applies throughout South Africa at present, but may be substantially altered as a result of recent legislation relating to the Transkei, which postulates the creation of a separate Division of the South African Supreme Court for that area, and provides, in addition, for the mandatory application, 'so far as is practicable', of customary law in 'all suits and proceedings involving or based on questions of Bantu custom'.[3] That this involves a radical departure from the system which operates in the remainder of the Republic will be evident from the fact that it permits the application of customary law as a matter of course by the High Court; makes its application mandatory rather than discretionary; and applies to all suits which merely 'involve' customary law.[4] But the provision as a whole has yet to be put into effect.

In the other countries of Southern Africa, the place of customary law within the general legal system has also been regulated by statute. In none of them has the South African system of discretionary application of customary law been reproduced. In most cases, indeed, the relevant rules were contained in early proclamations, were introduced shortly after annexation by Britain, and were later supplemented by

[1] Schreiner, J. A., in *Ex Parte Minister of Native Affairs* in re *Yako v. Beyi*, 1948 (1) S.A.L.R. (A.D.) at p. 399.

[2] For the details of these provisions, see S. M. Seymour, *Native Law in South Africa*, Chapters IV–VII, IX.

[3] Sec. 50(1) and 50(2)(b) of the Transkei Constitution Act, 1963.

[4] It would also appear to apply to criminal cases, though this is not relevant to the topic under discussion.

legislation concerned with the establishment of a separate system of customary courts.

The most elaborate provisions concerning the recognition of customary law in any of these countries are to be found in Rhodesia, and are set out in the Native Law and Courts Act of 1937, now Chapter 73 of the Laws of Southern Rhodesia. This Act, which establishes a separate system of Native Courts, defines 'native law and custom' as follows:[1]

' "native law and custom" means, in relation to a particular tribe, the general law and custom of such tribe, except in so far as such law or custom is repugnant to natural justice or morality or to the provisions of any statute law from time to time in force in the Colony:

'Provided that nothing in the statute law of the Colony relating to the age of majority, the status of women, the effect of marriage on the property of spouses, the guardianship of children or the administration of deceased estates shall affect the application of native law and custom except in so far as such statute law has been specifically applied to natives by statute.'

The effect of this proviso is to save a great deal of customary law from inroads by the Roman-Dutch or general law of Rhodesia, though two limitations are imposed on the scope of customary law by the definition: namely, the two aspects of the repugnancy clause, those dealing with statute law and 'natural justice and morality', respectively.[2] Section three of the Chapter, moreover, goes on to limit the application of customary law to suits involving Africans only.

The repugnancy clause has been widely used by the courts to limit the application of customary law, though it has been held that it 'should only apply to such customs as inherently impress us with some abhorrence or are obviously immoral in their incidence',[3] and to any custom which 'so outrages accepted standards as to create a sense of revulsion'.[4] The phrase has not been separated into its components, but has been used as a whole. It has, however, served to abolish a number of rules of customary law, such as those concerned with slavery,[5] and impotence as a ground for divorce at the instance of a wife.[6] It has also been used

[1] Sec. 2, Chapter 73, of the Laws of Southern Rhodesia.
[2] The phrase derives from earlier statutory provisions. See C. Palley, *The Constitutional History and Law of Southern Rhodesia*, pp. 504 et. seq.
[3] *Tabitha Chiduku v. Chidaro*, 1922 S.R. 55; *Vela v. Mandinika* and *Maguba*, 1936 S.R. 171.
[4] *Matiyenga and Mamire v. Chinamura and Others*, 1958 S.R.N. 553.
[5] *Mabigwa v. Matibini*, 1946 S.R.N. 117.
[6] *Rex v. Mchenji and Chargwi*, 1917 S.R. 69.

to alter the customary law of divorce, as a whole, through a decision that it would not be granted in the absence of 'just reason' for it between the spouses.[1] This has resulted in the abolition of divorce by consent or by unilateral repudiation under customary law. Since no specific grounds exist for divorce under customary law, another set of rules—those which justify the return of marriage consideration, or part of it—have been adapted by the courts for the purpose.[2]

No elaboration of the provision limiting the application of customary law to Africans alone is required, though mention should be made of Section 12 of the Act, which provides a procedure for the granting of certificates of exemption to Africans by the Government. The effect of the provision is that an exempted African is, 'for the purposes of this Act only, deemed to be not a native', which means that customary law is not applicable to him, though he may still fall within the provisions of other legislation relating to Africans.[3]

In general, the customary legal rules applied in the separate system of courts established under the Act are found—as they are in South Africa—in the previous decisions of the courts, through the evidence of assessors, or through writings on customary law. The Presiding Officers may also make use of their own knowledge of customary law. In the other courts which may be seized of customary law matters—on appeal by special leave, that is—assessors do not sit with the Judge, who is not normally able to take advantage of his own knowledge of customary law. The other methods of ascertainment of the customary law, however, are the same.

Rhodesia also has elaborate legislative provisions within the field of customary family law, which are contained in the 1950 Native Marriage Act and subsequent amendments to it in 1962. Thus rules are provided concerning the consent required of parties to a customary marriage, their competence to give evidence against one another, and the dissolution of marriage. There are also provisions concerning the need to register customary marriages, which are invalid unless registered— though not absolutely but only for the purpose of the customary law of succession, guardianship, and status; while an earlier provision rendering the contract for marriage consideration void in such circumstances was repealed in 1962. Frequent attempts have been made to establish a maximum for marriage consideration, the most recent being that of

[1] *Naomi and Chrimi v. Magara*, 1953 S.R.N. 331.
[2] e.g. desertion; adultery by a wife; barrenness of a wife; impotence of a husband; cruelty.
[3] e.g. Statutes relating to Native Marriages and Native Wills.

1950, but the 1962 Amending Act repealed these provisions as well.

The three other countries I propose to deal with under this topic— Lesotho, Botswana and Swaziland—do not differ greatly from those already described in regard to the provisions which deal generally with the recognition and application of customary civil law. Though the precise wording of the statutes differs,[1] each allows for the general recognition of customary law subject to a 'repugnancy' clause; and each provides for a separate hierarchy of customary courts, though the jurisdiction of the Superior Courts is not excluded in this regard.[2] The precise wording of the statutes leaves some uncertainty as to whether it is obligatory for customary law to be applied in all suits between Africans, but there seems to be little doubt that it is in fact applied in all such cases. A brief investigation of the (very few) reported cases on the customary law has not disclosed any major use of the repugnancy clause to oust the application of customary law. What the cases do reveal, however, is the very substantial reliance which is placed by the Superior Courts on the written material relating to the customary law, at least in the case of Lesotho and Botswana. In the former, a great deal of weight is attached to the rules which are embodied in the Laws of Lerotholi, a non-statutory code of *baSotho* law which, though by no means comprehensive, has achieved near-legislative authority; while, in

[1] The Swaziland and Botswana provisions are somewhat broader than those of Lesotho. The relevant provisions are:

Lesotho:
'The native law and custom prevailing in the Territory, so far as it is not repugnant to justice and morality or inconsistent with the provisions of any law in force in the Territory.' (Sec. 9(a), Native Courts Proclamation.)

Botswana:
'The High Commissioner in issuing such Proclamations shall respect any native laws or customs by which the relations of any native chiefs, tribes or populations under Her Majesty's protection are now regulated, except so far as the same may be incompatible with the due exercise of Her Majesty's power and jurisdiction.' (Sec. 4, General Administration Order in Council, 1891.)

Swaziland:
'Sec. 5 of the Swaziland Order in Council, 1903, contains identical wording to that used in Botswana.'

[2] The Superior Courts throughout Southern Africa may, however, be effectively made considerably less accessible by the application of the rule that costs will be awarded to the successful party on the lower scale appropriate to the courts of Bantu Affairs Commissioners. See L. I. Rubin, *The Law of Costs in South Africa*, pp. 163 *et. seq.*

the latter, the courts have been able to draw on the voluminous writings of Professor I. Schapera.[1] The evidence of witnesses, and of assessors, is also relied upon by the courts.

Given this outline of the place of customary law within the framework of the general law of Southern African countries, it remains for me to deal with a few of the problem areas within the field of the dualistic legal systems I have described. These arise for a variety of reasons, and concern the nature and details of the customary law to be applied. But they occur mainly because of the legislative enactments creating concurrent régimes in the field of marriage and succession (and, to a lesser extent, in regard to personal status); and because inadequate attention has been paid to areas of actual or potential conflict between them. Not all of the problems occur in each of the countries, but most of them arise in at least one of them. All that I can hope to do within the compass of the present paper is to indicate the nature of a few of them, and illustrate one or two with examples from particular countries.

One of the continuing areas of obscurity is that of the rules governing choice of law, as between different sets of customary law rules. There are no such rules prescribed by statute for Lesotho, Botswana or Swaziland; and, though the problems associated with this facet of conflict of laws are less likely to arise in the case of these largely mono-ethnic countries, this remains a serious gap—which is presumably to be filled by reference to the Roman-Dutch law on the subject. A similar, though not identical, situation obtains in Rhodesia, where the only provision on the subject is contained in Section 4(2) of Chapter 73, to the following effect:

'Where the parties to a civil case between Africans reside in areas where different African laws and customs are in operation, the African law and custom, if any, to be applied by the court shall be that prevailing in the place of residence of the defendant.'

This rudimentary rule is almost identical with that formerly in operation in the Transkei,[2] and has given rise to considerable difficulty in the Rhodesian courts, particularly in regard to cases involving members of tribes whose marriage rules differ, e.g. as between those which require marriage consideration and those which do not, which in turn gives

[1] e.g. *A Handbook of Tswana Law and Custom; Native Land Tenure in the Bechuanaland Protectorate; Married Life in an African Tribe;* and a large number of articles in various journals.

[2] In terms of Sec. 22 of Cape Colony Proclamation 140 of 1885.

rise to questions concerning the guardianship and custody of children on dissolution of marriage.[1]

A slightly less monistic approach to the subject is taken in South Africa, in terms of Section 11(2) of the Native Administration Act, which reads:

'In any suits or proceedings between natives who do not belong to the same tribe, the court shall not, in the absence of any agreement between them with regard to the particular system of Native law to be applied in such suit or proceedings, apply any system of Native law other than that which is in operation at the place where the defendant or respondent resides or carries on business or is employed, or if two or more systems are in operation at that place, not being within a tribal area, the Court shall not apply any such system unless it is the law of the tribe (if any), to which the defendant or respondent belongs.'

This section clearly relies heavily on the law of the defendant (which may be ascertained in a number of ways, principally from his place of residence), but it does at least make provision for the exclusion of the rules by agreement, and it does attempt to deal with what it terms 'non-tribal areas' as well as with a number of very limited avenues for the non-application of a system of customary law with which the parties are unfamiliar. But the rules are hardly free from obscurity, and could well do with elaboration and improvement.

Turning now to the substantive areas of conflict between the two prevailing systems of law, a few examples from the laws of marriage and succession should suffice to indicate the nature of the problem. Although the rule is not always explicit, as it is in South Africa in terms of the Native Administration Act,[2] a marriage in terms of the Roman-Dutch law takes precedence over a customary law marriage in all the countries of Southern Africa. It will normally dissolve or nullify an existing customary marriage, sometimes even where the two marriages are between the same persons (as is the case in Rhodesia[3]).[4] So much for the validity of customary marriages; but the question still

[1] See G. R. J. Hackwill, 'Southern Rhodesian Native Law: Conflict of Laws in relation to the guardianship of children after divorce' in *Rhodesia and Nyasaland Law Journal*, March 1961, and cases cited therein.

[2] The exclusion is contained in the definition of a customary union.

[3] *Rex v. Mshingura*, 1932 S.R. 67.

[4] But not in Swaziland—see the proviso to Sec. 7(1) of the Swaziland Marriage Proclamation, 1964, which specifically permits the marriage under the general law of persons already married under customary law.

remains whether the offence of bigamy exists in relation to such marriages. Here, as in so many cases, the law is obscure in most of these countries and the question has not arisen for decision in clear-cut form. In South Africa it seems certain that no such offence is committed; in Rhodesia—since the passage of an amendment in 1962[1] to the Native Marriage Act—the position is the same; though in both, and in Swaziland,[2] any subsequent marriage by customary law of parties married under the Roman-Dutch law does involve the commission of the offence.

Of greater interest—because less certainty prevails—are the problems arising from the conflicting legal rules of the two systems relating to the personal and proprietary consequences of marriage. An example of the former arises in cases where a suit brought under the Roman-Dutch law (because the parties are not all Africans, for instance) requires the rights of a party under the customary law to be established before a decision can be reached. Thus both South African and Rhodesian Courts have disallowed claims by a widow of a customary marriage against a White tortfeasor who caused the death of her husband—either because she has no claim at customary law for maintenance, or because the general law does not recognize the validity of the customary marriage and its consequences.[3] The matter has not come up for decision in any of the other countries.

The conflicting legal rules concerning the proprietary consequences of marriage offer a more serious set of problems. These arise primarily as a result of the institution of community of property and of profit and loss which result from the Roman-Dutch law of marriage, unless they are excluded by an ante-nuptial contract (though this is not the case in Rhodesia, where legislation provides for the opposite position; namely, that marriages are out of community of property in the absence of an ante-nuptial contract opting for community).[4] During the subsistence of a marriage in community of property, all property brought into the marriage by the parties, and acquired subsequently by

---

[1] Sec. 3, Act 2 of 1962.

[2] Sec. 7, read with Sec. 22, of the Swaziland Marriage Proclamation.

[3] See *S.A.N.T.A.M. v. Fondo*, 1960 (2) S.A.L.R. 467; *ex Parte Seti and others*, 1963 R. & N. 681. The anomaly whereby such an action was allowed by the Native Appeal Courts in South Africa (i.e. against an African tortfeasor) though it was not available against a White person under the general law has been removed by legislation (the Bantu Laws Amendment Act of 1963). There has been no such remedial legislation in Rhodesia.

[4] The Married Persons Property Act, Chapter 178, of the Laws of Southern Rhodesia.

them, forms a joint estate under the control of the husband. On the death of either party or dissolution of the marriage, one-half descends to the surviving spouse and the other half may be disposed of by will or by the rules of intestate succession. Clearly such an institution would make considerable inroads into the customary law of matrimonial property and succession. But it does not apply to all African marriages under the Roman-Dutch law, either in South Africa or in Rhodesia. In Rhodesia it is now well-established that the rights of intestate succession to all marriages by Africans are governed by customary law,[1] at least so far as movables are concerned.[2] As regards immovables, however, the Roman-Dutch law applies,[3] both *stante matrimomio* and on termination of the marriage, the marriage being treated as if it were out of community of property. It is therefore possible for a woman married under the Roman-Dutch law in Rhodesia to acquire separate property during the subsistence of her marriage. While this is probably not the case either in Lesotho or Botswana, a similar situation obtains both in South Africa and in Swaziland, at any rate so far as the rights of the parties during the subsistence of the marriage are concerned. The position in South Africa is governed by the terms of Section 22(6) of the Native Administration Act, which excludes the operation of community of property in the case of Africans married under the general law, but provides that they may choose to execute a contract prior to the marriage which applies such law to them.[4] Swaziland has recently enacted a provision with almost identical effect,[5] though the position is considerably complicated here by a failure to amend the provisions of

[1] *Vela v. Mandinika and Magutsa*, 1936 S.R. 171, and the provisions of the Native Law and Courts Act, Chapter 73.

[2] Section 14, Native Marriage Act, Chapter 79.

[3] *Komo and Leboho v. Holmes, N. O.*, 1936 S.R. 86, and *Dokotera v. The Master of the High Court*, 1957 R. & N., 697 (S.R.).

[4] The section reads: 'A marriage between Natives, contracted after the commencement of this Act, shall not produce the legal consequences of marriages in community of property between the spouses: Provided that in the case of a marriage contracted otherwise than during the subsistence of a customary union between the husband and any woman other than the wife it shall be competent for the intending spouses at any time within one month previous to the celebration of such marriage to declare jointly before any magistrate, native commissioner or marriage officer (who is hereby authorized to attest such declaration) that it is their intention and desire that community of property and of profit and loss shall result from their marriage, and thereupon such community shall result from their marriage except as regards any land in a location held under quitrent tenure such land shall be excluded from such a community.'

[5] Section 25 of the Swaziland Marriage Proclamation, 1964.

the Administration of Estates Act to bring it into line with this legislation. The result is that the Intestate Succession Proclamation applies to the estates of nearly all Africans—however married—and defeats the object of the legislation, by permitting a widow to succeed to the extent of £600 or one-half of the estate of her husband (whichever is the greater).[1]

These are but a few of the anomalies which arise within the field of customary family law in Southern Africa. No doubt they are capable of solution, either through the courts or by legislation. The same could be said of a large number of the others which have been alluded to, albeit briefly, in this paper. Far too often they have been ignored or allowed to multiply, so that confusion has been further confounded. Worse still, there has been unsystematic and haphazard borrowing by one group of legislators of provisions enacted elsewhere, which either do not solve the problems, or solve them inadequately—or even add to them.

It seems clear that there is a great deal of scope for further action, both by governments and outside bodies, designed to clarify and improve the rules which govern the shape and the scope of customary family law within the framework of the general Roman-Dutch law of Southern Africa. Specifically, there is a great need for further endeavour to ascertain the precise nature of the rules of customary law. Here the work of the Restatement of African Law Project of the School of Oriental and African Studies has already been of help in some of the countries; but more remains to be done. Similarly, there is a great need for the development of a more satisfactory system of integrated courts for the administration of the laws, and for the development of a coherent and comprehensive set of rules governing conflicts and choice of law. And there is certainly a need for the removal of some of the glaring anomalies that exist in the present dualistic legal structures of all the Southern African countries. Above all, there is a very strong case to be argued for the harmonization of the different (and differing) legal régimes, not only in order to avoid the unfortunate consequences of repeating one another's mistakes and experiments, but in order to draw more fully and more fruitfully on the common Roman-Dutch and customary legal traditions which they share.

[1] For a more detailed discussion of these provisions see N. N. Rubin, 'The Swazi Law of Succession: A Restatement' in *Journal of African Law*, Vol. 9, No. 2, pp. 94–6.

14

THE PERSONAL LAW OF THE PARSIS OF INDIA

PHIROZE K. IRANI

Lecturer in Indian and Pakistan Law, School of Oriental and African Studies

Though it governs probably the smallest group of people in the world, Parsi law is not without interest to the comparative lawyer. Unlike the great systems of Hindu and Islamic law that have flourished on the Indian sub-continent, Parsi law has no religious source. It is largely based on Hindu customary law and rules of the English common law compatible with Parsi circumstances. Its significance lies in the successful adoption of systems of personal law intended for people of different religions and cultures.

1. *Introduction*

The first Parsi immigrants came to India from Persia at the end of the seventh century to escape religious persecution by the Arab conquerors of that country.[1] They came largely from a Persian province called 'Pers' or 'Pars' (which gave the name 'Persia' to the whole country) from whence the name 'Parsi' is derived. The Parsi immigrants belonged to the same Aryan stock as the inhabitants of Northern India and cultural and trade contracts existed between the two races long before the Parsi migration to India. Darius Hystaspes, one of the greatest of Persian kings (521–485 BC), ruled an empire that included the Punjab and the whole Indus valley in India.

The first permanent Parsi settlement in India was established about the year 716[2] at a village called Sanjan (which is still in existence), which was then ruled by a Hindu chief called Jadi Rana, who gave the Parsis permission to reside on four conditions. These conditions were that the Parsis would adopt the language of the country, that they would not bear arms except at the behest of the ruler, that their women

[1] For the history of the Parsis in India, see D. F. Karaka, *History of the Parsis* (Vol. 1 & 2, 1884); D. Menant, *Les Parsis* (English ed. by M. M. Murzban, Vol. 1 & 2, 1917); S. K. Hodivala, *Parsis of Ancient India* (1920).

[2] There is some controversy about this date but this is the generally accepted one. See Karaka, op. cit. supra, Vol. 1, p. 30.

would dress in the Hindu fashion and that they would perform their marriage ceremonies after sunset in accordance with Hindu custom.[1] The Parsis have always scrupulously observed these conditions and have been influenced by them to adopt other Hindu customs.

The Parsis brought the oldest of extant religions with them to India —that of Zoroastrianism. The life and teachings of Zoroaster[2] are shrouded in legend as most of the historical records were destroyed during the Arab invasion of Persia. Estimates of the period during which Zoroaster lived and preached in Persia vary from 6,000 BC to 583 BC[3] but it is generally accepted by the Parsis that he founded his creed at least 1,300 years before Christ.[4] At one time, Zoroastrianism was the religion of the whole of Persia but its practice is now restricted to about 150,000 Parsis scattered all over the globe. It is founded on belief in one God and on the basic tenets of 'good thoughts, good words and good deeds'.[5] Though conversion is permitted and even enjoined by the Zoroastrian religion, the Parsis in India have never attempted proselytism out of respect for their Hindu hosts and it has been judicially accepted that conversion to the Zoroastrian religion is against the custom and usage of the Parsis in India.[6] A convert from Zoroastrianism ceases to be recognized as a Parsi, though his racial origin is unchanged, as the terms 'Parsi' and 'Zoroastrian' have traditionally been regarded as synonymous by the Parsis in India.

The first wave of emigration from Persia was followed by several others and emigration still goes on in a very small measure. For centuries after their first arrival in India the Parsis mainly followed the

[1] Karaka, op. cit. supra, Vol. 1, p. 34.
[2] The name Zoroaster is the Greek form of the old Persian Zarathushtra.
[3] See A. V. Williams Jackson, *Zoroaster: The Prophet of Ancient Iran* (1899), pp. 14–16. The wide disparity in dates is partly due to the fact that there were at least six philosophers at different periods in Ancient Persia who bore the name of Zoroaster, and scholars are in some doubt as to which of these was the Prophet Zoroaster.
[4] See Karaka, op. cit. supra, note 1, v. 2, pp. 147–9.
[5] The main tenets of the religion are to be found in 15 couplets or 'shlokas' believed to have been recited by the Parsi high priest to Jadi Rana. For an English translation of these couplets, see Menant, op. cit. supra, note 1, v. 1, pp. 90 to 100. Zoroaster's precepts are noted in hymns called *Gathas*, some of which are believed to have been composed by the Prophet himself. For a discussion of the tenets of the Zoroastrian religion, see I. Taraporweala, *The Religion of Zarathustra* (1926); R. Masani, *The Religion of the Good Life: Zoroastrianism* (1938); M. N. Dhalla, *History of Zorostrianism* (1938).
[6] *Sir Dinshaw M. Petit v. Sir Jamsetji Jijibhai* (1909), 11 Bom. L.R. 85; *Saklat v. Bella* (1925), 53 I.A. 42.

pursuit of agriculture. When the European powers established trading companies in India, the Parsis set themselves up as brokers to these companies but their real progress and prosperity came with the growth of Bombay as a great metropolis from the later eighteenth century and the foundation of their great wealth was laid in trade with China and the Far East till the middle of the nineteenth century. Since then, the Parsis have played a leading part in public life and in the trades and professions in India out of all proportion to their number. The Parsis have also acquired a reputation for benevolence by reason of the large number of cosmopolitan charities established by Parsi philanthropists.

The Parsis have been compared to the Pilgrim Fathers and the Jews —'a peculiar people, with no country of their own, no separate national life of their own, owing allegiance to no Parsi or Zoroastrian temporal sovereign, guests on sufferance of races, of peoples, who had nothing whatever in common with their religious organization'.[1] They have managed to survive and flourish in an alien land because of their great assimilative capacity and their strong religious faith. They readily adopted the habits and the customs of the Hindus among whom they found themselves and as readily adopted the western ideas and customs brought by the British. This commixture of east and west is the most distinctive characteristic of the Parsis.

The Parsis are biologically a stagnant race. The 1951 census of India placed the number of Parsis at 111,791 but in the 1961 census this number was reduced to 100,687 of whom about 70,000 lived in the City of Bombay.[2] The accuracy of the census figures has, however, been doubted. A common estimate of the present Parsi population of India is about 120,000. It is estimated that there are 17,300 Parsis in Iran, 5,400 in Pakistan, about another 2,000 in other countries of Asia and Africa[3] and, counting about 5,000 in the rest of the world, the total world population of Parsis is about 150,000. There are several reasons why the Parsis have not shared in the population explosion in India. The prohibition against conversion has prevented the influx of fresh blood. A large proportion of Parsis remain unmarried—in the City of Bombay about 50 per cent of Parsis are unmarried,[4] and, among those who do marry, the trend is towards late marriages and small families.

[1] *Sir Dinshaw M. Petit v. Sir Jamsetji Jijibhai* (1909), 11 Bom. L.R. 85, 152 (*per* Beaman, J.).

[2] See S. F. Desai, *Statistics of World Zoroastrians with Special Reference to Indian Zoroastrians* (1964), pp. 1, 2. For census figures from 1864 to 1911, see Menant, op. cit. supra, note 1, v. 1, pp. 268–84.

[3] Desai, op. cit. supra, p. 8.

[4] ibid., p. 11.

This is mainly due to economic reasons. The Parsis have a high standard of living and have not adopted the joint family system of the Hindus, which permits a pooling of family resources. A Parsi male generally postpones marriage until he is able to afford a home of his own. The high literacy rate of 90 per cent is also a contributing factor as, the longer the education, the later the prospect of earning a living. The Parsis themselves are keen to increase their number but, as long as the present way of life continues, there is little likelihood of doing so.

2. *The Development of Parsi Law*

The Laws of the Medes and the Persians, which governed Ancient Persia, have acquired legendary fame.[1] It is not clear whether the Parsis brought any of these laws with them to India or, if they did, whether they applied them for any length of time.[2] Little is known of the legal system governing the Parsis during the early centuries of their stay in India but it is clear that the Parsis had been gradually adopting Hindu customs and laws and had established a Panchayet, that is an assembly of elders, a body constituted on Hindu principles, to administer justice between them. This state of affairs continued till the British period. As late as 1825, a British observer noted:

> 'The Parsis have no laws; for such books as they had before they emigrated from Persia were at that time all lost; and the rules, which, by their engagement with the Hindu Chief of Sunjan, they bound themselves to obey, form, together with the custom of the country which they insensibly picked up in their intercourse with the people, a body of rules or common law differing in few respects from that custom of the country founded on Hindu law which regulates the whole of a Hindu's life.'[3]

Authority over the Parsis in all religious matters was vested in the priests and in all civil and criminal matters in the Panchayet. Only capital offences were referred to the ruler for his consideration and

[1] For an account of these laws see S. J. Bulsara, *The Laws of the Ancient Persians* (1937).

[2] A code of Zoroastrian religious laws called the *Vendidad* has been preserved but it is not certain whether the Parsis brought his code with them when they migrated to India or acquired it later from Persia. One view is that the work was brought to India from Persia by a Parsi priest in 1184 (see Karaka, op. cit. supra, note 1, v. 1, p. 38). In any event, the rules of the *Vendidad* seem never to have been applied by the Parsis in India to their secular affairs.

[3] Statement by Mr Borrodaile (later a member of the First Indian Law Commission) quoted in *Mithibai v. Limji Nowroji Banaji* (1881), I.L.R. 5 Bom. 506, 521.

decision.[1] The Panchayet exercised strict control and imposed penalties for transgressions of the laws. The severest punishment was excommunication from the caste. Fines were also imposed as well as a beating with shoes in public.[2] The Panchayet at Bombay was the paramount authority and its rulings were followed by the other Panchayets. This Panchayet, however, gradually lost its authority as it ceased to be a properly elected body and also began to be criticized for administering one law for the rich and another for the poor. The Bombay Panchayet made an effort to recover its position in 1838 by petitioning the Legislative Council of India for legal power to enforce its authority. The petition was referred to the Judges of the Supreme Court of Judicature at Bombay for their opinion but they recommended against any such grant on the ground that it would lead to the same kind of collision between the Panchayet and the courts of law as had taken place between the spiritual and temporal courts in England. The petition was, thereupon, rejected and, since then, the Bombay Panchayet performs only the function of acting as trustee of the charitable funds and properties of the community.[3] The recommendations made by the Panchayet in religious and secular affairs are, however, treated with deference and respect by the Parsis in India.

The judicial system established by the British in India created a difference between the personal law applicable to the Parsis in the Presidency towns of Bombay, Calcutta and Madras and that applicable to Parsis outside these towns, i.e. in the mofussil areas. The Mayors' Courts established in 1726 in the three Presidency towns applied English law in all civil matters before them.[4] The Mayor's Court in Calcutta was succeeded in 1773 by the Supreme Court of Judicature at Fort William, which was enjoined under its Charter in 'all matters arising out of inheritance and succession to land and goods, and all matters of contract and dealing between party and party', to apply Islamic laws and usages in the case of Muslims and Hindu laws and usages in the case of Hindus and the laws and usages of the defendant if only one of the parties was a Muslim or a Hindu.[5] Parsis thus con-

[1] See Menant, op. cit. supra, note 1, v. 1, p. 7.

[2] When the Panchayet at Bombay found it difficult to enforce this mode of punishment it petitioned the Governor of Bombay in 1778 for legal authority to inflict this punishment, which was granted. See Karaka, op. cit. supra, note 1, v. 1, pp. 218–19.

[3] For an account of the working of the Bombay Panchayet, see Karaka, op. cit. supra, note 1, v. 1, pp. 217–41.

[4] See M. P. Jain, *Outlines of Indian Legal History* (1952), p. 39.

[5] ibid., p. 115.

tinued to be governed by the English civil law. The Mayors' Courts in Bombay and Madras were succeeded in 1797 by the Recorders' Courts, which were required to apply the same law in the specified matters as the Supreme Court at Calcutta. These courts were replaced by the Supreme Court at Madras in 1801 and the Supreme Court at Bombay in 1823 but the same law continued to be applied in matters relating to succession and contract. Ultimately, the three Supreme Courts were succeeded by the High Courts of Bombay, Calcutta and Madras in 1862 but there was no change in the law applicable to the specified matters.

In the mofussil areas, the position was different so far as Parsis were concerned. The Judicial Plan of 1772 promulgated by Warren Hastings established Diwani Adalats as the highest civil courts in the districts and provided that in all cases of inheritance, marriage, caste and religious matters, the laws of the Koran were to be applied to Muslims and the laws of the Shaster to Hindus. As a matter of justice and equity, the Adalats applied their personal laws to the other communities also, including the Parsis.[1] This state of affairs continued till 1827 when Regulation IV of that year promulgated by the Governor-General laid down (sec. 26) that the law to be applied in the trial of all suits in the mofussil was: 'Acts of Parliament and Regulations of Government applicable to the case; in the absence of such Acts and Regulations the usage of the country in which the suit arose; if none such appears the law of the defendant; and, in the absence of specific law and usage, justice, equity and good conscience alone.'[2]

The position, therefore, was that, in personal matters, the Parsis in the Presidency towns and in the mofussil were governed by two sets of law. The former in common with other British subjects, except Hindus and Muslims, were governed by the rules of the English common law, while the latter were governed by Parsi customary law, in so far as it existed. Only if there was no such customary law were the mofussil Parsis to be governed by the rules of 'justice, equity and good conscience', which were construed to mean 'the rules of English law if found applicable to Indian society and circumstances'.[3]

The difficulty and inequity of applying English law to the personal affairs of the large majority of Parsis, who lived in the City of Bombay, was felt at an early stage. To appreciate the problem, it is necessary to

---

[1] See M. P. Jain, *Outlines of Indian Legal History* (1952), p. 445.

[2] Cf. Government of India Act, 1915, sec. 112.

[3] *Waghela Rajsanji v. Shekh Masludin* (1887), 14 I.A. 89, 96. On the application of the doctrine of 'justice, equity and good conscience' in India, see Derrett, in *Changing Law in Developing Countries* (ed. Anderson, 1963), pp. 114, 129ff.

note that the Supreme Courts were applying not only the common law but also English statutes up to 1726 and the Civil Law as it obtained in the Ecclesiastical Courts in England.[1] The direct cause of the first piece of legislation affecting the Parsis was a claim based on English law. In 1835 a Parsi died intestate leaving considerable immovable property in Bombay and his eldest son filed a suit in the Supreme Court of Bombay claiming the whole of the property by virtue of the English rule of primogeniture. Alarmed at this claim, the Parsis appealed to the Legislature and the result was the Parsi Chattels Real Act of 1837, which provided that all immovable property within the jurisdiction of the Supreme Courts should, as far as succession to the estate of a Parsi was concerned, be deemed to be of the nature of chattels real and not of freehold.[2] The Act was repealed in 1868 after other legislation had been enacted.

Following the success of this move, the Bombay Parsis appealed again to the Legislature in 1838 for exemption from the English Statute of Distribution in case of intestacy and from the common law rule that a wife could not exercise disposing control during the life of her husband over any property whatever, not even over that which she obtained from her family.[3] Nothing, however, came of this appeal.

These events and the feeling among the mofussil Parsis that judicial decisions based on unwritten usage were too uncertain and led to speculative litigation directed the attention of the Parsis to the need for a code of laws relating to marriage, inheritance and succession. This movement, however, did not go far at first owing to differences between the Bombay and the mofussil Parsis as to what the laws should be. It was not until 1855, when a Parsi Law Association was established to make a systematic study of Parsi customs and usages and put forward concrete proposals to the Legislature, that the movement finally got off the ground.

This Association had hardly begun its work when the Judicial Committee of the Privy Council gave an opinion that caused consternation among the Parsis and gave an added impetus to the movement for legislation. This was the case of *Ardaseer Cursetjee v. Perozeboye* in 1856.[4] The wife in this case had been deserted by the husband, who had contracted a dubious polygamous marriage with another woman. She filed a suit on the Ecclesiastical Side of the Supreme Court of Bombay

---

[1] See Jain, op. cit. supra, note 19, p. 129.

[2] For the text of the Act, see Karaka, op. cit. supra, note 1, v. 2, p. 297.

[3] See P. L. Paruck, *Indian Succession Act* (4th ed. 1953), p. 63.

[4] (1856) 6 M.I.A. 348.

for restitution of conjugal rights and maintenance. The Charter of the Supreme Court provided that the law to be applied on its Ecclesiastical Side was the same as 'is now used and exercised in the Diocese of London in Great Britain'. The husband contested the jurisdiction of the court to pass any order against him. The Chief Justice and a puisne judge, who heard the suit, disagreed, the former holding that the court had jurisdiction and the latter that it had not, and, in accordance with the practice of the Supreme Court, the opinion of the Chief Justice prevailed.

On appeal, the Privy Council stated that English Ecclesiastical law is founded exclusively on the assumption that all the parties litigant are Christians. Since the husband was either lawfully married a second time or was living in adultery, an order to take the first wife back was unheard of in English Ecclesiastical law. The Privy Council accordingly held that the Supreme Court had no jurisdiction to entertain the suit, as there existed such a difference between the duties and obligations of a matrimonial union among Parsis and that of Christians, that the court, if it made a decree, had no means of enforcing it, except according to the principles governing the matrimonial law in Doctors' Commons, which were in such a case compatible with the laws and customs of the Parsis. The Privy Council went on to state that the Supreme Court of Bombay, on its Civil Side, might possibly administer some kind of remedy for the violation of the duties and obligations arising out of a matrimonial union between Parsis.

Though this decision applied to a suit for restitution, its principle could be extended to any form of English matrimonial relief, which could be considered incompatible with a Parsi marriage. The Parsis were thus in the position of having practically no matrimonial law at all as English law did not apply and there was hardly any Parsi customary law to speak of.

The Parsi Law Association submitted a Draft Code on inheritance, succession and matrimonial matters to the Legislative Council of India in March 1860 and, at the request of the Council, the Government of Bombay appointed a Parsi Law Commission, headed by an English judge of the Bombay Supreme Court, to inquire into the usages recognized as law by the Parsis and the necessity of special legislation in respect of Parsi personal matters. The Commission took both written and oral evidence and made its report on October 13, 1862.[1] It had been urged before the Commission that there should be separate laws of

[1] For a summary of the report, see Karaka, op. cit. supra, note 1, v. 1, pp. 256–72.

inheritance and succession for Bombay and mofussil Parsis, as their customs varied, but the Commission rejected this suggestion.[1] The result of these developments was the enactment of two statutes in 1865— the Parsi Marriage and Divorce Act[2] and the Parsi Intestate Succession Act.[3] An Indian Succession Act was also enacted in 1865 but the Parsis were exempted from those of its provisions dealing with intestate succession, which were covered in the Parsi Act. Both the 1865 statutes have been re-enacted with modifications. The Marriage Act has been replaced by the Parsi Marriage and Divorce Act of 1936 and the Succession Act has been re-enacted in Chapter III of Part V of the Indian Succession Act 1925.

In matters which fall outside the scope of these two statutes, the old schism continues. The Parsis in the town and island of Bombay are governed by the common law of England in so far as it is compatible with the circumstances of the Parsis.[4] Speaking in 1911, a judge of the Bombay High Court said: 'I am afraid it is too late in the day now to raise the question as to whether the Common Law of England does or does not apply to the Parsis who inhabit the town and island of Bombay.'[5] He went on to hold that solicitors acting for a Parsi wife in a divorce action could recover their costs from the husband under the common law rule that the wife is entitled to pledge her husband's credit and defend herself at his cost in a divorce action. The common law doctrine of the presumption of advancement to an heir has been held to be applicable to Parsis[6] and a Parsi wife has been held to be entitled to the deserted wife's so-called equity in the matrimonial residence.[7] On the other hand, the common law right of the repudiation of an infant marriage has been held to be inapplicable to Parsis as Parsi custom countenances such marriages.[8] A common law rule may also be rejected if it is of special origin or nature. Thus, the rule in *Shelley*'s case has been held to be inapplicable to Parsis as 'it is a law of property or tenure based on feudal considerations'.[9] In the case

---

[1] See Paruck, op. cit. supra, note 26, p. 64.

[2] For the text of the Act, see Karaka, op. cit. supra, note 1, v. 2, pp. 298ff.

[3] For the texts of the Acts, see ibid., pp. 316ff.

[4] *Naoroji Beramji v. Rogers* (1867), 4 Bom. H.C.R. 1; *Hirabai v. Dinshaw* (1926), 28 Bom. L.R. 391.

[5] *Payne & Co. v. Pirojshah* (1911), 13 Bom. L.R. 920, 929.

[6] *Bharucha v. Bharucha*, Judgment of Coyajee J. dated April 1, 1953, in Bombay High Court Suit 271 1953 (O.S.) (unreported).

[7] *Banoo v. Jal Daruwalla* (1963), 65 Bom. L.R. 750.

[8] *Peshotam v. Meherbai* (1888), I.L.R. 13 Bom. 302.

[9] *Mithibai v. Limji Nowroji Banaji* (1881), I.L.R. 5 Bom. 506. Affirmed in appeal (1882), I.L.R. 6 Bom. 151.

of mofussil Parsis, it is the custom of the community which is primarily applicable, and they are put in the same position as the town Parsis only in the absence of any custom, by being subjected to English law on the basis of justice, equity and good conscience.[1]

When the statutory law has been unified for a century, there is no rational basis for the continuation of this distinction between the town and mofussil Parsis. As has been noted, the origin of this distinction lies in the historical accident of separate sets of civil courts in the Presidency towns and in the mofussil, but the judiciary was unified as far back as 1862 so this reason no longer exists. Besides, the uncertain application of common law principles can hardly conduce to the orderly management by Parsis of their personal affairs. No other community in India suffers from such an anomaly. It is high time that all Parsis were brought under a unified system of law in all matters. This can be done by making the statutory laws as comprehensive as possible and, where lacunae are still found to exist in such law, by the judiciary developing a uniform system of law for all Parsis, based on the recognized customs and usages of the community, which would, of course, include the common law principles already received.

3. The Application of Parsi Law

Some difficulty has arisen about the application of Parsi law because of the failure of the Indian legislature to define the term 'Parsi'. Hindu or Islamic or Christian law is applicable on a religious basis, but there is no such thing as a Parsi religion, though loose references to this effect are sometimes made. Technically, as has been judicially noted,[2] it is possible to conceive of a Parsi Hindu or a Parsi Muslim or a Parsi Christian and the Parsi Marriage and Divorce Act 1936 impliedly recognizes this fact by defining 'Parsi' to mean a 'Parsi Zoroastrian'.[3] Among Parsis, however, there is no such confusion. No one who is not a Zoroastrian would be recognized as a Parsi. The panchayets of the community are called 'Parsi' panchayets, the fire-temples and towers of silence are declared to be open only to 'Parsis' and the charitable trusts of the community are for the benefit of 'Parsis'. By the usage of the community

[1] *Mancharsha v. Kamrunisa Begam*, 5 Bom. H.C.R. 109; *Kuberdas v. Jerkish Naoroji* (1941), 43 Bom. L.R. 981. If there is no rule of English law applicable to the facts of a particular case, the court will attempt to do substantial justice between the parties. *Robasa Khanum v. Khodadad Irani* (1946), 48 Bom. L.R. 864, 879.

[2] *Sir Dinshaw M. Petit v. Sir Jamsetji Jijibhai* (1909), 11 Bom. L.R. 85, 112–13; *Yezdiar v. Yezdiar* (1950), 52 Bom. L.R. 876, 882.

[3] S. 2(7).

as well as by statutory recognition, Parsi law applies only to Parsi Zoroastrians. As noted below, difficulty has, however, been caused by the question whether all Zoroastrians are Parsis.

The problem of what exactly is meant by the term 'Parsi' first came to be judicially considered in 1909 in the case of *Sir Dinshaw M. Petit v. Sir Jamsetji Jijibhai*[1] by a division bench of the Bombay High Court consisting of Mr Justice Davar, a Parsi judge, and Mr Justice Beaman, an English judge. The event leading up to this case, which was in the nature of a *cause célèbre*, was that Mr Ratan Tata, a leading industrialist, had married a French lady who purported to be converted to the Zoroastrian religion by going through the necessary ceremonies. She claimed thereafter that she had become a Parsi, professing the Zoroastrian religion, and was entitled to the benefit of all charitable and religious funds and institutions of the Parsis including the fire-temples and the towers of silence. The Trustees of the Parsi Panchayet of Bombay refused to countenance the claim. The community was torn between rival factions and a suit was filed by certain members of the community as relators to test the validity of the claim. Opportunity was taken of the suit to challenge the competence of certain Trustees of the Panchayet, who had been appointed by the surviving Trustees, to hold office. The suit was really two suits rolled in one but the court decided, in view of the importance of the questions involved to the whole community, to overlook this procedural difficulty as well as the further difficulty that the lady, whose interest was affected, was not a party to the suit.

On the question of removal of the trustees, the court held that they had been illegally appointed as they were not elected by the members of the community but the court re-appointed them trustees as they were men of high character and standing. The main question before the court was: who were entitled to the benefit of Parsi Funds and Trusts, which had been provided for the use and benefit of 'the members of the Parsi community professing the Zoroastrian religion'?

The court pointed out that the word 'Parsi' has only a racial signifi-cance and has nothing whatever to do with religious faith[2] and that the Parsis in India had started out as a religious community but, in course of time, had changed into a caste or tribal society due to two reasons, namely, the immemorial Indian caste sentiment which surrounded them and their own growing prosperity.[3] The court noted that there was no

[1] (1909) 11 Bom. L.R. 85.
[2] ibid., p. 112 (*per* Davar, J.).
[3] ibid., pp. 154–5, 162 (*per* Beaman, J.).

instance in ancient or modern times of anyone but a Parsi professing the Zoroastrian religion and that Parsis and Zoroastrians had become synonymous.[1] The court held that, though conversion was permitted and even enjoined by the Zoroastrian religion, it was against the custom of the Parsis of India to permit conversion to the Zoroastrian religion.[2] The court finally held that the Parsi community in India consisted of:

> Parsis who are descended from the original Persian emigrants, and who are born of both Zoroastrian parents, and who profess the Zoroastrian religion, the Iranis from Persia professing the Zoroastrian religion, who come to India, either temporarily or permanently, and the children of Parsi fathers by alien mothers who have been duly and properly admitted into the religion.[3]

This exposition of the law remained undisturbed till 1950 when it was partly upset by another division bench of the Bombay High Court consisting of Chief Justice Chagla and Mr Justice Gajendragadkar, later Chief Justice of India, in the case of *Yezdiar v. Yezdiar*.[4] This was a suit for divorce by the wife against the husband under the provisions of the Parsi Marriage and Divorce Act, 1936. The parties were both Zoroastrian immigrants from Iran and had been married in Bombay under the provisions of the Parsi Marriage Act. In the trial court, the husband contended that the court had no jurisdiction to try the suit as the parties were not domiciled in India. To understand this argument, which found favour with the trial judge, it is necessary to look at two provisions of the Parsi Marriage and Divorce Act, which, it is submitted, were overlooked by both the trial and appeal courts. Sec. 52(2) of the Act provides that a Parsi, who has been married under the Act or the 1865 Act, will remain bound by the provisions of the Act, even though he changes his religion or domicile, so long as the spouse is alive or the marriage has not been dissolved or declared null and void by a competent court having jurisdiction under the Act. Sec. 4 provides that no Parsi, whether or not he changes his religion or domicile, can contract a marriage under the Act, or any other law, if he is already married to a Parsi or non-Parsi, unless the marriage has been lawfully dissolved or declared null and void and, if the marriage was contracted under the Act or the 1865 Act, was dissolved or declared void under the provisions of the Act. The purpose of this provision was to prevent

---

[1] (1909) 11 Bom. L. R., pp. 114, 115 (*per* Davar, J.).
[2] ibid., pp. 109, 110 (*per* Davar, J.).
[3] ibid., p. 128 (*per* Davar, J.).
[4] (1950), 52 Bom. L.R. 876.

polygamous marriages, which, following Hindu customary law, were permitted by Parsi custom.

The crucial test, it is submitted, is whether the marriage was contracted under the provisions of the Parsi Marriage and Divorce Act. If so, it can only be dissolved under the provisions of the Act by a court established under the Act. The factors of religion, domicile or even nationality are immaterial for the purpose of vesting jurisdiction in the court.

The trial judge declined to exercise jurisdiction on the ground that the parties were not domiciled in India, even though the marriage had been contracted under the provisions of the Act. The wife appealed. The Appeal Court chose to follow a strange procedure. Without considering the question of domicile, which was the only issue raised in the court below, it raised the issue of whether the parties were 'Parsis'. The husband had never raised this contention and the issue did not arise on the pleadings. The court held that the term 'Parsi' has a racial and not a religious significance and is restricted to those only who are the descendants of the original Zoroastrian emigrants from Iran. It went on to say that 'an Iranian, who temporarily resides in India, who is registered as a foreigner and whose domicile continues to be Persian does not become a Parsi merely because he is a Zoroastrian and his race is the same as that of the Parsis in India'.[1] The court brushed aside the observation in the *Petit* case that Iranis, who are temporarily or permanently in India, are Parsis, on the ground that it was *obiter*. It went on to state that if an Iranian changes his domicile and becomes an Indian subject, he may be considered as a Parsi as he belongs to the same race as the Parsis originally belonged to.

It is difficult to accept the reasoning of the court, particularly as it fails to consider Secs. 4 and 52(2) mentioned above. The court conceded that Zoroastrians from Iran belong to the same race as the Parsis of India but insisted that they can only qualify to become Parsis if they change their domicile and nationality. This is not only at variance with the Act and the custom of the Parsis but against the historical evidence which shows that the term 'Parsi' was in use in Persia to describe Zoroastrians even before the first emigration to India. The judgment in the *Petit* case, which had been good law for more than forty years, had been lightly brushed aside. The incalculably harmful effects of the decision for the so-called Irani Zoroastrians on questions such as the validity of marriages, the legitimacy of children, vested inheritance rights and the use of Parsi fire-temples and trusts were not even considered or com-

[1] (1950), 52 Bom. L. R., p. 883.

mented upon. Fortunately, these effects were greatly mitigated by the attitude of the Parsis, who continued as if nothing had been changed and even made an unsuccessful attempt to obtain a legislative definition of the term 'Parsi' according to the observations in the *Petit* case.

The issue came again before the Bombay High Court after a few years in the case of *Jamshed Irani v. Banu Irani*.[1] The facts in this case were similar to those in the *Yezdiar* case, except that the suit was by the husband and the husband claimed to possess an Indian domicile, and the contentions raised on behalf of the defendant-wife were based on the judgment in that case. The case was tried by a single judge. On behalf of the plaintiff, the Court was urged to ignore the *Yezdiar* decision on the ground that it had failed to consider Secs. 4 and 52(2) of the Act and to follow the observations in the *Petit* case. The court allowed expert evidence of historians, Persian scholars and Parsi priests on the meaning of the term 'Parsi' and was satisfied, on the basis of this evidence, that the term 'Parsi' was commonly understood to refer both to the Zoroastrians of Iran and the Zoroastrians of India. The court held that the *Yezdiar* decision was not good law, as Secs. 4 and 52(2) of the Parsi Marriage Act had not been brought to the notice of the court in that case. On the general meaning of the term 'Parsi', the court followed the principle of the *Petit* case. The court accordingly held that it had jurisdiction to try the suit and found in the plaintiff's favour on the merits. An appeal from this decision was subsequently withdrawn.

The position then is that the Parsi law of India applies to three categories of Zoroastrians: persons who are descended from the original Persian emigrants and are born of Zoroastrian parents; children of Parsi fathers by alien mothers, who have been admitted to the Zoroastrian religion, and Zoroastrians from Iran, who are either temporarily or permanently residing in India. Zoroastrians, who come to India from other countries, would fall under one or other of these groups, as they would necessarily be descended from the racial stock in Iran or in India. While this accords with the wishes of the Parsi community, the question cannot be regarded as free from doubt as long as it can be re-agitated in a court of law. Only a legislative definition in terms of the present position can remove this uncertainty.

4. Parsi Matrimonial Law
Prior to the 1865 statute, there was hardly any Parsi matrimonial law and, for many years, no forum to grant relief to Parsis in matrimonial

[1] (1966) 68 Bom. L.R. 794.

matters. The Panchayet had performed this function but it had ceased to be an adjudicating tribunal in the early part of the nineteenth century and the courts were powerless to grant any relief as the English law, which they administered, was unsuitable to the rights and obligations of Parsi marriages.[1] The Parsis had adopted the undesirable Hindu practices of infant and polygamous marriages. The Parsi Marriage and Divorce Act of 1865 went a long way in removing these evils.

The most important effect of the Act was the prohibition against polygamous marriages, which was in consonance with the sentiments of the majority of Parsis. In fact, the Panchayet had attempted to put a curb on such marriages by insisting that such a union could be formed only with its sanction and after a proper case had been made out. The Act provided that no Parsi could contract a second marriage without the dissolution of the first union and that Parsis would be subject to the penal law of bigamy from which they had hitherto been exempt.[2] It left infant marriages undisturbed and the courts, while recognizing that it was an injurious practice and against the tenets of the Zoroastrian religion, reluctantly held that they were permitted by Parsi custom and were not of such an inchoate probational character as to allow of repudiation.[3] The Act did, however, provide that the consent of the father or guardian was necessary if a party to a marriage was under 21 years of age.[4]

The Act provided for the registration of Parsi marriages and established special courts in the Presidency towns and in the mofussil to try Parsi matrimonial matters. As the majority of judges at the time were Englishmen, who were unfamiliar with Parsi customs, they were to be assisted by Parsi delegates, whose function was to decide questions of fact.

The Act provided for five kinds of matrimonial relief: declaration of nullity, dissolution of the marriage, divorce, judicial separation and restitution of conjugal rights. A nullity decree would be granted if one of the parties was a lunatic at the time of the marriage and this fact was not known to the other spouse and if the consummation of the marriage was impossible from natural causes.[5] The Act, however, made no distinction between void and voidable marriages. A decree of dissolution was obtainable if one of the spouses had been absent and not heard

[1] See *Ardaseer v. Perozeboye* (1856), 6 M.I.A. 348.
[2] Secs. IV and V.
[3] See *Peshotam v. Meherbai* (1888), I.L.R. 13 Bom. 302.
[4] Sec. III.
[5] Secs. XXVII and XXVIII.

of as being alive for seven years.[1] In the matter of divorce, the Act differentiated between the rights of the wife and the husband. The husband could only obtain divorce on the ground of adultery but, in addition to this ground, the wife could rely on adultery coupled with bigamy or with cruelty or with wilful desertion for two years or more as well as the commission by the husband of rape or an unnatural offence.[2] Judicial separation could be demanded only by the wife, the grounds being that the husband was guilty of cruelty or personal violence or of such conduct as to cause apprehension to the wife of danger to life or serious personal injury or that he openly brought or. allowed a prostitute to remain in the matrimonial abode.[3] A decree for the restitution of conjugal rights was obtainable by either spouse on the ground of desertion and failure to comply with such a decree entailed fine and/or imprisonment.[4]

While the Act did not provide a minimum age for marriage, it prevented the grant of any relief unless the husband was at least 16 and the wife 14 years of age.[5] It empowered the court to make such orders as it thought fit for interim and permanent alimony[6] and custody of children.[7]

The Act was a far-sighted piece of legislation, based largely on English law, which was considered most suited to the circumstances of the Parsis; and it served the needs of Parsis satisfactorily for more than seventy years, when it was revised to remove some anomalies revealed by experience and to bring it more in line with the changing views and circumstances of the community. The basic framework of the Act was, however, retained.

The main improvements in the 1936 Act were that it put husband and wife on an equal footing so far as divorce and judicial separation were concerned; added new grounds for divorce; made, in line with English law, judicial separation obtainable on the same grounds as divorce; and substituted a ground for divorce instead of punishment as the penalty for failure to comply with a restitution decree.[8] It also provided that not

[1] Sec. XXIX.
[2] Sec. XXX.
[3] Sec. XXI.
[4] Sec. XXVI.
[5] Sec. XXVII. There is a similar provision in the present 1936 Act (Sec. 38).
[6] Secs. XXVIII to XXXV.
[7] Sec. XXXIV.
[8] Under O.21, R.32, and R.33 of the Civil Procedure Code 1908, which Rules apply to all the communities in India, a decree for restitution may be enforced by attachment and sale of the judgment-debtor's property and a wife may alternately enforce a decree by obtaining such periodical payments from the husband as the Court may fix.

only a subsisting Parsi marriage but also a non-Parsi marriage would be a bar to a marriage under the Act and, in order to prevent desertion of wives, added a new provision that a Parsi would remain bound by the Act even if he changed his religion or domicile. The Act did not, however, prohibit infant marriages[1] or make a distinction between void and voidable marriages, which were two of the defects in the old Act.

The present Parsi matrimonial law, as based on the 1936 Act, may now be considered. The Act defines a 'Parsi' to mean 'Parsi Zoroastrian'.[2] There are three conditions for the validity of a Parsi marriage.[3] First, the parties must not be related to one another in any of 33 degrees of prohibited relationship mentioned in Schedule I to the Act. Secondly, the marriage must be solemnized according to the Parsi form of ceremony known as 'Ashirvad' by a Parsi priest in the presence of two Parsi witnesses. 'Ashirvad', which literally means 'blessing', includes a prayer or exhortation to the parties to observe their marital obligations. As has been noted,[4] it would be senseless if addressed to infants and yet the Act countenances this anomaly besides ignoring the fact that the minimum age for marriage according to the Zoroastrian religion is 15 years.[5] Thirdly, if a party to the marriage is under the age of 21, even if he has changed his or her religion or domicile, the previous consent of the father or guardian is essential. It is difficult to understand the provision regarding change of religion, as a Parsi who changes his religion ceases to be a Parsi within the meaning of the Act and hence becomes incapable of contracting a Parsi marriage. A marriage which contravenes any of these three conditions would presumably be void.

There is provision for the appointment of Registrars of Parsi marriages and the maintenance of Registers of such marriages, which are open to public inspection, and a duty is cast on the officiating priest to certify the marriages in the prescribed form and to send such certificate to the Registrar at the place where the marriage is solemnized.[6] The Act provides, however, that no marriage shall be deemed to be invalid

---

[1] Though infant Parsi marriages are valid, a male above 18 who marries a female under 15 and a parent or guardian and a person performing, conducting or directing the marriage of a male under 18 or a female under 15, are punishable with imprisonment and/or fine under the provisions of The Child Marriage Restraint Act, 1929, which applies to all the communities in India.

[2] Sec. 2(7).

[3] Sec. 3.

[4] In *Peshotam v. Meherbai* (1888), I.L.R. 13 Bom. 302, 211.

[5] See Karaka, op. cit. supra, note 1, v. 1, p. 170.

[6] Secs. 6 to 8 and 12 to 16.

solely because of failure to certify or to send the certificate to the Registrar or on the ground of a defect in the certificate.[1] In such cases, the marriage can be proved by other relevant evidence.[2]

The Act continues the system of special courts and adjudication of questions of fact by delegates, established under the 1865 Act. These courts are known as the Parsi Chief Matrimonial Courts in the Presidency towns and the Parsi District Matrimonial Courts in the mofussil. A Judge of the High Court presides over the former and a District Judge over the latter.[3] In the trial of cases under the Act, the judge is assisted by seven delegates selected from a panel appointed by the State Government after consulting the wishes of the Parsis of the locality.[4] Under the old Act, delegates were appointed for life but they are now appointed for a period of ten years. All questions of law and procedure are to be decided by the judge, and of fact by a majority of the delegates; but, if the delegates are equally divided (as, for instance, if one delegate abstains from voting), the judge has also to decide questions of fact.[5]

The jurisdiction of the different matrimonial courts is governed by Sec. 29 of the Act. A suit must be brought in the first instance in the court within the limits of whose jurisdiction[6] the defendant is residing at the time of the institution of the suit. If the defendant has left India, it is the court at the place where the parties last resided together. The court is empowered in any case to grant leave for a suit to be brought at the place where the plaintiff is residing or where the parties last resided together. In the *Yezdiar* case,[7] it was held that Sec. 29 merely indicates the proper court in which a suit must be brought and postulates that the suit is one which can be tried by a Parsi Matrimonial Court. Appeals may be made within three months to the High Courts from the decisions of the Matrimonial Courts on grounds of law[8] and the High Courts also exercise the same power of superintendence over these courts as they exercise over inferior courts and tribunals under Article 227 of the Constitution.[9]

[1] Sec. 17.
[2] *Awabi v. Khodadad*, A.I.R. 1921 Bom. 189, 190.
[3] Secs. 18 to 20.
[4] Secs. 19, 20 and 24.
[5] Sec. 46.
[6] These limits are coterminous with those of the ordinary original civil jurisdiction of the High Court or the district as the case may be. Secs. 19 and 20.
[7] (1950) 52 Bom. L.R. 876.
[8] Sec. 47.
[9] Sec. 51.

The only ground of nullity is non-consummation from natural causes.[1] Lunacy, which was formerly a ground for nullity, is now a ground for divorce, presumably to save the children of such marriage from becoming illegitimate. The other grounds for divorce are: non-consummation for one year owing to wilful refusal, adultery, bigamy, the commission of rape or an unnatural offence, the causing of grievous hurt,[2] the causing of infection with a venereal disease, the suffering of a sentence of imprisonment for seven years or more, desertion for three years or more, the lapse of three years after an order for judicial separation or separate maintenance, failure to comply with a restitution decree for one year and conversion from Zoroastrianism. The husband has the additional ground of pregnancy of the wife by another man, which was unknown to him at the time of the marriage, and the wife the additional ground of being forced into prostitution.[3] A time limit is prescribed for suits on certain grounds as there was some doubt on this question under the old Act. Cruelty is not a ground for divorce but only, in addition to all the grounds for divorce, for judicial separation.[4]

Desertion, which is a ground both for divorce and restitution, is only defined to mean desertion without reasonable cause and without the consent of the wronged party.[5] Parsi Matrimonial Courts have, therefore, had to fall back on English law to determine the legal meaning of 'desertion' and have followed the English cases including those that propound the doctrine of 'constructive desertion'.[6]

The English practice of making the third party a co-defendant in an action for adultery and imposing a liability for costs on such party has been adopted.[7] However, no damages are recoverable from the co-defendant. In addition to the regular forms of relief, there is provision for a decree of dissolution when a spouse is absent for more than seven years.[8] Divorce would not be an appropriate relief in such a case, as the absent spouse is presumed to be dead.

A Parsi Matrimonial Court will not grant any relief if there has been condonation or connivance by the plaintiff or if the parties are colluding or if there has been improper delay in claiming relief or if there is

[1] Sec. 30.
[2] 'Grievous hurt' is defined in Sec. 2(4) of the Act.
[3] Sec. 32.
[4] Sec. 34.
[5] Sec. 2(3).
[6] *Khorshed v. Muncherji Kapadia*, A.I.R. 1938 Bom. 86, 87.
[7] Sec. 33.
[8] Sec. 31.

any other legal ground for refusing relief.[1] The court is empowered to make such orders as it considers reasonable for interim or permanent payment of alimony by the husband to the wife so long as the wife remains chaste and unmarried,[2] for the disposal of the joint property of the parties[3] which under Parsi custom consists of presents given to the parties between the time of betrothal and marriage, and for the interim or permanent custody or maintenance of the children of the marriage under the age of 16.[4]

The effect of a decree of divorce or nullity or dissolution is that the marriage is treated as if it had been terminated by death and the parties are free to remarry after the time for appealing against the decree has expired or any such appeal has been dismissed.[5] There is no provision in the Act as to whether divorce terminates the affinity relationship created by the marriage or causes a reverter to the wife's maiden surname. It is submitted that English law would be followed on these questions whereby divorce does not have such effects.

The present Parsi matrimonial law is based on English matrimonial law as it prevailed at the end of 1934, when the Bill, which was enacted as the 1936 Act, was prepared.[6] Since then, there have been considerable changes in the English law, both statutory and judicial, but there have been no corresponding changes in the Parsi Act. Further, Parsi Matrimonial Courts have built up a considerable body of case-law, based on English law, which ought to be statutorily incorporated to obviate reagitation in the courts.

Most dissatisfaction has, however, been felt with the delegate and special court systems. There was some justification for the introduction of the delegate system in 1865, when a large majority of the judges were English and Parsi customs and usages were largely unknown, but for a long time these reasons have ceased to exist. Such a system does not operate in the administration of the personal law of any other community in India and, in the interest of the uniformity in personal law which the Constitution enjoins,[7] should be dispensed with. There have been instances of perverse verdicts by delegates and judicial criticism of the system. Moreover, when the jury system, on which it is obviously

[1] Sec. 35.
[2] Secs. 39 to 41. There is no provision for payment of alimony by the wife to the husband as in the Hindu Marriage Act 1955, sec. 25.
[3] Sec. 42.
[4] Sec. 49.
[5] Sec. 48.
[6] The 1865 Act was modelled on the English Matrimonial Causes Act of 1857.
[7] Art. 44.

modelled, has been abolished throughout India,[1] there is less justification for the existence of the delegates.

A special court, forming part of a High Court or a District Court, was established in 1865 to try Parsi matrimonial cases, because Parsis wanted their disputes to be decided by the highest court in the local area. In practice, it has proved to be a costly and cumbersome procedure. The Parsi Chief Matrimonial Court of Bombay, which, as the vast majority of Parsis lives in the City of Bombay, is by far the busiest of these courts, meets twice a year in April and October. There are usually about 30 to 35 cases on its board for disposal. As most cases are uncontested, the sittings of the court rarely last for more than two or three days and are sometimes completed in a single day. There is no justification for maintaining a special court for this kind of work. The matrimonial disputes of all the other communities are decided by the subordinate civil courts with, of course, a right of appeal to higher courts and this arrangement has proved quite satisfactory. Further, as the Parsi court meets only every six months, there is frequently delay in obtaining relief from it, which does not happen in the ordinary civil courts, which take up matrimonial cases as part of their regular work. As it is, the ordinary civil courts already have power to try one type of Parsi matrimonial case which is outside the competence of the special Parsi court. This is a case where a declaration is sought that there has been no marriage at all.[2]

A comment is called for on the grounds for divorce. The 1936 Act provides liberal grounds for divorce and has removed the invidious distinction in this matter between husband and wife which existed under the old Act. Most Parsi divorce actions are uncontested. Divorce by mutual consent has been part of Indian law since 1954, when this ground was introduced in the Special Marriage Act,[3] which applies to all the communities. There is no reason why a similar provision should not be included in the Parsi Act.

Enlightened Parsi opinion is in favour of the reforms discussed above. There are several factors, however, militating against their introduction. First is the unfortunate Parsi habit of disagreeing on questions affecting the community, which delayed for so long the salutary legislation of 1865 and which prevents a consensus of Parsi opinion that alone can bring about legislative change. Second is the strong orthodox element in the community which is against any reli-

---

[1] The jury system used to apply only to criminal cases in India.

[2] *Peshotam v. Meherbai* (1888), I.L.R. 13 Bom. 302.

[3] Sec. 28.

gious or social change. Then, like the British, the Indian legislature has proved unwilling to disturb the personal laws of the minority communities.

It remains to note an interesting problem that has not yet come up for judicial decision. The Parsi Act provides that a Parsi marriage can be terminated only by a decree under that Act.[1] The Special Marriage Act, which is a liberal piece of legislation, applies to marriages between persons of different, as well as the same, religion, and provides for marriages celebrated in other forms and under other laws to be registered under the Act, in which case the marriage is deemed to be solemnized under the Act.[2] A Parsi marriage can, therefore, be registered under the Special Marriage Act and will then be treated as if it was a marriage under that Act and can be terminated under the provisions of that Act, which prescribe other grounds for divorce including mutual consent. Can the provisions of the Parsi Act be evaded in this manner? While it is difficult to predict what view a court of law would adopt, it is submitted that such evasion is not possible, as the provisions of the Parsi Act, which is a special law, would prevail over those of the Special Marriage Act, which is a general law.

5. The Parsi Law of Succession

Prior to 1865, when the Indian Succession and Parsi Intestate Succession Acts were introduced, the Parsis in the Presidency towns of Bombay, Calcutta and Madras were governed in matters of inheritance and succession by the English law and the Parsis in the mofussil by the ascertained usage[3] of the community.[4] Thus, the Parsis in the Presidency towns were governed by the English Statute of Distribution by which a third went to the widow and the residue was divided equally among the children and their descendants, and by the English common law rule that married women had no right to hold or dispose of any property during coverture. Up to 1837, when the Parsi Chattels Real Act abolished this rule, they had also been governed by the common law rule of primogeniture as regards immovable property. The mofussil Parsis, following Hindu custom, excluded females from a share in

[1] Secs. 4 and 52(2).
[2] Secs. 15 and 18.
[3] In applying usage, the courts modified it by rules of equity and good conscience and, for this purpose, followed the practice of the English Equity Courts with necessary modifications. See *Shapurji v. Dossabhoy* (1905), 7 Bom. L.R. 988, 991.
[4] For a historical account of the development of the Parsi law of succession, see Paruck, op. cit. supra, note 26, pp. 62–72.

the estates of male intestates and gave them only a right of maintenance and, adopting the common law rule, denied married women the right to hold or dispose of property during coverture.

Thus, Parsi women in the mofussil were in an inferior position to those in the Presidency towns in matters of inheritance. As regards testamentary succession, the Privy Council had held in 1856 that there was no restraint upon the testamentary power of disposition by a Parsi[1] but, since 1865, Parsis are subject to the same restraints imposed by the Indian Succession Act as are the other communities. The Parsis were unsuccessful in obtaining exemption from the restrictions in the Indian Succession Act on bequests to religious or charitable uses,[2] which were based on the English Statute of Mortmain.[3]

With the enactment of the two succession statutes in 1865, Parsis in all areas came under a uniform and comprehensive code in matters of inheritance and succession. The Parsi Law Commission, which provided the framework of the Intestate Succession Act, rejected the proposal of the mofussil Parsis that there should be separate laws of intestate succession for town and mofussil Parsis as also that females should be excluded from rights of inheritance and that married women should have no disposing power. It accepted, however, the suggestion of both sets of Parsis that the English Laws of Succession and Property as between husband and wife were totally unsuited to the requirements of the Parsi community.[4] So strong is the aversion in mofussil areas to females having inheritance rights that even today, a hundred years after they have been emancipated, there are instances of Parsi women in mofussil areas being deprived of their legitimate shares in the estates of their fathers and husbands and accepting such injustice out of ignorance of the protection which the law gives them.

In matters of testamentary disposition, the procedure for obtaining representation to the estate of a deceased person and all matters except the devolution of an estate on intestacy, Parsis are governed today by the general provisions of the Indian Succession Act 1925. The Parsi Intestate Succession Act of 1865 was repealed and re-enacted as Chapter II of Part V (Secs. 50 to 56) of the Indian Succession Act 1925. This Chapter was considerably modified by an Amending Act in 1939[5] 'in order to remove doubts, supply deficiencies, incorporate as far as

---

[1] *Modee Kaikhoosorow Hormusjee v. Cooverbhaee* (1856), 6 M.I.A. 448.

[2] Sec. 105 of the 1865 Act and Sec. 118 of the present 1925 Act.

[3] See Paruck, op. cit. supra, note 26, pp. 64, 65.

[4] ibid., p. 64.

[5] Statement of Objects and Reasons of the Amending Act. Ibid., p. 70.

possible the judicial decisions which the community has accepted, introduce changes commonly desired and make the arrangements more systematic'. As the Parsis have a comprehensive code, there is no longer any scope for the application of common law rules to them in matters of inheritance and succession. The Bombay High Court has held, for instance, that Parsis are not subject to the English law regarding testamentary settlement of estates.[1]

There are three general principles in the present Parsi law of intestate succession. These are that there is no distinction between a living and a posthumous child for inheritance purposes, that a share will be attributed to a pre-deceased child only if he or she has left a spouse or a lineal descendant, and that a widow of a relative of an intestate, who has remarried in the lifetime of the intestate, gets no share.[2]

A Parsi is deemed to die intestate in respect of all property of which he has not made a testamentary disposition which is capable of taking effect.[3] The primary heirs of a Parsi male intestate are his widow, children, and parents.[4] The widow and a son get twice the share of a daughter, while the father gets half the share of a son and the mother half the share of a daughter.[5] The position of widows and daughters has been improved as, under the old Act, the son received twice the share of the widow and four times the share of a daughter. In the case of a Parsi female intestate, the parents receive nothing. The widower and children share alike and, if there is no widower, the whole estate is divided equally among the children.[6] Under the old law, the share of the widower was twice that of a child.

In the case of a pre-deceased child of a Parsi intestate, the share attributed to such child is divided in the same manner as above except that the widower of a pre-deceased daughter gets no part of her share.[7] Under the old law, the widower had a share.

If a Parsi dies leaving a widow or widower but no lineal descendant, the widow or widower takes half and the other half is divided among certain relatives in a specified manner. If there is a widow of a lineal descendant, the widow or widower takes one-third, the widow of the lineal descendant takes one-third and the residue is divided among the specified relatives. If there is no widow or widower, the widow of the

[1] *Dadabhai v. Cowasji* (1922), 24 Bom. L.R. 1,111, 1,123 (*per* Marten, J.).
[2] Indian Succession Act 1925, Sec. 50.
[3] ibid., Sec. 30.
[4] Under the old law, the parents had no share.
[5] Indian Succession Act 1925, Sec. 51.
[6] ibid., Sec. 52.
[7] ibid., Sec. 53.

lineal descendant gets one-third or, if there are two or more, two-thirds and the remainder goes to the relatives.[1] In the absence of the heirs mentioned above, the relatives divide the property in a specified manner.[2] In the absence of any of the specified relatives, the property of the intestate is divided equally among those of the relatives in the nearest degree of kindred.[3]

It is important to note that the heirs of a Parsi need not be Parsis themselves. Thus, an alien spouse or a child of a Parsi mother and an alien father, who cannot be Parsis, can succeed to the estate of a Parsi intestate. There was a custom of adoption of sons, similar to the Hindu one, among the mofussil Parsis but this custom was not recognized in the Intestate Succession Act of 1865 and a son, purported to be adopted, cannot succeed to the estate of a Parsi male intestate.[4] A step-child also has no right of inheritance.

There is an interesting question with respect to succession to agricultural land, which has not yet been judicially tested in the case of the Parsis. When the present Parsi law of intestate succession was enacted in 1939, the Central Legislature had no power, under the Government of India Act 1935, to make a law in regard to the devolution of agricultural land. This was within the exclusive competence of the Provincial Legislatures.[5] Under Sec. 292 of the 1935 Act, all existing laws were to continue in force until altered or repealed or amended by a competent legislature. Thus, the Central Legislature had no power in 1939 to repeal or alter the provisions of Chapter III of Part V of the Indian Succession Act 1925 in so far as they applied to the succession to agricultural land among Parsis.

A similar question arose with respect to the Hindu Women's Rights to Property Act 1937, which was also a central piece of legislation. The question whether it affected the devolution of agricultural land was referred to the Federal Court for opinion. The answer of the court was in the negative on the ground that the Central Legislature was not competent to enact legislation affecting the devolution of agricultural land.[6]

Under the Constitution, the transfer and alienation of agricultural land can be regulated only by the State Legislatures. The word 'de-

---

[1] Indiad Succession Act 1925, Sec. 54.
[2] ibid., Sec. 55.
[3] ibid., Sec. 56.
[4] *Kersaji v. Kaikhushru* (1929), 31 Bom. L.R. 1,081.
[5] Government of India Act 1935, Entry 21, List II, Seventh Schedule.
[6] In *Re Hindu Women's Rights to Property Act* 1937, A.I.R. 1941 F.C. 72.

volution' is omitted in the corresponding entry in the Legislative List.[1]
It may well be, therefore, that Parliament can control the devolution of
agricultural land but Parliament has not re-enacted the provisions of
the 1939 Act. Under Art. 372 of the Constitution, all laws existing at
the commencement of the Constitution continue in force until altered or
repealed or amended by a competent legislature. The question then is:
what was the Parsi law of intestate succession with respect to agricultural land at the commencement of the Constitution?

Anomalous as it seems, it would appear that this law is the original
Chapter III, Part V, of the 1925 Succession Act before its re-enactment
in 1939. If so, Parsis still continue to be governed by the old law in
respect of succession to agricultural land.[2]

By and large, the Parsis are satisfied with their present law of succession. It is felt by some, however, that a daughter should be given a
share equal to (and not as at present half) that of a son in the estate of
the father, as among the Hindus[3] and the Christians.[4] The mofussil
Parsis have long since been reconciled to the surrender of their cher-
ished customs. The spread of education in mofussil areas would in any
case have brought changes without legislative reform and, when
Hindu women have been emancipated, it would have been impossible
to have kept Parsi women in their former lowly status.

There was some dissatisfaction among Parsis that the privileges
accorded to other communities to claim the property of a deceased
person without obtaining representation to the estate,[5] and to obtain a
succession certificate to make legal recovery of debts due to the estate
of a deceased person,[6] were denied to Parsis. This anomaly was removed in 1962 and Parsis now enjoy these privileges.[7]

6. The Future of Parsi Law

The Parsis have come a long way since they forsook their homeland
almost thirteen centuries ago. The fact that they brought no laws with
them or, if they did, allowed them to fall into desuetude and perforce
had to adopt the laws and customs of the people around them, undoubtedly helped to assimilate them to their new environment. The
historical accident, that subjected them to the English common law at

[1] Constitution of India, Entry 8, List II, Seventh Schedule.
[2] A similar view is expressed in Paruck, op. cit. supra, note 26, p. 71.
[3] Hindu Succession Act 1956, Sec. 10.
[4] Indian Succession Act, Sec. 37.
[5] ibid., Secs. 212, 213.
[6] ibid., Sec. 370.
[7] By Act 16 of 1962.

a time when they were laying the foundations of their wealth and influence, brought them the benefits of Western civilization. Certainly, in the case of the Parsis, law created a profound social change.

How long the separate systems of personal law will continue to exist in India is a moot point. The legislature is armed with a constitutional directive[1] to prescribe a uniform system of personal law for all the communities in India but seems reluctant to carry it out.[2] There is no doubt that the separation in personal laws has been a divisive factor when national integration is the urgent need. If and when uniformity comes, there is no reason to feel that the Parsis will find it difficult to accept the change. They have always been an adaptive race and the success with which they absorbed two alien and widely differing systems of law bodes well for the future.

In the meantime, their thoughts must turn to improving the present system of law. In a country of 485 million, which is embarked on a vast programme of social legislation, it is not easy to seek redress for the grievances of 120,000 people. The lead for changes in Parsi law has always come in the past from the Parsi Panchayet of Bombay and it is this body which must give the lead again. Fortunately, the Panchayet is aware of the need for reforming Parsi law and has recently appointed a Parsi Law Reform Committee to make recommendations.[3]

The reforms that are necessary in the present system of law have been pointed out. There is need for a legislative definition of the term 'Parsi' to perpetuate the present judicial view. It is a hundred years since the Parsis have had a statutory body of law and it is possible to make it comprehensive enough to obviate recourse to the common law with the unpredictability of judicial attitude which this involves. To depend on a system of law, which will be applied only if compatible with Parsi circumstances, is to make the law uncertain. There is need for reform in the matrimonial law along the lines suggested above, particularly in the method of adjudicating upon disputes. Except for the mode of intestate succession, with which they are generally satisfied,

[1] Constitution of India, Art. 44.

[2] On the feasibility of a uniform law of divorce in India, see S. S. Nigam, 'A Plea for a Uniform Law of Divorce', 5 J.I.L.I. pp. 47–80 (1963).

[3] This Committee (of which the writer is a member) is considering, among other things, the desirability of legalizing adoption among Parsis. The possibility of a separate Parsi law of adoption may not arise as the Indian Conference of Social Work and other welfare organizations have been urging the enactment of a uniform adoption law for all the communities, as a solution for the problem of homeless children, and have prepared a Draft Adoption Bill for submission to Parliament.

there is little the Parsis can do to change the law of succession, which is of general application. The Law Commission of India, which is reviewing the whole Indian statute-book, will no doubt have something to say about the forty-year-old Succession Act.

The Parsis are a drop in the sea of Indian humanity. That they have been able to retain their separate identity and traditions is due as much to their system of law as to their religious faith. It is on these two pillars that they must build for the future.

WORKS RELIED ON IN CHAPTER 6

ALLOTT, A. N. *The Akan law of property.* Unpublished Ph.D. thesis. University of London, 1954.

ALLOTT, A. N. The Ashanti law of property (1966). 68 Zeitschrift für vergleichende Rechtswissenschaft 129-215.

ASANTE, S. K. B. Fiduciary principles in Anglo-American law and the customary law of Ghana—a comparative study (1965), 14 ICLQ 1144-1188.

BENTSI-ENCHILL, K. *Ghana land law*, London, 1964. Sweet & Maxwell.

COKER, G. B. A. *Family property among the Yorubas*, 2nd ed. London, 1966. Sweet & Maxwell.

FORTES, M. *The dynamics of clanship among the Tallensi*, London, 1945. OUP.

LLOYD, P. C. *Yoruba land law*, London, 1962. OUP.

OBI, S. N. C. *The Ibo law of property*, London, 1963. Butterworths.

OBI, S. N. C. *Modern family law in Southern Nigeria*, London, 1966. Sweet & Maxwell.

OLLENNU, N. A. *Principles of customary land law in Ghana*, London, 1962. Sweet & Maxwell.

OTTENBERG, S. Inheritance and succession in Afikpo. In *Studies in the laws of succession in Nigeria*, ed. J. D. M. Derrett, OUP, 1965, pp. 33-90.

SARBAH, J. M. *Fanti customary laws*, 2nd ed. London, 1904. Clowes.

SMITH, M. G. *The economy of Hausa communities of Zaria*, London, 1955. HMSO

SMITH, M. G. Hausa inheritance and succession. In *Studies in the laws of succession in Nigeria*, ed. J. D. M. Derrett, OUP, 1965, pp. 230-281.

TAIT, D. *The Konkomba of Northern Ghana*, London, 1961. OUP

WOODMAN, G. R. The acquisition of family land in Ghana (1963). JAL, 136-151.

For Product Safety Concerns and Information please contact our EU
representative GPSR@taylorandfrancis.com
Taylor & Francis Verlag GmbH, Kaufingerstraße 24, 80331 München, Germany

www.ingramcontent.com/pod-product-compliance
Lightning Source LLC
Chambersburg PA
CBHW050702280326
41926CB00088B/2421